FRENZY!

FRENZY!

HEATH, HAIGH & CHRISTIE

The First Great Tabloid Murderers

Neil Root

preface
publishing

Published by Preface Publishing 2011

10 9 8 7 6 5 4 3 2 1

Copyright © Neil Root 2011

First published in Great Britain in 2011 by Preface Publishing

20 Vauxhall Bridge Road
London, SW1V 2SA

An imprint of The Random House Group Limited

www.randomhouse.co.uk
www.prefacepublishing.co.uk

Addresses for companies within The Random House Group Limited
can be found at www.randomhouse.co.uk

The Random House Group Limited Reg. No. 954009

A CIP catalogue record for this book is available from the British Library

ISBN 978 1 84809 317 1

The Random House Group Limited supports the Forest Stewardship Council® (FSC®),
the leading international forest certification organisation. All our titles that are printed on
Greenpeace approved FSC® certified paper carry the FSC® logo. Our paper procurement
policy can be found at www.randomhouse.co.uk/environment

Typeset in Dante MT by Palimpsest Book Production Limited,
Falkirk, Stirlingshire
Printed and bound in Great Britain by Clays PLC, St Ives

For Lorna and Len

INTRODUCTION

In the twenty-first century the society in which we live is a twenty-four-hour television news and Internet culture. Breaking news is on air and online within hours, sometimes minutes or even seconds. This is especially true when it comes to murder cases, the dark and sensational details of the extraordinary actions and sad misfortunes of others keeping viewers and surfers gripped. This has in turn put pressure on the tabloid press, its readership drifting away to the new media. Pages and pages in newspapers are devoted to gruesome events and tales, sometimes with a level of detail that is truly chilling. Just how did we get to this incredible level and detail of murder coverage?

Murder has transfixed the popular press since the mid-nineteenth century, a statement which says a lot about human nature and society, as tabloids mirror their readership. Editors know what people want and deliver it, week in and week out. Murder is the rarest form of crime and yet it gets far more coverage than any other. Why is this? The answer must be because the public wants to read about it. In the second half of the twentieth century murder saturated front pages as never before. Three British serial killers caught and executed in the few years after the end of the Second World War provoked a level of coverage never seen before, the precursor to the press frenzies which surround serial murder today. Neville Heath, a 'charming' sadist who killed two women; John George Haigh, the acid bath killer, who killed between six and nine men and women; and John Christie, the ineffectual necrophile who killed between six and eight women – modern news coverage was born with the stories of these three men who crime historian Donald Thomas called the 'post-war psychopaths'.

HEATH IN CLUB PARTY – WITH ALL CHARM TURNED ON
Daily Mirror, Friday, 27 September 1946

VAMPIRE HORROR IN LONDON SW7
Daily Mirror, Thursday, 3 March 1949

CHRISTIE SAYS "FIRST I GAVE THEM GAS."
Daily Express, Wednesday, 24 June 1953

Post-war London was a bleak and ravaged city, blitzed and scarred by German bombs. The chaos and savagery of war had desensitised people and in many ways cheapened human life. The population of cities all over Britain but particularly London had seen and experienced terrible things. Almost everybody had lost a loved one.

In the midst of this devastation, the underworld thrived and the crime rate shot up. As Colin Wilson points out in *A Criminal History of Mankind*, in 1946 crime was at twice the level of 1939, a doubling of robberies, burglaries, rapes and crimes of violence. Although in 1954 overall crime was lower than in 1945, only robbery and burglary had fallen sharply, due to greater affluence. Violent offences and sex crimes had doubled again since the end of the war.

Between 1946 and 1953 serial killers Neville Heath, John George Haigh and John Christie became the macabre pin-ups of their age and set the tone for the news frenzy which surrounds multiple or gruesome murders today. Heath mutilated and murdered two young women with a brutal ferocity not seen in Britain since Jack the Ripper, with the possibility of a further victim. Haigh killed between six and nine men and women for financial gain, dismembering and dissolving them in acid baths, and perhaps drinking blood from their necks. Christie strangled between six and eight women, performing necrophilia on their bodies and burying them in his garden or under the floorboards, or storing them in a kitchen cupboard.

The police files on Neville Heath (closed extract: 260 pages and fourteen photographs) have never been declassified. This author made a Freedom of Information request for the files in November 2010, but after long consideration it was decided by the Freedom of Information assessor that they could not be released to the public. This is because of an exemption clause to access. To quote the assessor, 'This exemption applies to information in the extract that relates to an unconnected murder that remains unsolved, and this information may be used to reinvestigate this case in the future.' This tells us that Neville Heath was a strong suspect for a further murder during the police investigation of June–July 1946, something which has not until now been known. We may never know if indeed Heath did claim a third victim, but this tells us that it is possible.

The crimes and lives of these murderers have been documented before. The most recent biography of Neville Heath was published in 1988, the last of John George Haigh in the 1950s, although he was the subject of the 2002 television drama *A is for Acid*. John Christie is by far the most notorious, largely because of the miscarriage of justice which resulted in the execution of his upstairs neighbour Timothy Evans in 1950 for the murder of his wife and baby. Ludovic Kennedy's 1961 book *Ten Rillington Place* is the definitive work on Christie and Evans, and updated editions were produced. However, under the Freedom of Information Act, more information has been obtained from the archives, details that shine new light on the extraordinary crimes of Heath, Haigh and Christie. All of this material is included in this book and helps us get closer to the truth.

An angle that Ludovic Kennedy did not cover on the Christie–Evans case was the effect of the massive media interest at the time on the charging, conviction and execution of Timothy Evans. The pressure on the police and judiciary meant that Evans was not given a fair trial. The proof of this is that Ludovic Kennedy's book, which was prefaced by an open letter to the Home Secretary of the day, gained Evans a posthumous pardon in 1966. The contribution of tabloid news coverage to this infamous miscarriage of justice will also be explored here.

Heath, Haigh and Christie (and Evans) were not the only names to emerge from this darkness. Albert Pierrepoint, Britain's number-one executioner, hanged all four of these men, and no exploration of the role of the tabloids would be complete without him. As the popular newspapers warmed to their newfound ability to scandalise and sensationalise, he himself became a celebrity. Executioners were required to be discreet and to conduct themselves in a respectful manner and above all avoid any contact with the press. However, when Pierrepoint retired in 1956 over what he regarded as unpaid fees, he went to *Empire News* and the *Sunday Chronicle*, who paid him in excess of five hundred thousand pounds in today's money for a series of sordid stories called *The Hangman's Own Story*. In 1974 Pierrepoint published his autobiography in book form.

Tabloids were also directly involved in payments to Heath, Haigh and Christie. The *Sunday Pictorial* (later the *Sunday Mirror*) paid huge sums for the inside stories of both Neville Heath in 1946 (although the *Daily Mail* got the initial story) and John Christie in 1953, and paid their legal costs. The *News of the World* did the same for John George Haigh in 1949. Incredibly, it was the *News of the World* that got the full confession from Haigh, not the police. As a direct result of the cavalier and intemperate press coverage of the murders, laws governing the payment of the legal fees of victims and criminals, the withholding of evidence and many other aspects of how the media cover such crimes were changed.

The tabloid journalists of the 1940s and '50s are an intrinsic part of this story. Crime correspondents had a minor celebrity of their own in the days when the tough crime novels of Raymond Chandler and Mickey Spillane were flying out of bookshops. In the famous *Picture Post* magazine in 1947 there was a photographic feature on 'Fleet Street's Murder Gang', accompanied by a photograph of the legendary *News of the World* crime correspondent Norman Rae. The photograph shows him with his ear to an old-fashioned telephone 'phoning in his latest scoop'. Rae is part of this story. It is a little-known fact that he arranged to meet Christie without the knowledge of the police while the killer was on the run.

In the end Rae missed his scoop: Christie's story was ghost-written for the *Sunday Pictorial* in 1953 by the equally legendary Harry Procter, who had also got the scoop on Neville Heath in 1946 for the *Daily Mail*. Incredibly, Procter had actually met Heath twice before his first murder, but it was the *Sunday Pictorial* which got the full inside story from Heath's mouth from his death cell, the paper which Procter would move to in the 1950s. Rae was responsible for the 'confessional' story of John George Haigh in 1949, and he was the source of many other crime scoops in a long career. Rae and Procter did more than anybody else to stir up the tabloid frenzy around Heath, Haigh and Christie, with the authority of their editors and the expense accounts of their newspapers behind them. Harry Procter would later write his memoirs about his career in Fleet Street entitled *The Street of Disillusion*. The title says it all. The roles played by members of Fleet Street's Murder Gang are a key strand of this tale.

Other members of the Murder Gang in this period included Hugh Brady of the *Daily Mail*, who died in 1949; Charles Leach of the *Exchange Telegraph Co.*; Jimmy Reid of the *Sunday Dispatch*; Cecil Catling of the *Star*; Victor Toddington of the *Evening Standard*; E. V. Tullet of the *Sunday Express*; Fred Redman of the *Sunday Pictorial*; Percy Hoskins of the *Daily Express*; Gerald Byrne of *Empire News* (who wrote books on Heath and Haigh soon after they were executed); Reginald Foster of the *News Chronicle*; Sam Jackett of the *Evening News*; William Ashenden of the *Daily Graphic*; Stanley Bishop of the *Daily Herald*; W. G. Finch of the Press Association; Arthur Tietjen of the *Daily Mail*; and Harold Whittall of the *Daily Mirror*. But it is Norman 'Jock' Rae and Harry Procter who concern us here.

This was the first time killers had been paid for their stories while in custody, the money going to their families after they were hanged. This was especially important to John George Haigh, who was very close to his mother and wanted to give her a substantial amount of money to improve her life. Never before had the public been exposed to so much sensational information about serial murder. The more the tabloids printed, the more the public lapped it up. The more horrible the better. It was the dawn of a new age. Ludovic Kennedy wrote in *Ten Rillington Place*, 'Christie was in the papers every day eclipsing in interest even the death of Queen Mary.' Heath, Haigh and Christie cultivated their notoriety and basked in their fame. Heath made prodigious efforts to look his best at his trial; Haigh thrived on his perverse celebrity and vampire revelations, and contemporary photographs show him smiling and waving at the crowds outside various courts; and Christie boasted about his murder count being higher than Haigh's.

WOMEN STRUGGLE TO SEE HAIGH CHARGED
Daily Mirror, Tuesday, 19 July 1949

The coverage of these three psychopaths and their crimes was the true beginning of contemporary tabloid murder reporting. It was also the birth of the serial murderer as criminal celebrity in Britain. Whipped into a frenzy of excitement by the newspapers, women in particular crowded to catch glimpses of these dangerous men, many fainting at the sight of them in court. This book tells the stories of these serial killers against the backdrop of the tabloid frenzy that surrounded them.

PROLOGUE

30 March 1953, very early morning

A man sits in the front passenger seat of a Ford Anglia E494A motor car directly outside Wood Green town hall in north-east London. He is built for comfort rather than speed, wearing a heavy black overcoat over his crumpled double-breasted suit, the white display handkerchief in his left breast pocket obscured. His hat has a lighter band sitting above the rim encircling the black felt, covering his closely cropped grey hair and balding pate. If this were a cartoon, the man would have a 'Press' sign tucked into his hatband, but this is very much real life. Next to him is a driver, assigned to him by his newspaper. Few hacks have a personal driver, and this shows he is something special.

It's wet and windy in the after-midnight darkness on the High Road. The town hall looming above the car, an imposing building partially revealed by the street lights, was originally a private residence known as Earlham Grove House with grounds covering twenty-eight acres. The man is sweating, and not just because of his heavy clothes. He is anxious: he is taking a huge risk.

It's possible a passer-by might recognise the man if he were not sitting slouched in his seat and they could see his face, but the streets are almost deserted. Six years earlier a photograph of him had appeared in the *Picture Post*, showing him placing a telephone call in a betting office, the sign above his head reading 'BETTING, WRITING OR PASSING SLIPS STRICTLY PROHIBITED'. The caption of the picture read, 'Fleet Street crime reporter Norman Rae of *News of the World* phones the news desk with the latest scoop.' The article entitled 'Fleet Street's Murder Gang' had appeared on 17 May 1947. But if nobody recognises Norman Rae tonight, most will be familiar with his name. The *News of the World* has a circulation of eight million a week and, as now, is only published on Sundays. Rae is the paper's chief crime correspondent.

Norman Rae is a living legend in Fleet Street. Born in Aberdeen in 1896, he is a no-nonsense gruff Scot. He joined the *News of the World* in the early 1930s, after lying about his age to serve in the Highland Division in the First World War. Since then he has built a reputation as *the* crime reporter in Fleet Street, a man who can sniff out and secure the most sensational murder stories. An earlier break was getting the inside story on Dr Buck Ruxton in 1936, an Indian doctor practising in Lancashire who killed his wife in a jealous rage and murdered their housemaid because she witnessed the crime. Ruxton then dismembered the bodies, packed the parts into parcels and threw them randomly from a train

travelling through Scotland. He was caught because the newspaper he had wrapped the body parts in included a supplement
only published in a small part of Lancashire. Rae met Ruxton
several times and got the inside scoop, making his name.
Since then many other exclusives have followed, the most
memorable being the full story of acid bath killer John
George Haigh in 1949.

Rae is now fifty-six years old and a veteran of tabloid
murder. It is almost 1.30 a.m., and his Ford Anglia, a two-door
black saloon, is filling up with the pungent smell and whirling
smoke of Rae's Player's cigarette and his driver's Craven A.
As the windows are closed against the heavy rain outside,
visibility is not good from the car. It's almost the time of the
rendezvous. Rae has arranged to meet John Reginald Halliday
Christie, who has been on the run from the police for seven
days, since the trussed-up bodies of three women were discovered in a papered-over alcove in his kitchen at 10 Rillington
Place in Notting Hill, west London. Christie has been staying
in a fleapit hostel in King's Cross, wandering aimlessly through
the smoggy city by day.

Three years earlier his upstairs neighbour Timothy Evans
was hanged for the murder of his wife Beryl and baby
Geraldine. Christie will later confess to murdering Beryl, and
it is highly probable that he killed Geraldine too. Norman Rae
covered the arrest, trial and execution of Evans for the *News
of the World*, and Christie kept newspaper cuttings of his work.
The previous day – in fact, just two hours ago at 11.20 p.m.
– Christie had telephoned the newspaper from a public phone
box and asked for Rae. Christie was out of money, cold, wet
and hungry, and wanted to sell his story in return for a hot

meal. Rae agreed, as long as Christie undertook to surrender himself to the police immediately afterwards. Rae knows the huge risks he is taking in meeting Christie. There is a huge manhunt on for the serial killer and all the papers are following it. But Rae's bloodhound instinct for a big scoop overrides any moral qualms he may have had.

It's now 1.30. Rae nods to his driver, steps out of the car and braves the rain on the pavement. Just then and purely coincidentally, a policeman on the beat walks past. Rae cannot believe his bad luck. He hears rustling in some bushes in the near-blackness and knows that it's Christie making his escape. He will be caught just two days later by a policeman next to Putney Bridge in south-west London and Rae will never get his scoop. Christie will sell his full story to Rae's rival, the equally legendary Harry Procter of the *Sunday Pictorial*, who had secured the story of the sadistic killer Neville Heath in 1946.

15 July 1953, Pentonville Prison, London

It was less than three weeks since Mr Justice Finnemore had donned the black cap and, shedding tears of pity for humanity, sentenced John Christie to death for multiple murder, adding the traditional 'May God have mercy on your soul,' mercy which Christie had not shown his victims. In the condemned cell the balding and stooped fifty-five-year-old, his huge domed forehead creased with tension, ineffectual and pathetic and indistinguishable in a crowd if it were not for his depraved crimes, was brought to his feet as the execution party arrived. It was a few minutes before nine o'clock in the morning.

A chaplain had spent the last hour with Christie in quiet contemplation, but now God's representative was sidelined as Britain's chief executioner Albert Pierrepoint entered the cell, followed by his assistant, the chief prison officer and another officer. In silence Christie's glasses were removed and his hands pinioned tightly behind his back. Pierrepoint and his assistant had arrived at the prison the afternoon before and observed Christie from a distance to weigh up the length of drop required, and tests had been carried out, with a bag of sand standing in for Christie, to confirm the gallows were in good working order. That bag of sand had been left hanging all night to stretch the rope.

Christie hadn't been held at Pentonville before and during his trial, but at Brixton. While there he was examined by a succession of psychiatrists, all of whom felt nauseated and repulsed by him. At Brixton Christie had bragged about his murders to other inmates, comparing himself to another serial killer hanged just a few years before, acid bath killer John George Haigh. Like Haigh, Christie had killed at least six people, but said that he had been aiming for twelve victims. This bravado was totally at odds with his nondescript personality and appearance. His trial had lasted four days, and the jury took just an hour and twenty minutes to unanimously find him guilty. After he was condemned to death and sent to Pentonville to await execution, he was very withdrawn. One man who had known Christie during the First World War visited him just two days before his execution. Christie told him, 'I don't care what happens to me now. I have nothing left to live for.'

Christie was quiet as he was led to the gallows, the prison

officers on either side of him. The sheriff, the prison governor and the medical officer were waiting as Christie came in and was escorted to stand on the trapdoors through which he would drop, the spot marked in the interests of speed and efficiency. Christie's feet were placed directly across where the trapdoors divided. Pierrepoint then put a white cap over Christie's head and placed the noose around his neck, while his assistant pinioned his legs to prevent him from trying to jump off the trapdoors. Everything ready, Pierrepoint pulled the gallows lever. Christie went down swiftly and smoothly. The medical officer then inspected his broken body in the pit below the trapdoors and satisfied himself that he was medically dead. After the body was left hanging for an hour, an inquest on Christie took place before he was buried in the prison grounds in an unconsecrated grave.

CHAPTER

I

9 September 1944, Gloucester Road Underground station, London.

It's late evening and the weather is cool but not unpleasant and the crowds are bustling in and out of the station entrance. Outside, the newspaper boy has long since shut down his stand for the night, the late edition of the twopenny *Evening Standard* already on its way to wrapping tomorrow's fish-and-chip supper. Soldiers on leave walk past the Edwardian splendour of Bailey's Hotel just south of the station with girlfriends on their arms. A tin-hatted air raid warden crosses the road, his torch pointed down and covered with tissue, obeying his own instruction 'Put that light out!' The white band on his arm matches the stripes painted down the middle of the road and the horizontal stripes daubed on the lamp posts to help drivers unable to use their headlamps in the blackout.

The war is still raging. Just the day before, the first V2

rocket, Hitler's new secret weapon, had hit the area of Chiswick a few miles south-west of Gloucester Road. Travelling at 3,000 miles an hour and carrying a ton of explosive, the V2 was even more powerful than the V1 'doodlebugs' that had brought terror to the streets of London that summer, reminding Londoners of the sustained devastation of the Blitz four years earlier.

Two men walk briskly down Gloucester Road. They are fortified in the chilly air by the beer they have drunk at tenpence a pint at the Goat, a gaudy Victorian pub in nearby High Street Kensington. One is tall and slim, the other slightly shorter but well built. They are both thirty-five years old, smartly dressed in well-cut suits and ties, two youngish men about wartime town. The taller man with the angular face and styled mop of dark hair and pencil moustache is William McSwan, a Scot known to his friends as Mac. The man next to him is John George Haigh, whom Mac counts as his trusted friend and drinking buddy. Haigh has always been known within his family as George, but Mac calls him John. They have known each other for eight or nine years, although they lost touch for much of that time and only recently met again.

Haigh first met Mac in late 1935, when Mac's father Donald advertised for a secretary / chauffeur. Donald McSwan had previously been a local government minister in Scotland, but relocated to London with his wife Amy and son William to join the London County Council. Soon after he invested some of his savings in an amusement arcade in Tooting, south-west London, and his son William was employed as manager of the arcade, which operated pinball tables. Haigh quickly became trusted by the McSwans, especially Mac, the two of them frequenting the Goat in the evenings. Haigh was always able to impress those around him. When Haigh moved on, he and the McSwans lost contact. It was only in the late summer of 1944 that Mac ran into Haigh again in the Goat, a meeting that Haigh no doubt wanted and perhaps planned to happen, and not just to rekindle the friendship.

For the previous two weeks they have spent a great deal of time together in the evenings. Haigh is now a salesman and bookkeeper for a small company, Hurstlea Products Ltd, in Crawley, West Sussex. His patter and personable manner are key assets in selling products, and his shrewd mind is adept at figures. But his expensive lifestyle is beyond his average salary. He is now running out of funds and seeking an opportunity to make some quick cash.

Mac has no idea that his friend was released from HM Prison Lincoln the previous year after serving a sentence for fraud and forgery. Nor that while in prison Haigh had done experiments on mice with sulphuric acid he stole from the prison tinsmith's workshop, observing how the creatures dissolved. These tests had a purpose – little that Haigh does lacks a purpose, whether menial gestures or life decisions. His easy manner belies the fact that even his smiles are not spontaneous. Mac may know about Haigh's car accident a few months before, when he suffered a head injury that caused bleeding into his mouth. But as they approach their destination, Mac is relaxed and grateful to his friend. Firstly, Haigh, always good with his hands, has promised to repair a broken pin table for him, although Mac's father has already sold the amusement arcade, a fact not lost on Haigh over the previous fortnight. Secondly, and far more importantly,

Haigh has promised to help his old friend with a pressing problem. Mac has been worried for some time. He is due to be conscripted into the army but is not a natural soldier and he has no wish to die. Haigh has promised to help him disappear until the war is over, leaving his business and personal affairs in the capable hands of his jovial friend. Mac has no idea how completely his drinking partner wants to help him.

Haigh is the dominant party in the friendship – socially at ease, interesting and proactive in conversation, the milder-mannered Mac happy to laugh along at his daring jokes and ideas. Haigh's side-parted hair remains immaculately slicked back even though he wears no hat in the breezy night, his thin lips pursed between smiles, the upper topped by a small moustache that the vain Haigh likes to think makes him resemble the popular matinee idol Ronald Colman. If ever Mac wondered that his friend was not what he seemed, the clue is in his eyes. Slightly Asian in shape, his dark pupils stare out like fish eyes. Even when his lips are parted in a mechanised smile, those eyes are cold and scheming.

They chat cheerfully as they arrive at their destination directly opposite the Underground station, a basement room at 79 Gloucester Road which Haigh rents as a workshop. The bonhomie continues as Haigh thrusts out his arm to gesture his friend to go first. Mac is happy tonight, as with the help of his friend he is going to avoid being sent to war. As they walk down the steps into the small basement yard, fingering the ornate wrought-iron railings as they descend, Mac sees the blacked-out window complying with wartime regulations. Haigh knows what war is about, having experienced death at first hand. A few years before, during an air raid, he was chatting to a nurse and when the explosions got close took refuge in a doorway. A few minutes later he saw the nurse's head rolling along the street. As they reach the door of the basement, little does Mac know that he is seeing his last natural light, the dark milky sea turning pitch black above him his last experience of open sky.

Inside, the basement room is sparsely furnished: a wooden work table, an oil drum, some small machine parts and tools. Mac doesn't know that the forty-gallon oil drum is meant for him or that his friend has been accumulating quantities of acid by posing as 'Technical Liaison Officer' to 'Union Group Engineering' and suddenly acquiring a science degree on his business card. The carboys of acid may or may not be there that night. The focal point of the room is a drain in the middle of the floor, and this is impossible for Mac to miss. They continue to chat, Haigh showing Mac something he is working on.

Mac doesn't see it coming. He's hit with great force from behind on the back of the head. Once on the ground, two further blows make certain he is dead, the third transmitting to Haigh a 'squashy' feeling. The weapon is a blunt instrument – perhaps a leg removed from a pin table or more likely a piece of heavy metal piping that Haigh had procured in advance. Haigh then strips Mac of his watch, wallet and National Identity Card. Haigh's eyes are still staring and intense, the windows to a clinical coldness and a frozen soul, but there are no smiles any more.

There are two theories about what happens next. In the first, Haigh panics and locks the door of the basement, hails a taxi and goes to a late-night drinking club in nearby

Bayswater, where a few drinks calm him down. He then returns to the basement at about 2.30 a.m. and begins to clear up. This is when he possibly made an incision in Mac's neck and gathered a cup of blood which he then drank, but this may well not have happened. The mice experiments demonstrating the effect of acid on animal tissue have given Haigh his big idea. If there is no body, there can surely be no murder charge. It takes Haigh two or three days to order the acid, and by then Mac is beginning to smell. The body worries Haigh, but it's not a guilty conscience. This is Haigh's first murder, and his panic is due to fear of hanging for murder rather than any belated compassion. When the acid arrives, Mac is placed in the oil drum and Haigh waits over-night for his friend to dissolve. The sludgy remains are then poured down the cellar drain.

The alternative theory is that Haigh buys a mincing machine from a shop called Gamages in Holborn and some swimming trunks (to wear while he works) in Bayswater. Then he greases the floor of the basement to prevent blood-stains. He cuts Mac into small pieces over the following three days, before chopping up the bones and boiling and mincing them. The floor is then washed with hot caustic soda to remove any evidence and it all goes down the drain. There is little to support this story, but the occupants next door to 79 Gloucester Road later say that the basement was very noisy at this time. The truth may be a mixture of the two versions.

After Mac's disappearance Haigh wastes no time. Sending letters to Mac's parents, Donald and Amy, apparently from their son in hiding, he manages to secure large sums of money from them over the following months which they think he is passing on to their son. Haigh's cunning mind and beady eyes are now working overtime, revelling in his own ingenuity. Corpus delicti: no body, no proof of murder. These will not be the last dealings that Haigh has with the McSwan family. Mac's murder has desensitised him, made him feel invincible. As he walks jauntily down the Gloucester Road with a spring in his step every day, perhaps whistling a favourite tune, nobody knows that the well-dressed man of business is a mercenary psychopath. But then why should they? Mac knew him well for years and had no idea at all.

Pointing at a small bluish scar on his forehead, John George Haigh's father John spoke in an austere voice as he delivered one of his parables to his young son.

'This is the brand of Satan. I have sinned, and Satan has punished me. If ever you sin, Satan will mark you with a blue pencil likewise.'

'Well . . . mother isn't marked,' said the rapt son after a moment's thought.

'No, she is an angel,' said his father.

Years later the son would learn that the cause of his father's scar was a fragment of burning coal spat from the fire, but in John George Haigh's eyes, his mother Emily would never fall from her angelic pedestal.

When John George was born to John and Emily Haigh in Stamford, Lincolnshire on 24 July 1909 Emily was already forty, and he was her only child. John had lost his job as a foreman at an electricity plant in Stamford just three months before his son's birth. Emily would later say that the financial and emotional instability this caused at the time had affected her son in the womb and twisted his mind. John and Emily called their newborn George at home to avoid confusion with his father.

Soon after his son was born, John Haigh managed to find work further north at the Lofthouse Colliery in Wakefield, West Yorkshire, and they soon relocated to a small village called Outwood close to Wakefield. This was not such a wrench for them, as John and Emily were originally of Yorkshire stock, sturdy and strong-minded. Significantly in the light of later events, there was not a shred of mental illness in the family history, but a strong case could be made for religious mania. The Haighs were devout members of the Plymouth Brethren, an evangelical, non-ritualistic and anti-clerical branch of Protestantism. The Haighs followed the inflexible strictures of the sect to the very letter and line of the Old Testament. The household that John George Haigh was born into was therefore different from most homes of the time. His grandparents had been among the pioneers of the Brethren, holding informal assemblies instead of worshipping in church. Ascetic and God-fearing, the Brethren's piety shut them off from the world at large, which they considered full of sinners and dangerous to their souls.

John Senior spoke in negatives: 'Thou shalt not . . .'; 'Do not . . .' No entertainment or sport of any kind was allowed. No magazines or newspapers, just the Bible in its oldest, purest form. This strong sense of sacrifice and austerity was the source of the Brethren's strength, and control the means of building it. John Senior promised that to behave right-eously 'would please the Lord'. Heaven and the afterlife were the reward for obeying; eternal damnation and descent into Hell the punishment for disobedience. 'It is a sin to be happy in this world,' John Senior was fond of saying. The next life mattered far more than this. Young George, his only child, was steeped in this rhetoric from the moment he could grasp meaning. 'The worms that will destroy this body' were irrelevant if a life of sacrifice were followed, John Senior told his son, and the soul was all that mattered. But from an early age George began to develop his own idea about eternal sleep – physical death meant nothing, merely being another sacrifice.

With evil and corruption from the outside world being devilish threats and temptations to be steadfastly avoided, John built a ten-foot (three metre) fence around their garden. Young George was truly penned in. There were no peering or prying eyes, no chatting neighbours. His mother Emily was George's beacon, his light; all of his trust went into her. He loved John Senior, but feared him in equal measure. The two emotions dominated the young boy: love of his parents and their beliefs, tempered by fear, a microcosm of his love and fear of God. His enforced separation from his peers (as far as possible) added to the strength of his beliefs, just as John and Emily wished. When George became John George Haigh the man, he would stay on deeply loving terms with his parents, especially his mother, until he died.

George loved animals as a little boy, nurturing the rabbits he was allowed, as they were God's creatures, and even secretly feeding the dogs of strangers in the street. He was also prone to accidents, like many young children. At the age of seven he hit his ear hard on a wardrobe in the bedroom, drawing blood, and a few years later cut his scalp when he fell down the stairs. On neither occasion was medical help sought, Emily's caring hands keeping it in the family. Also aged seven, George entered a private preparatory school with a strict disciplinary regime, no doubt to John's satisfaction. It was at about this time, during the First World War, that John and Emily took their son on his first holiday to the seaside. However, while there a German Zeppelin raid occurred, and George was so disturbed by the destruction he saw that the family rushed home to Outwood and the high fence.

In 1920 at the age of eleven George entered Wakefield Grammar School, meant for children in the area with the most academic potential, remaining there until the age of seventeen. His teachers later remembered him as a 'mischievous boy', undoubtedly trying to find a semblance of individuality outside the parental home. Flashes of the later John George Haigh were beginning to appear. He had a quick mind, and his parents' strictures meant that he was always very well groomed and dressed, a habit that remained a lifelong one for him. He was also becoming a good liar, seeking to avoid the displeasure and reprimands of John Senior for minor misdemeanours which to a Brethren father were major lapses.

John George was also developing a deep passion for music, becoming entranced by the sound of the imposing pipe organ in Wakefield Cathedral, and soon he was playing the piano very well himself. John George had a good voice too, and this led to him being awarded a choral scholarship to the cathedral choir. The angelic image of the choirboy suited him in the context of his family, even though churchgoing in the conventional sense was not the Brethren way. The irony of this phase in his life would later seem almost grotesque, but there was an element to the time he spent in the cathedral that was less innocent than appearances suggested.

He would later say that he spent many hours in the cathedral staring at a statue of the bleeding Christ, a physical embodiment of the Messiah he had avidly read about and whose life and teachings his father had drummed into his head. But this could also be early evidence of John George Haigh's unhealthy interest in blood. He also claimed that he drank his own urine from the age of eleven, but this has never been verified. Much of what Haigh said later must be viewed with caution – he was an expert manipulator, and would soon start putting that to profitable use.

As a teenager, John George began to have religious or at least spiritual dreams, although perhaps this is not surprising considering how much of his waking life was consumed with such matters. In some Christ would appear, and in one a ladder featured and helped him climb to the moon. John and Emily naturally saw this as religiously significant. Was he subconsciously trying to escape the strictures of his family? It does show that he had a vivid imagination and a strong inner life. He was also living in two worlds: the repressed one of his parents and the Brethren, and the world of the cathedral, where his real personality could manifest itself. This got him into the habit of living his life in compartments, concealing aspects of himself when it suited him in order to gain the confidence of people.

When he was seventeen, in 1926, Haigh left Wakefield Cathedral. Alongside his musical talent and passion, he was interested in machines and so went to work for a motor engineering firm to train as a mechanic, although after a while the physical labour the job entailed began to pall. Fastidious in appearance and lazy by nature, even the lure of learning how engines worked was not enough, and he took a desk job with an insurance company. He did well there, and soon found that his shrewd and calculating mind made him a natural at sales. In 1930, at the age of twenty-one, Haigh moved on to work for a company specialising in insurance, estate agency and advertising. This venture was quickly very successful, and Haigh proved himself an excellent broker, securing a £30,000 contract to insure a dam-building project in Egypt. However, his future tendencies came to the fore, and he was fired after being suspected of stealing money from an office cash box. The irrepressible Haigh then founded an advertising agency, Northern Electric Newspapers Ltd, and this was even briefly floated on the London Stock Exchange.

The year 1934 was a watershed for Haigh. Three weeks short of his twenty-fifth birthday, on 6 July he married twenty-one-year-old beauty Beatrice Hammer. He moved out of his parents' house in Outwood and stopped attending Brethren assemblies. What they thought of this is not recorded, but it is unlikely they were happy about it, having controlled him for so long. This was the real beginning of his waywardness, his disposition for dishonesty starting to grow. Haigh had realised there were easier ways of making money than working for a living.

A newspaper article about a car swindle inspired him to have a go himself. These were the Depression years, and while Britain did not suffer as greatly as the USA, they were times of great hardship. Many businesses got into trouble or closed down and unemployment was rising. Haigh approached a garage in financial difficulty and through it bought cars, paying in instalments. He would forge the signatures and handwriting of real people he didn't know but probably found in a telephone directory, and then sell the cars on after only one or two small payments had been made. Haigh discovered that he possessed a natural ability for forgery and this would become the focus of his future criminal career. It worked well for a few months, and he made a lot of money, but then he was caught. On 22 November 1934 he was sentenced to fifteen months for fraud and forgery at Leeds Assizes.

'May God give me time to redeem the past, and to make you happy in your later years,' wrote Haigh to his horrified parents from prison. While incarcerated he received a letter from the Plymouth Brethren politely ostracising him, as he had brought shame on them. He was shocked and devastated, this having been the very centre of his existence since he was a baby. His mother Emily later thought that this embittered her only son and changed him, but of course he was already a convicted criminal when he received the letter. For John and Emily, finding reasons for their son's criminality would prove increasingly difficult. In their eyes he had been brought up strictly, correctly and in a God-fearing environment. It was not their nurture but the world that had ruined him, diseased his pure nature, the very reason John had erected that fence years earlier.

Haigh was released on 8 December 1935 and returned to live with his parents. While he was in prison, Beatrice – they had been married just over four months when he was convicted – had discovered she was pregnant, had the baby, given it up for adoption and left him. John and Emily now gave him the money to start a dry-cleaning business with a financial partner. This was immediately successful, Haigh's natural sales ability being a great asset. Soon after the first shop opened, it was cleaning over 2,000 garments a week, but fate then dealt a cruel blow. Haigh's partner was killed in a car accident and, short of money, he was forced to put the firm into voluntary liquidation. In 1936, he went south for the first time, to London.

There he answered an advertisement for a secretary / chauffeur to the McSwans, a family then living in Wimbledon who would play a major part in Haigh's life over the next ten years, and be for ever linked to his name. As we have seen, he impressed them and became great friends with the son, William or Mac. After some months working for the McSwans, Haigh moved on, turning criminal again. He set up fake solicitor's offices using the name of reputable real firms and sold imaginary shares in genuine companies at below-market prices, hooking the greedy. Deposits for share options flooded in, and Haigh often bought goods with the proceeds so as not to have too much unexplained cash, then swiftly moved on. He was now a fully fledged confidence man, a 'grifter', repeating the scam in different locations in and around London. But once again Haigh was caught – in Guildford, Surrey. On 24 November 1937 he was sentenced to four years at Surrey Assizes for dishonestly obtaining over £3000, a small fortune then.

Haigh was in prison when the Second World War broke out in September 1939, not being released until 13 August 1940, on licence, just before the Battle of Britain and the Blitz started. He became a fire warden in Victoria, central London, not far from the Houses of Parliament. It was during this time that he saw a nurse he had been talking to decapitated by a German bomb. In February 1941 Haigh, like every fit young man, registered for military service, although he never intended to fight and in 1943 would fail to attend a military medical board. He had just been released from prison yet again. On 11 June 1941, still on licence, he was sentenced to twenty-one months hard labour for stealing household goods and sent to Lincoln Prison, not far from his birthplace Stamford.

'If you are going to go wrong, go wrong in a big way, like me. Go after women – rich, old women who like a bit of flattery. That's your market, if you are after big money,' Haigh is reported to have said to other prisoners. He may not have followed his own advice yet (at least there is no proof that he had) but this would prove to be his eventual modus operandi. He got on well with the other prisoners – he was gregarious, boastful and mischievous, the Brethren boy nowhere to be seen any more. Inmates on outside work duty would supply him with field mice they caught, but they probably did not know what he was doing with them. Haigh's work duty was in the prison tinsmith's shop, and he dissolved the mice in sulphuric acid he obtained there. He found that within ten minutes the acid darkened and the temperature rose to one hundred degrees Celsius. After thirty minutes only black sludge remained of the mice.

Haigh lost some remission from his sentence for being involved in a post trafficking ring and was finally released on 17 September 1943. He moved back in with his parents for a few weeks and then returned to London. He was thirty-four years old now, a mature man who had done three stretches in prison, all for dishonesty. There had been no violence yet, but that was about to change. He began work as a salesman and bookkeeper for Hurstlea Products in Crawley, West Sussex and lived simply in a small rented room in Queen's Gate Terrace in the affluent district of South Kensington in west London. He also rented a basement room at 79 Gloucester Road, outwardly for business purposes but most probably in preparation for murder. He had a method and a location; now he just needed a victim.

He continued to be a successful salesman, even having a close friendship with his boss's daughter Barbara, who was much younger than him. Haigh's passion for music had not left him and they went to concerts together. This relationship was purely platonic. In early 1944 he had a car accident, suffering a two-inch-long cut to the left temporal region of his scalp which bled into his mouth, giving him a taste of blood that he would make much of later. Then, in the late summer of 1944, Haigh walked into the bar of the Goat on High Street Kensington, running into an old friend with whom he had spent many evenings there eight years previously. As we have seen, he probably planned to bump into William McSwan, the son of his former employer. They became reacquainted over the next fortnight, and on the night of 9 September left the Goat together for the last time. The rest is murderous tabloid history.

John George Haigh had broken the Sixth Commandment of the Old Testament: 'Thou shalt not commit murder.' He had broken other commandments many times before, but this was something else. There was no going back now.

CHAPTER
2

While John George Haigh is busy milking the McSwans for Mac's money, less than a kilometre away another man has a female visitor. The house she is visiting is worlds away from the affluence of Gloucester Road, however. It is a cul-de-sac with ten terraced houses on each side facing each other. Close to the Portobello Road street market, which bustles with furniture, antiques and other curiosities, Rillington Place is definitely on the poorer side of Notting Hill, in the shadow of Ladbroke Grove Underground station, making it almost deafeningly noisy when a train passes. Little better than a slum, some windows are boarded up and the paint on the houses is hanging off as if it has melted in the heat of war, although it is natural decay. There is no fading glamour here, no hint of an affluent or haughty past. Number 10 is small like all the houses, tall with three floors but very narrow and divided into three flats. The facade is workmanlike, solid but ugly, the ridge tiles on the roof serrated like the jagged edge of a knife.

It is some time in October 1944, and the pallor of the sky is somehow suited to the bleakness of the war, which now has only seven months left to run. John Christie is in the kitchen of number 10 Rillington Place with his visitor. He and his wife Ethel live in the ground-floor flat sharing an outside toilet with the two flats above them. Ethel has gone to see her brother in Sheffield in the north of England. Christie and the woman sit at the kitchen table, he in a hardback chair, she in a fraying deckchair. Christie looks older than his forty-six years, balding and very thin. There is an air of defeat about him, but he minimises this with a calm, patient and controlled manner. If he were a medical man (he does claim to have medical knowledge) he would be described as having a good bedside manner. Muriel Eady is in her early thirties, an attractive and respectable woman with dark wavy hair. She sips her drink, but she is there for more than tea and a chat. They both work at the Ultra Radio Works in Acton, in far-west London, where they assemble radio components. He has promised her that he can cure her catarrh, from which Muriel suffers terribly.

That explains the rough breathing device there on the table, which Christie himself made. It is a glass jar, square in shape and with a screw top. There are two holes in the lid and a rubber tube is inserted into one of them. They sit and chat amiably, Christie's voice little more than a whisper, the way he has spoken since being gassed in the trenches in the First World War. Then he tells Muriel that he is ready to give her the 'treatment' now.

★   ★   ★

John Reginald Halliday Christie was not from London and the life journey that brought him to the kitchen that day was an arduous one. He was born on 8 April 1898 at the very end of the Victorian era in the countryside around Halifax, West Yorkshire, not so far from Wakefield, to where the Haighs would move eleven years later. Also like John George Haigh, Christie's father was very dominant. Ernest John Christie was a designer of carpets, a man quick with his hands but also with his temper. His marriage to Mary Hannah Halliday was a fruitful one – they had seven children, of which Christie was the fifth. He had a brother and five sisters; another sister died when she was a baby. Within the family, Christie was called by his middle name, Reggie.

Ernest was a stern father who would punish his children for the most minor offence, often giving them beatings. Reggie was a sickly boy, thin and delicate, and his mother Mary's maternal instinct was very strong towards him. She almost suffocated him with affection, and this led to Reggie not developing enough confidence, becoming withdrawn. The beatings from his father and the pampering by his mother confused the boy and he began to develop a private, internal world.

When Reggie was six or seven, the family moved to an inner district of the city of Halifax, where their house overlooked a graveyard. He would spend hours wandering among the tombstones, a deathly playground. He would also peer into a broken vault at the coffins laid out within. This fixation on death intensified further when he was eight years old when his grandfather died. Reggie had always been terrified of his mother's father, who was distant and forbidding, as many men of the Victorian era were. Reggie was taken in to view the dead body in the open casket, and he was full of wonder at how harmless and ineffectual his granddad was now that he was dead. He would later explain how the corpse had transfixed him, strengthening his fascination with death.

A year or two later another strand in the development of his unusual personality originated. A much older sister, who was already married, unknowingly showed Reggie her naked leg as far as the knee when she was putting on a shoe. This sent a sexual thrill through him; like most boys in those times he had never glimpsed such a thing. Reggie's shyness meant that his siblings also bullied him, and this secret peek gave him a sense of power over his dominant sister, a feeling that he had covertly violated her. A strange and obsessive combination of death, sex and the need to feel power was now brewing in Reggie, and all three would later become disastrously intertwined into a conscious impulse.

In 1909, at the age of eleven, Reggie gained a scholarship to Halifax Secondary School. Reggie had a logical brain, excelled at mathematics and was reasonably bright – he was later found to have an IQ of 128. He did well at school, getting good reports, although his classmates later remembered him as odd and withdrawn. Like Haigh, Reggie also sang in the choir, but not to the same standard. He became a Boy Scout and rose to become assistant scoutmaster, a position that empowered him and became a peg on which to hang his identity, the uniform visual evidence of his status.

As was often the way then, Reggie Christie left school at fifteen in 1913, and went to work as an assistant projectionist at a cinema. One night with some friends he went to a little lane in Halifax known to be popular with courting couples, and the boys went off with a girl each to get to know each other better. Something happened that evening that would have a huge impact on Christie – he could not perform, whether through nerves or a medical problem is not known. But word soon spread, and the grapevine gave him the demeaning names of 'Can't-do-it-Christie' and 'Reggie-no-dick'. This made him feel repulsive and sapped the little confidence he had with girls. The sense of inferiority would stay with him into adulthood.

The following year the First World War broke out. Christie did not join up until September 1916, and in April 1917 he was assigned to the 52nd Nottinghamshire and Derbyshire Regiment. Exactly a year later he was sent to France as a signalman attached to the Duke of Wellington's Regiment. He was just twenty years old. In June 1918 Christie was gassed on the front and sent to a military hospital in France, where he stayed a month. Christie later said that the mustard gas had blinded him and left him mute for three and a half years. However, there is no proof he was ever blind, and it is doubtful that he lost his voice for anywhere near that long. But he would always speak in a soft whisper thereafter. This may well have been a psychological effect rather than a physical one. Christie was always something of a hypochondriac and liked attention. At the end of the war he was discharged with a token disability pension.

Christie returned to his family in Halifax and went back to his projectionist's job, before becoming a clerk in a mill. On 10 May 1920 he married Ethel Simpson Waddington from Sheffield. She was safe and domesticated, and unlikely to taunt or humiliate him about his sexual shortcomings. They moved to Sheffield to be nearer Ethel's family, but Christie began to get in trouble with the police. On 12 April 1921 he was sentenced to three months in prison for stealing postal orders while working as a postman. In January 1923 Christie was briefly imprisoned and put on probation for a year for obtaining money on false pretences and violent conduct. In September 1924 he was given consecutive three- and six-month sentences for larceny. Ethel was shocked and dismayed by her new husband's criminal tendencies. In late 1924 they separated after just over four years of marriage. Ethel moved in with relatives in Sheffield, and Christie decided to make a fresh start in London when he was released.

In London Christie's criminal career continued. Like Haigh his early offences involved dishonesty and stealing, but unlike Haigh some violence occurred in one or two of these apprentice crimes. He also got into the habit of using prostitutes. In May 1929 Christie was living with a prostitute in Battersea, south London when he was arrested for hitting her over the head with a cricket bat. The judge called this 'a murderous attack', a prescient remark. He served six months' hard labour. His last term of imprisonment came in 1933 when he stole the car of a priest he knew and received three months in prison. When he was released Christie was thirty-five years old. He had written to Ethel in Sheffield from prison – they had never divorced – begging her to come back to him and join him in London after he was released. Ethel was bored and lonely, and finally agreed. The stability that Ethel gave him kept Christie away from crime for some time, but his secret use of prostitutes continued when his wife went to visit her family. Like Haigh, he was adept at concealment and living his life in compartments, no doubt a psychological trait stemming from his childhood.

In December 1938 Christie and Ethel rented the run-down ground-floor flat at 10 Rillington Place, Notting Hill. It was cramped even for two people – a living room, a kitchen and a bedroom – although the Christies had the small back garden, where there was a wash house and shared toilet. A near-blind ex-railway worker, Charles Kitchener, lived in the first-floor flat, while the top flat was empty at that time. Christie had been working as a ledger clerk, but he continued to flit from job to job. When Britain entered the war in September 1939 he applied to the Metropolitan Police for work as a special (war reserve) constable – not a fully fledged police officer, but with some powers and a uniform. He should never have got this position due to his criminal record, but because of the wartime chaos and the shortage of able-bodied men, the necessary checks were not made and he was accepted.

He would continue in this post until the end of 1943, and he thrived in it. Just as the Boy Scout uniform had lifted his self-esteem years before, Christie, now in his early forties, loved the power the job gave him, and he became officious and pedantic about the law – this from a man who had served several prison terms. It was not long before he became known in the vicinity of his home as the 'Himmler of Rillington Place', a satirical comparison with the infamous head of Hitler's SS. But Christie was also using his position to associate with petty criminals, sometimes taking bribes to turn a blind eye, and accepting freebies from prostitutes. Part of the job was removing corpses from bombed buildings, and this fed his dark fascination with death – the control he had over the dead. All of this enhanced his sense of status, and his uniform gave him great confidence.

However, all of this was threatened when he began an affair with a younger married woman at Harrow Road police station, where he was based. If his superiors had found out, he would have been dismissed immediately. It is almost incredible to imagine Christie being able to attract younger women, but his new status as a special constable helped and he was a good listener – his patient and attentive manner could be seductive to women used to more masculine men. Christie was also manipulative. The woman's husband was a serving soldier. When he returned home in the middle of 1943, he heard some gossip about his wife, caught them together and beat Christie black and blue. It is difficult to imagine how Christie explained his injuries to Ethel and his superiors, but he probably fabricated some story about his police work. Christie was deeply humiliated by the beating. He had been shown to be physically weak and ineffectual, the image created by his uniform shattered. It may have also been the trigger to what happened next.

In August 1943, just a couple of months after his beating, the violence he hadn't displayed since attacking the prostitute with a cricket bat in 1929 resurfaced in the darkest way possible. Ruth Fuerst was an Austrian nurse who had arrived in London at the age of twenty-one. She was poor, had few friends and worked in a war munitions factory not far from Rillington Place. She also worked part-time as a prostitute, and this is how Christie picked her up. She came back to the flat, as Ethel was visiting relatives in Sheffield. It was a business transaction and it is unknown if Christie used his police uniform to get a discount on this occasion. Christie later told the police and the *Sunday Pictorial* what happened next: 'I got on the bed and had intercourse with her and strangled her with a rope . . . She was completely naked. I tried to put her clothes back on her. She had a leopard skin coat and I wrapped this around her. I took her to the bedroom and put her under the floorboards.'

The contradiction of being 'on the bed' and that he later 'took her to the bedroom' is typical of Christie's statements. He also tried to give the impression it was an impulsive act, but if so would he have had a rope handy? Ruth Fuerst was reported missing, but she was an immigrant who had few friends or acquaintances in London to worry about her disappearance. Before Ethel returned from Sheffield, Christie reburied her on the right-hand side of the garden one night.

Fourteen months later Christie's work colleague Muriel Eady sits in the kitchen of 10 Rillington Place, ready for her catarrh treatment. Christie is calmly explaining how his breathing device works. She trusts and believes him. He has spent weeks building that trust. He gives the end of the tube connected to the glass jar to Muriel, and she begins to sniff, inhaling the strong whiff of Friar's Balsam that will unblock her congested nose. What she does not know is that Christie has secretly attached another tube to the jar, which is connected to the gas point in the wall.

Sniff, sniff. Ahhh . . . Her nose is beginning to run already.

While her eyes are closed, Christie undoes a clip on the second tube, and the Friar's Balsam is gradually diluted by coal gas. Slowly the gas overpowers the balsam. Muriel begins to feel woozy. Her head drops. Christie is smiling weakly. His device is working. The Austrian prostitute had struggled, and he hates to fight. Now he will have Muriel all to himself, at his command. Finally Muriel passes out and slumps down in the deckchair.

Christie wastes no time. He picks her up and, trembling with both her weight and the excitement, he carries her to the bedroom, where Ruth Fuerst had temporarily resided under the floorboards. Once on the bed, Christie lifts up Muriel's skirt and removes her underwear. He decides to leave the rest of her clothes on. Dressing the Austrian prostitute had been an effort. He touches and molests her, has intercourse with her, a salivating vulture descending on his prone prey, at the same time pulling the rope around her neck tighter until she is strangled. Oh, the power, the power. He's not Can't-do-it-Christie any more. He will later explain how he felt: 'Once again, I experienced that quiet, peaceful thrill. I had no regrets.'

After dark, Christie moves Muriel's body into the outside wash house, where it stays for a while, but before Ethel comes back from her brother's in Sheffield he buries Muriel fully clothed in the garden next to Ruth Fuerst. 'I planned it all out very carefully,' Christie later says about Muriel's murder.

Muriel Eady will be reported missing by friends and family, but in the chaos of that summer and autumn's V1 and V2 bombs, it is believed that she may have been killed in an air raid, her body like one of those that Christie had pulled out of the rubble in his police uniform. On her return from Sheffield, Ethel suspects nothing.

Within a few months John Christie will resign from his post as a special constable. Within nine years he will be notorious, a dark tabloid sensation.

CHAPTER
3

2 July 1945

The war in Europe has been over for almost two months. Victory in Europe (VE) Day was on 8 May, festivities, cheering and parades taking place in and around Whitehall in central London. Winston Churchill came out on to the steps of the prime minister's home 10 Downing Street to give his famous V for victory two-fingered salute, cigar in the corner of his mouth. Meanwhile, at 10 Rillington Place in Notting Hill an insignificant man called John Christie has two women buried in the garden, and in nearby Gloucester Road a sociopath called John George Haigh can confidently say that there is no trace of his old friend William 'Mac' McSwan, who has vanished off the very face of the earth. The war in the Pacific against Japan is still struggling on, but in Europe there is a collective sense of relief, especially in London which suffered so badly from air raids. The war is almost over. But in west London violent death is still very much alive.

John George Haigh will later claim that he murdered another between Mac's dispatch and today. She was apparently a middle-aged woman from Hammersmith, but her killing will never be verified and no victim is ever identified. Haigh has also moved into the more up-market Onslow Court Hotel in South Kensington, a short walk from his workshop at 79 Gloucester Road, taking a room there as a long-term resident, although keeping his small room at 38 Queens Gate Terrace. Every pretence has been maintained that Mac is alive and well – but absent. Just five months ago on 6 March Haigh typed a letter to the Amusement Caterers' Association to keep up his victim's membership. Haigh wrote, 'Mr McSwan is not in business at all at present and I am merely keeping his membership alive in his absence.'

Haigh has already made a tidy sum from Mac's disposal, fleecing his old friend's parents and his own former employers, Donald and Amy McSwan, by posing as Mac's middleman while he is in hiding from the army authorities. Much of this money has come from Mac's considerable assets, but the war is over now, and Haigh knows that Mac cannot hide for ever. Sooner rather than later he will have to reappear. Only Haigh knows that this is impossible.

Donald and Amy received a visit from Haigh soon after William disappeared. Haigh used his reassuring charm to explain why Mac had gone into hiding. His parents understood and were pleased that William would not be going to war. So many people had lost sons. They have also received several forged postcards from their son over the last nine months, postmarked Scotland, their trusted ex-employee Haigh making trips to Edinburgh and Glasgow to facilitate the subterfuge. They have no reason to doubt Mac has gone there: as a Scot, it is a natural place to hide. But they don't know that Haigh is a master forger or that he has served prison terms for that very offence. Haigh knows that the end of the war means that he has to act and he has been making preparations for a few weeks. Haigh is as always adaptable to circumstances, his calculating mind working unpaid over-time, and he knows that a larger payday is coming.

William's last letter informs Donald and Amy that William is returning to London, and that they can meet him at Haigh's basement workshop in Gloucester Road. But they must come at night, as William does not want to be seen in public just yet. Please come on 2nd July, Haigh has written in William's handwriting. That night is now here.

It has been a hazy summer's day with a few showers of rain. The sun has finally gone down. The sky over Gloucester Road is approaching darkness as Haigh climbs the steps from his basement workshop at number 79, although the street lamps are on now, the blackout a thing of the past. He walks across the road to the Underground station opposite and, sure enough, Donald, aged seventy, and sixty-five-year-old Amy McSwan are waiting for him, elegantly dressed and distinguished-looking. They are excited at the prospect of seeing their son after ten months. How has he been keeping? Has he lost any weight from his already thin frame? Little do they know that there is nothing of him left, only his name, memory and assets.

Donald and Amy have come from their flat in Claverton

Street, Pimlico, near Victoria. Haigh has been there before – Mac took him there several times to see his parents. Haigh was nervous about talking to them after Mac's murder, but since the postcards and letter have been accepted without question, his irrepressible confidence has returned. After pleasantries, Haigh reassures them that their son is waiting for them. He tells Donald and Amy that it would be better if they came to the workshop separately to arouse as little attention as possible. They understand, and Haigh leads ex-local politician Donald across Gloucester Road while Amy waits outside the still-busy station.

Haigh and Donald McSwan walk down the steps of number 79 and enter the basement workshop, just as Donald's son had in September the previous year. The war was raging then, but although it isn't now, the effects of bombing, rationing and shortages are still visible all around. Haigh shuts the door behind them. The workshop has had one or two additions since Mac was there – Haigh has been refining his technique. There is a steel bathtub, which has been painted to make it more corrosion-resistant, a stirrup pump and some makeshift face masks made of tin. Haigh truly has thought about his method, a professional to the last detail, assiduous about his own health and safety.

Haigh hardly gives Donald time to ask where his son is but hits him on the head from behind with an iron bar known as a blackjack. The elderly Donald goes down immediately. His body is shifted out of view, and then Haigh composes himself, straightening his jacket before going to meet Amy. As she enters the workshop she has no idea that she is the last of her family of three still alive. Haigh knows, after that night's work, that there will be no more questions about Mac's where-abouts, and most importantly there will be nobody to stop him getting his hands on the rest of Mac's property.

Amy is blackjacked just like her husband. After removing valuables, keys and money from the McSwans, he dissects Donald first, having changed into his swimming trunks to avoid bloodstains on his street clothes. Haigh then uses the stirrup pump to fill the bath with acid. Sulphuric is the main component, as before, but Haigh has discovered that adding a quantity of hydrochloric acid speeds up the process. What remains of them goes down the drain in the centre of the room, following their son the previous year. Haigh will later say that he felt no fear or nerves, and that neither Donald nor Amy 'suffered' before they died, although he could not be sure that they were medically dead before dissection began, but they were certainly unconscious. The McSwan family is no more, and Haigh is very pleased with himself. His careful preparations have gone exactly to plan.

The following two days, 3 and 4 July, Haigh lets himself into the McSwans' rented flat in Claverton Street, using their keys, while the McSwans themselves are rapidly vanishing. On both days Haigh leaves notes for the McSwans' landlady, informing her that they have 'gone away to America', and do not know when they will return. Haigh is brazen with confidence now, tying up all loose ends before putting the final part of his plan into action.

By the time Haigh travels north a week later the McSwans are just a memory, but Mac's assets are on his mind. In Carlisle, close to the Scottish border on 16 July, he writes and sends a letter to an old friend saying that he feels at home in the north, perhaps remembering his childhood and youth. Anybody reading the letter could have no idea of his depraved crimes. A true sociopath, Haigh apparently functions perfectly normally, with his immaculate clothes, slick hair and moustache and plausible salesman's swagger, but in his mind he is completely focused on his next move and the pound signs at the end of it. He is getting low on funds, and knows that he has to act swiftly.

Two days later on 18 July in Glasgow, where Mac is supposed to be hiding, Haigh walks into a solicitor's office posing as him and forges his signature expertly on a power of attorney, later reproduced in the *News of the World*: 'BY POWER OF ATTORNEY I William Donald McSwan of Claverton Street London, S.W.1. APPOINT John George Haigh of Thirty-eight Queens Gate Terrace, London S.W.7., and of the Onslow Court Hotel, Queens Gate, London S.W.7., my attorney for me and in my name to execute all or any of the following acts, deeds . . .'

This is duly approved and stamped by the solicitor. Haigh now has control of the McSwan family's possessions and power over three freehold properties in Mac's name in Kent and in Wimbledon, south-west London. A few months later, on 9 October 1945, Haigh forges another deed, this time bearing Amy McSwan's signature, transferring another freehold property in her name to her son William, and therefore to Haigh. In all, from the three murders of the McSwan family, from properties, possessions and gilt-edged securities, Haigh gains between five and six thousand pounds, an enormous sum: in 1945 a Ford Anglia car costs £293 new, an average house £540.

John George Haigh will be in funds for a while now, but this doesn't stop him dabbling in other scams, such as setting himself up as a fake patent liaison officer, starting offices in several towns. He will also later say that in the months following the end of the McSwan family he disposed of a young man called Max from Kensington, but like the woman from Hammersmith he also claims to have murdered, the police will never identify or trace Max. Haigh has gone up in the world now: at least a triple murderer, in funds, living a comfortable life at an expensive hotel and able to leave his sales and bookkeeping job at Hurstlea Products Ltd.

Captain Neville Heath, also known as Lord Dudley, Colonel Armstrong, Bruce Lockhart (a Cambridge blue), Captain Selway MC, Lieutenant Colonel James Cadogan Armstrong, Captain Blyth, Major Danvers, Squadron Leader Walker and Group Captain Rupert Brooke DFC (after the First World War poet) is about to enter the story. Heath is in South Africa, serving in the air force. Younger than Haigh, with matinee idol looks and devastating charm, the term ladykiller could have been invented for him. Soon he will descend on London, checking into a hotel just a ten-minute walk from 10 Rillington Place, where John Christie lives with his wife Ethel and two visitors who never left. Like Haigh and Christie, Neville Heath is heading for tabloid infamy for the terrible crimes he is about to commit.

CHAPTER
4

20 June 1946, Dive Bar at the Falstaff pub, Fleet Street, London

The bar is scattered with people, mostly men, many of them journalists from the nearby newspaper offices: the *Daily Sketch*, *Daily Express*, *Daily Mail* and *Sunday Pictorial* among others. Men in suits with notebooks in breast pockets, many hatted inside despite the warm afternoon, trilbies jauntily angled on heads. This bar and many others are an extension of their offices, where contacts are made and leads found and followed. Everybody knows that most of them won't see sixty, and for some reaching fifty will be a push. Their smoking and drinking will put paid to that, along with unstable lives and unsociable hours, living on their wits. Like bloodhounds they can sense a kill, a story, a scoop, which will give them prestige with their news editors for a few days until the story is forgotten. A week might be a long time in politics, but for these men, and occasionally women, an hour is an eternity.

Propping up the bar, pints of bitter half-empty, rarely half-full. Hard-bitten looks and the infrequent weary smile, perhaps even a punctuated laugh as they chatter and whisper, spread gossip and stories, leads and misleads. There is a dense fog of tobacco smoke, cloying and acrid in the still air. It appears homely and a home from home, but everybody knows the rules here: when it comes to a story, friendship means nothing, the lead everything. The war has been over for more than a year, but austerity still bites on the ravaged streets outside, every bombsite a reminder of Hitler. Bread and meat are still heavily rationed. There has recently been talk that bread rations will be further cut, but now it's thought that might be avoided because of a good wheat crop in America. Some shops sell horse meat, 'No Coupons Required', but many would never serve it at their tables; others do so without telling anyone.

One of the men standing at the bar stands out. Tall and broad, he doesn't slouch like many of the others, some of whom he regales with stories of the war and service as an RAF fighter pilot. Often he carries his flying helmet or goggles, but this afternoon he doesn't. This man with the well-styled dark-blonde wavy hair and sparkling blue eyes, square jaw and cleft chin is called Neville Heath, but he has been known by many other names in his twenty-nine years. He is the life and soul, a man's man also very attractive to women. The hacks and the barman hang on his words – he is used to an audience – but it is unlikely they believe all of his stories. Heath is relaxed and at ease, as he always is, full of charm and grace, moving his fine physique with natural elegance. He is hardly a man in need of Sanatogen nerve tonic food, which is very popular. The mustard-brown sports jacket, grey flannel trousers and RAF tie sit well with this confidence. He is a man who knows who he is. At least it appears so to those around him.

Some customers who can be made out through the cigarette haze still wear their 'demob' suits. Available in many sizes and several styles, as well as the option of sports jacket and trousers, they can be easily spotted. Not that Neville Heath's attire is demob. Everyone can see that his clothes are of the highest quality and entirely suitable for the ex-officer that he is. Heath has already had a skinful that day, his usual routine recently. He frequents many bars in the area and is a mixture of barfly and gadfly, but never drinks alone, as he is a magnet for company. He has a large amount of cash on him today, and this has only increased his confidence. Yesterday a *Daily Mail* journalist gave him the princely sum of thirty pounds to be flown to Copenhagen. Little does the hack know that Heath has no plane, or indeed a commercial flying licence. That same day he had also been drinking with Harry Procter, the *Daily Mail*'s ace reporter (later with the *Sunday Pictorial*), who within a week will be writing about him.

Earlier today Heath had lunch in a small cafe in Theobalds Road. While sitting under a common poster reading 'Don't ask for bread unless you really want it' Heath characteristically struck up a conversation with an attractive young woman. 'Why don't you get yourself dolled up and come out with me this evening?' he asked her. She turned him down, a rare occurrence for Heath. She didn't let strangers in cafes pick her up, no matter how charming and attractive they might be. But Heath was hardly fazed as he already has a date set up for this evening, a young woman with less caution whom he already knows intimately.

Heath finally leaves the Falstaff Dive Bar, saying a cheerful cheerio to his drinking acquaintances. He walks with a military bearing and an athletic confidence. He's a looker, and he knows it. Women look at him in the street. With his charm and cache of RAF stories, he's quite the catch. He is inebriated but shows no sign of it. He walks past a billboard bearing a poster for a film 'COMING SOON', *The Big Sleep*. On it are pictured Humphrey Bogart and Betty Bacall, looking at each other, she wistfully and he with a steely toughness. If Heath had made the effort to glance at the poster of the film based on the Raymond Chandler novel, he might have been interested. Heath is fond of mystery novels, although he tends to prefer British ones. He loves escapism. He has a short attention span and needs constant stimulation. But little does Heath know that he will never be able to see *The Big Sleep* even if he wanted to.

He is on his way to Mayfair to meet an ex-public schoolboy, Leslie Terry, a friend. They will both then head for Knightsbridge, where Heath will meet his date for the evening.

When Heath and Terry arrive at the Trevor Arms in Knightsbridge, Heath's date, Margery Gardner, at thirty-three almost four years older than him, is already there. They first met in April and spent the night together sometime in May, when it later came out they enjoyed some sado-masochistic sex. The Trevor Arms is one of her regular haunts. Margery Aimee Brownwell Gardner is five feet four inches tall with a medium build and dark brown hair, attractive and dressed a little provocatively. She is by no means a prostitute, but she has a bohemian and reckless lifestyle, sometimes sleeping with men soon after meeting them, especially recently since she split up with her husband, a wine salesman, who is back in Sheffield with their child. She is artistic, having written part of a novel, and has appeared as an extra in one or two films. Margery Gardner is broadminded, and Neville Heath is just the kind of company she likes, impulsive and living for today. There is also another reason she likes Heath, and this is sexual. Her life has also become very transient, moving from room to room and boarding house to boarding house, due to financial necessity. That very morning she had to borrow fivepence from a friend for her fare to Knightsbridge.

According to what his friend and companion Leslie Terry later recalled, Neville Heath has drunk an amazing twenty-four pints of beer by the time they arrive at the Trevor Arms that evening. In fact the last pub they visited had run out of beer. The alcohol is beginning to tell a little on Heath now, but at the Trevor Arms he goes on to have four more pints. Heath and Margery Gardner then leave Terry and walk off together to the Normandie Hotel, also in Knightsbridge, where Heath has left his flying helmet. He needs it as he plans to fly the *Daily Mail* journalist to Copenhagen the next day. No doubt his charm will somehow get him a plane.

After recovering his helmet, they have dinner at the Normandie before going on to the Panama Club in South Kensington. It is a classy establishment, and there is a party tonight. Heath is well known at the Panama, as he has frequented it many times over the past few weeks. Heath and Gardner dance and drink until just after midnight, when they leave and hail a taxi. The taxi takes them to nearby Notting Hill, where Heath is booked into the Pembridge Court Hotel in Pembridge Gardens, close to the Underground station. As requested by Heath, the taxi drops them just down the road from the hotel. There is no night porter, and Heath has his own key. Heath and Gardner are so drunk that they have to prop each other up as they walk towards the hotel. The taxi driver is the last person to see Margery Gardner alive. Apart from Neville Heath, that is.

Born into a comfortable middle-class family, Neville George Clevely Heath arrived in the world in 1917 in Ilford on the far outskirts of east London, actually in the county of Essex. His father was a barber by trade, and his mother an imposing woman who was the real power in the family. His early years were spent at a local Catholic school, and it later came out that he was something of a bully there and also sometimes enjoyed being cruel to animals. This is the only early evidence of his later extreme personality, the Mr Hyde to his affable Dr Jekyll side. By his teens the family had moved to leafy suburban Wimbledon in far south-west London, the home of the world-famous tennis tournament. He then went to Rutlish, then a grammar school but operating very much like a public school. Later alumni include the future prime minister John Major, who attended from 1954 to 1959.

Neville Heath was no academic, but he excelled at sports, especially rugby and athletics, and this helped develop the perfect physique he acquired. By his mid-teens he was very good-looking and many thought he would become a film star. He was also very self-assured and this only added to his personality. The comfortable life he led as a schoolboy – playing sports and taking girls to dances – would continue into adulthood, but then of course he had to fund it himself, by any means necessary. The fact is, Heath was never truly to grow up, despite his manly appearance and charm. He left Rutlish at the age of seventeen in 1934, having managed to gain his School Certificate, despite failing some exams. He then worked for a short time in a warehouse packing goods, but this was never going to be enough for the adventurous Heath. He soon enlisted in the Artists' Rifles, a territorial regiment founded in 1859 which had played a notable part in the Boer and First World Wars.

The structure and status of service life appealed to Heath, and he signed up for a short-service commission with the Royal Air Force in February 1936. He trained as an officer cadet at Cranwell, and proved to be a good pilot, something that undoubtedly pleased the image-conscious Heath, as pilots possessed the most glamour among servicemen. But he was soon to begin a wayward and then criminal phase which would continue for the rest of his short life. He was somebody who could have succeeded conventionally if he had applied himself, but something in his personality prevented this.

He was made sports officer at RAF Duxford and stole mess funds while there, although this was not found out until after he had left. Between March and June 1937 Heath went absent without leave from RAF Mildenhall; he was arrested back in

Wimbledon on 22 June 1937. He then escaped and stole – or
'borrowed without permission' – a car owned by an officer,
and there were also rumours that he had flown a plane under
a bridge. Heath wrote to his commander while on the run
offering to resign his commission to 'save dragging the name
of a decent squadron in the mud'. He was clearly criminally
inclined, but there was also a touch of charm and class about
him. He was court-martialled in August that year. On 20
September 1937 Heath was dismissed from the RAF, just
seventeen months after receiving his commission. His criminal career now began in earnest.

He now began to impersonate both real and imaginary
people, a habit that would continue on and off for the
remaining decade of his life. Heath was now twenty, but his
physique and confidence allowed him to pass as older (as
well as enabling him to pose as a Cambridge blue), and he
now moved to Cambridge, where he stayed at the Lion Hotel.
He was now using the name Jimmy Dudley, registering his
addresses as c/o The House of Lords and Trinity College,
Cambridge. He moved on again swiftly. In November 1937
he was arrested and charged with obtaining credit by fraud
at a hotel in Nottingham (the Sherwood Inn) and fraudulently
trying to buy a car from the hotel owner by use of a forged
cheque. By now he was impersonating very grand people
indeed. Jimmy Dudley had become Lord Dudley, who really
existed and was a close friend of the Duke of Windsor (Heath
also pretended to be Lord Nevill at one time). As Francis
Selwyn recounted in his book *Rotten to the Core*, the following
conversation took place in the hotel bar when a man
approached Heath.

'Excuse me, sir. Are you Lord Dudley?'

'As a matter of fact, old man, I am,' said Heath.

'Then I must tell you that I am Inspector Hickman of Nottingham CID.'

'In that case, old man, I am not Lord Dudley,' said Heath.

Heath was lucky. The magistrates gave him two years' probation, putting his criminal acts down mainly to youthful indiscretion. Back in London, Heath managed to stay out of trouble for a short time and in May 1938 even managed to work for two weeks. This was as an assistant in the draper's department of the John Lewis department store in Oxford Street, although he had forged references to get the job. But in July 1938 he was arrested again. This time he had broken into a house in Edgware, north-west London, which belonged to a friend, stealing fifty-one pounds' worth of jewellery, and then accepted the same man's hospitality by staying with him in Brighton. This showed a ruthless streak: friendship obviously meant little when it conflicted with gain. He was also accused of stealing a car, false pretences and forging cheques and a banker's order for twenty-seven pounds' worth of clothes.

Fraud and theft had become Heath's stock in trade. He was sent to borstal for three years, and held at the Hollesley Bay Colony, near Woodbridge in Suffolk, so named because it had previously been a training establishment for 'young colonial gentlemen'. By the time Heath arrived there in 1938, it had been handed over to the Prison Commission, and was undoubtedly a tough environment for offenders. But Heath never served his three years, the outbreak of the Second World War coming to his rescue in September 1939. As a fit

young man with previous pilot training, he joined the Royal
Army Service Corps (RASC).

Heath started in the ranks but on 23 March 1940 he was
commissioned as an officer and sent to the Middle East to
help guard the Haifa–Baghdad pipeline. He was now an
acting captain, a remarkable achievement, from borstal to
responsible officer in six months. This can be explained by
the shortage of manpower, but also undoubtedly by Heath's
ingratiating and charming manner; he was always able to
impress those around him. But his criminally dishonest
tendencies emerged again, made possible by that same charm
and persuasiveness. In July 1941 he was court-martialled and
cashiered by the army and deported back to England on the
Mooltan, a troopship. The charges against him were buying
his brigadier's motor car with a dud cheque before selling it,
and stealing a second army paybook, so that he was paid
double. He had also gone AWOL, during which time he had
used his extra funds to explore Egyptian brothels. It would
later emerge that he had indulged in sado-masochistic acts
in these dens, a fact relevant to later events. Heath had
boasted to a fellow officer (a superior) that he had enjoyed
such acts with two sisters in Cairo. However, everything that
Heath said had to be taken with a very large pinch of salt,
as he was such a good liar.

But Heath never arrived back in England, escaping from
the ship at Durban in South Africa and travelling to
Johannesburg. Ever resourceful, he adopted a new persona:
Captain Selway MC – the decoration awarded for incredible
bravery – of the Argyll and Sutherland Highlanders. In this
guise he even added a limp, no doubt difficult to keep up,

but a useful prop to his role of war hero. One does wonder if Heath had used his looks more conventionally whether he could have been a good actor, but he had already proved himself unable to follow the straight and narrow. His early career bears a jaunty resemblance to that of Eddie Chapman, known as Agent Zigzag, whose war service as a spy redeemed him, making him a lovable rogue. But then of course Chapman never went on to commit the crimes that Heath did. While he was Captain Selway MC, Heath also passed forged cheques again.

Then Heath changed roles yet again. Enlisting in the South African Air Force, he was now James Robert Cadogan Armstrong, a rugby and boxing Cambridge blue, his athleticism again facilitating his new persona. When his record was checked, Heath was found to be an impostor, but as he had worked hard, proved a useful pilot and become popular in the SAAF, he was allowed to remain, another example of his charm working. He flew Tomahawks and Hurricanes in this period, and was to rise to the rank of captain. He also met an heiress to the Pitt-Rivers fortune. The Pitt-Rivers family had been famous for its interest in archaeology and ethnology, and a museum bearing its name still exists in Oxford. Heath married the heiress in February 1942, and money no longer seemed an issue. But the restless Heath would not settle.

Heath's South African Air Force Squadron was then attached to 180 (Bomber) Squadron of the Royal Air Force and posted to RAF Finmere, from where he took part in bombing attacks on the Ruhr in Germany, flying American B-25 Mitchell bombers. The number of missions that Heath flew is debatable because he forged his logbook to make himself seem more impressive and daring, especially to females. Some records show that he only flew for a few hours. What is known for sure is that on 29 October 1944 his plane suffered a hit and caught fire. Heath ordered his crew to bail out and managed to fly the aircraft back behind Allied lines. In the meantime he showed his charitable side, raising money for the Merchant Navy, and the people whom he worked alongside grew very fond of him. Still James Armstrong, Heath was then sent back to South Africa, as the European war was coming to an end.

Back in Durban, Heath was given a twenty-five-pound fine for fraud by magistrates in July 1945. He then posed as Major Danvers, Lieutenant Colonel Graham and Captain Blyth, as well as James Robert Cadogan Armstrong, who was now a colonel with the Order of the British Empire (OBE) and a Distinguished Flying Cross (DFC). The scandal of the magistrates' court trial effectively brought his marriage to an end. He was court-martialled for the third time on 4 December 1945, six charges of conduct prejudicial to good order and military discipline, and wearing decorations without entitlement being brought against him. He was dismissed from the military yet again. In the same month his wife divorced him for desertion. Heath would later say that the divorce traumatised him and led to a darkening of his personality, but again this is questionable.

Heath arrived back in Southampton, England on 5 February 1946 and went to live with his parents in Merton Hall Road in Wimbledon. Just over two weeks later Heath and an unnamed young woman were thrown out of the elegant art deco Strand Palace Hotel in central London. The house

detective had heard a woman's screams and on entering a
room found her naked and tied to the bed with Heath caning
her. Minutes later the detective saw Heath and the woman
leaving with their arms around each other. It had obviously
been a consensual act. In April he was fined ten pounds by
Wimbledon magistrates for wearing decorations and a
uniform to which he was not entitled. For a while during
this period the police watched him as he was suspected of
being a cat burglar.

Donald Thomas relates in his book *Villain's Paradise* that
a photograph was displayed of Heath for years in a Fleet
Street pub. It was a souvenir of perhaps Heath's greatest
confidence trick. In the spring of 1946 Heath conned Prime
Minister Clement Attlee and Foreign Secretary Ernest Bevin
into sharing their official box with him and his crowd at an
international rugby match at Twickenham. The photograph
apparently showed the group smiling, but it cannot be traced
now. This shows how fearless and effective Heath could be.
He had posed as Squadron Leader Walker of the South
African Rugby Union.

This was the period when Heath hovered around pubs and
clubs, staying on and off in various hotels, offering to fly
people abroad for money, borrowing cash and obtaining
funds by dishonesty. He stayed for a while at the Normandie,
and during this time the hotel wall safes were robbed. Heath
may have been involved. The fact that Heath socialised with
Fleet Street journalists at this time is startling, as just weeks
later they would be writing about him and chasing his story.
He may have liked the excitement around them, or just seen
them as potential marks for his piloting scam. As already

mentioned, Heath had no commercial licence or plane at his disposal, but little things like that didn't stop him. He wanted readies and acted impulsively to get them. It was almost as if his life was speeding up. He was becoming more reckless, trying to cram everything in before it was over. He was increasingly showing the impulsiveness of a psychopath, although he was as charming and affable as ever.

On the evening of Saturday, 15 June 1946 Heath met Yvonne Symonds, a woman of nineteen, ten years his junior, at a Women's Royal Naval Service (Wrens) dance in Chelsea. Symonds was temporarily staying at the Overseas Club, but she came from Worthing, Sussex, where her parents still lived. Heath introduced himself to her as Lieutenant Colonel Heath and his charm and assured manner soon impressed. He and Symonds were just one of many dashing demobbed serviceman and attractive young woman couples twirling around the floor, the drink freely flowing as ever. It was a time of war reunion parties, and many ex-servicemen and -women were still spending their war gratuities, a contrast to the tight rationing all around. The long after-party of VE Day the previous year had still not finished that summer.

From the dance Heath took her to a favourite haunt, the Panama Club in South Kensington. She did not stay with him that night, but they spent all Sunday together, and then Heath proposed to her. She accepted and agreed to stay with him that night at the Pembridge Court Hotel in Notting Hill. Heath checked them in as Lieutenant Colonel and Mrs N. G. C. Heath of Black Hill Cottage, Romsey (Hampshire). They were given room 4 and enjoyed the night together. Yvonne Symonds had no interest or penchant for sado-masochism, and Heath made no demands on her in that direction.

Wednesday 19 June 1946, lunchtime

Harry Procter sits in the saloon bar of the City Club just off Fleet Street. He has a strong full face, handsome and with intelligent features, which looks grave when not amused. He is of above-average height and well built, his dark brown hair swept back from his forehead, flicked over and longer on the right side of his head, held in place by Brylcreem. Procter is twenty-nine years old but like most men of his generation can pass for older. His dark brown herringbone tweed jacket gives him gravity. His dark eyes have already seen a great deal, but they are just this side of cynical, although very discerning and shrewd. He can weigh somebody up very quickly and is seldom wrong. One of the key assets he has is the ability to spot the weaknesses of those who do wrong and then goad them into making a confession to him, even if they would never spill everything to the police. He calls these exposures, and they are increasingly becoming his bread and butter, although he actually prefers lighter stories. But crime is where he is making his name, and he is becoming a leading light of Fleet Street's Murder Gang, just like Norman 'Jock' Rae of the *News of the World*.

Harry Procter is getting used to writing about murderers for the *Daily Mail*. His crime scoops are increasing the paper's circulation, and in the intense rivalry between papers he is seen as a key weapon. Lindon Laing, news editor of the *Daily Mail*, who will later also be Procter's boss on the *Sunday*

Pictorial, knows his worth. When the *Daily Express* bought a helicopter to get to stories faster, Laing wasn't fazed. 'The *Express* may have a helicopter, but we've got a Harry Procter,' said Laing. This means something, as Laing has a reputation for deadpan understatement, calling almost everybody he knows Mister no matter how well he knows them. One of Procter's biggest scoops so far was when he tricked his way onto a US battleship and managed to be the only journalist present at a secret meeting between President Harry Truman and King George VI. Procter is tenacious, tough, cunning and very resourceful, and will only suffer fools if it is in his interest to do so. He is a moral man in his private life, but when it comes to getting a story inhabits grey areas.

Procter is also starting to believe that other hacks hate him, jealous of his consistent ability to get big stories. He will write in his 1958 memoirs *The Street of Disillusion* of how it is lonely at the top of Fleet Street, but by then he has become cynical, the title of his book saying it all. In reality, his peers admire him greatly, and just like his friendly rival, Norman Rae of the *News of the World*, Procter is swiftly becoming a legend. Richard Dimbleby reigns on the BBC; Duncan Webb is making a name for himself exposing organised crime, the likes of the London gangsters Jack 'Spot' Comer and Billy Hill; while murder is largely the realm of Norman Rae and Harry Procter. Thousands of readers write to them personally every week, and they are close to being household names.

Harry Procter was born in Leeds, Yorkshire in 1917, making him an exact contemporary of Neville Heath. When he was a teenager he worked in the rat-infested basement of a shoe shop near Leeds City Market, dreaming of being a reporter on Fleet Street, reading as much as he could. His greatest inspiration was *The Street of Adventure* by Philip Gibbs, published in 1909, the title of Procter's own memoirs almost five decades later a homage to this early spur. Gibbs, who had been a major reporter during the First World War, wrote the book as a semi-autobiographical/semi-fictional account of his first steps in journalism in the late nineteenth century, and gave Fleet Street – or Grub Street – a sense of glamour and excitement.

At the age of sixteen Procter himself took his own first step in journalism when he became a reporter on his local paper, the *Armley and Wortley News*. This was the traditional route via provincial newspapers: those with talent and ambition could work up towards London and Fleet Street, and the best of those would flourish there. At eighteen Procter became chief reporter on the *Cleveland Standard* in Redcar, North Yorkshire, and then moved to Middlesbrough's *Northern Echo*. When he was made redundant during cutbacks, it was his first setback. But he was soon a reporter on the *Yorkshire Evening News* back in Leeds, and while there he got a temporary job for a week during his holidays on London's *Daily Mirror*. The *Mirror* then took him on permanently. At the age of twenty-two Procter had arrived in Fleet Street, and his drive had got him there. In 1939, at the outbreak of war, he volunteered for the RAF, before becoming the war correspondent of the *Daily Mail*, for which he still works.

A pint of bitter in front of him, Harry Procter chain-smokes as he talks to the man sitting opposite him. Procter later wrote in his memoirs, 'I liked Neville Heath from the very first beer we had together. He was without doubt one of the most handsome men I ever saw, and he had great personal charm.' But there is something about Heath that Procter finds strange. He wears his leather flying helmet around his neck, and Procter asks him why: 'A doctor does not carry his stethoscope with him when he goes for a drink.' Heath's reply is unknown, but we know that it is part of his persona as an ace pilot. Procter is meeting Heath because he has lent the considerable sum of twenty-five pounds to a colleague on the *Daily Mail* so that the colleague can pay Heath to fly him to Copenhagen that Friday. The colleague wants Procter to OK 'Colonel' Heath. Little do Procter or his colleague know that Heath has a string of fraud convictions.

That evening Harry Procter bumps into Neville Heath again, this time in the Nag's Head on Kinnerton Street in Knightsbridge, where coincidentally John George Haigh also sometimes drinks. It is incredible to think that Heath and Haigh knew each other and probably stood at this bar together, even though Haigh had a low opinion of Heath's abilities, as we shall see. Heath buys Procter a pint of bitter, his usual poison, and they stand at the bar drinking and chatting. Then the barman calls Heath to the telephone. He is in pubs so much that he gives their numbers out to contacts. When he comes back from the telephone, Heath tells Harry Procter that he has just spoken to a woman who has agreed to go out with him the next evening. Heath is in a hurry to leave now and has to decline Procter's offer of a drink in return, but before he leaves they arrange to meet again at the home of a friend of Procter in Stanmore, Middlesex that Saturday, so well have they got on.

Harry Procter does not know that Heath's date for the next night is called Margery Gardner, or that he will be writing about Heath and Gardner for the next few months. For her part, Margery Gardner, when she arranges that date with Heath, probably knows it is going to be another wild night out, followed by extreme sex, which both of them enjoy. But like most people Margery Gardner has limits, whereas Neville Heath does not.

21 June 1946

The Pembridge Court Hotel is a family-run business, a detached stucco villa built in 1859 in the Italianate style then popular, classy and elegant. Notting Hill Gate Underground station is just a short walk away. The hotel has nineteen rooms for guests spread over four floors, and there is also a basement. Grand, the white hotel towers above the entrance, the Georgian windows and period features adding to the impression. Heath still occupies room 4, where he entertained his 'fiancée' Yvonne Symonds the previous Sunday night. There are three other rooms very close to his. Nobody saw Heath and his female companion Margery Gardner return last night after midnight. Heath has his own key, and he let them in, both of them almost falling-down drunk.

Mrs Alice Wyatt runs the Pembridge Court with her father-in-law. It is a very warm day, and the windows in the lobby are open to let in some air. Alice Wyatt is getting ready for the weekend, which is due to be busy. It is just after two o'clock in the afternoon. She carries out her normal routine but wonders when Colonel Heath will appear. His good looks have made an impression on Mrs Wyatt, who thinks he's dishy. It's true he usually sleeps late – he's not a breakfast-taker – but not this late. Alice Wyatt finally gives her chambermaid instructions to go up and clean his room, reminding her to knock first.

The chambermaid duly goes up to room 4 with her cleaning materials. She knocks on the door. No answer. And again. No response. She turns the handle and pushs the door open. All is quiet inside. The blinds are still down, but shafts of sunlight penetrate the room from where they don't fully cover the windows. Then she sees something on one of the twin beds. Somebody is lying on it, face down. When the chambermaid looks closer, she sees that the person has their face buried in a pillow. Then she sees the naked back of a woman with deep marks and scars all over it. The woman's tangled hair is saturated in blood. The chambermaid runs from the room, calling for Mrs Wyatt. There is no sign of Neville Heath.

Alice Wyatt rushes upstairs, and on reaching the room turns on the light. This reveals some of the woman's injuries but not the full sadistic horror of the mutilations. There are heavy bloodstains all over the sheets and on the floor around the bed. She also sees that the woman's legs are tied together. Alice Wyatt almost vomits, but she gathers herself and telephones for the police. Sergeant Averill of F Division (Notting Hill) arrives within a very short time. He calls for senior backup, Superintendent Cherrill and Inspector Symes. By this time the identity of Margery Gardner has been established from her wartime identity card found in the room, and a solicitor who knew her later confirms this.

It is Inspector Symes who signs the fingerprint report (declassified in 1999) and gives a brief description of the woman and the time of the discovery of her body, which is given as 2.30 p.m. but was undoubtedly a little earlier. The divisional surgeon is also called. Photographs of the body are taken from all angles and the room swept for fingerprints. Bloodstains are also discovered under the covers of the other bed. The injuries are considered so serious that the Home Office pathologist and lecturer in forensic medicine at Guy's Hospital, Dr Keith Simpson, is called to the scene. Simpson is arguably now Britain's number-one pathologist, as Sir Bernard Spilsbury is ill and will commit suicide on 17 December 1947.

Dr Keith Simpson finds that Margery Gardner's body is still warm, the room temperature being sixty-three degrees Farenheit, while her vaginal temperature is eighty-four degrees F. He judges that she died at about midnight or in the very early hours of the morning. This means that she was killed not long after arriving in room 4, as Gardner and Heath arrived at around 12.15 a.m.

Dr Simpson's post-mortem report on thirty-three-year-old Margery Gardner is gruesome reading. This very experienced pathologist will later describe her injuries as 'appalling'. Simpson concludes that the flagellation started off as consensual, but then the killer escalated into frenzied beating and then mutilation. There are deep teeth marks all over the breasts and her nipples are almost totally bitten off. Both the front and back of her body is torn and bruised, and there is also heavy bruising on her face and throat. There are no less than seventeen purple scars showing a criss-cross pattern.

Simpson says that a woven whip is likely to have made these deep marks. There are nine lash marks on her back between the shoulder blades, in the small of her back and on her buttocks. Six marks cover the right side of the front of her body – on the breast, chest and abdomen. There are also two lash marks on the head, over both eyes. Marks are also present on Margery Gardner's wrists, which indicate that her hands were also tied, but they are not tied when she is found, unlike her feet. The most brutal wound is to her vagina, which is seven inches in length, a long object having been thrust up into the wall of the womb and turned violently. Most of the blood undoubtedly poured from this wound.

The most disturbing of Dr Simpson's findings is that all of these injuries (including the deep vaginal wound) were inflicted while Margery Gardner was still alive. The pain would have been absolutely excruciating, and she might have passed out, but this cannot be said for sure. Simpson puts the eventual cause of death as suffocation. She was gagged (obviously to stifle her cries of pain and for help) but the gag has been removed by the killer, and this is not thought to have caused her death. It is likely that suffocation was brought about by her head being pressed hard into a soft object like a pillow, exactly as she was found. Neither the details of her injuries nor the cause of death by suffocation are given to the press.

Reporters and press photographers are beginning to gather outside the hotel, as there has been a tip-off that something major has happened. They watch as an undertaker and his assistant pull up in a hearse and then carry an unvarnished coffin into the hotel and later out again. On the opposite side of Pembridge Gardens, behind the press, a group of neighbours stand, waiting for news of what has happened so close to their homes.

The murder of Margery Gardner is the work of a sexual sadist. The barbarity of the murder is probably the worst seen in Britain since Jack the Ripper almost sixty years earlier. Heath is not such a charming rogue any more, but a very dangerous and sick man.

Harry Procter coincidentally lived just round the corner from the Pembridge Court Hotel, another strange connection between Heath and the *Daily Mail* journalist. It should also be remembered that they had been drinking together in Fleet Street, near Procter's workplace, and in Knightsbridge, but not in Notting Hill. These connections would help Procter when he was chasing the scoop on Heath.

In *The Street of Disillusion*, published twelve years later, Procter recounted how he had discovered that a significant murder had occurred so close to where he shared a flat with a newspaper colleague. He wrote that he had been walking home in the evening when he saw the gaggle of reporters still grouped outside the Pembridge Court Hotel. When he asked Sydney Brock, a fellow reporter whom he knew well, what had happened, Brock replied, 'Looked like a murder. But it turns out to be an abortion.' Abortions were of course illegal at the time and performed in anonymous residential streets by bent doctors and unqualified charlatans. The case of John Christie of Rillington Place – just a ten-minute walk from the Pembridge Court Hotel – provides an example.

But then Procter wrote that he went into one of his local

pubs, the Sun and Splendour, where a policeman he knew was drinking. The policeman asked Procter if he was covering the murder, and Procter replied that it wasn't a murder but an abortion. To which his policeman friend is recorded as responding, 'Then it's the queerest abortion I ever heard of. The dead woman has seventeen ugly whip-marks on her back. And her ankles are tied with a handkerchief.'

Harry Procter had been in Oxford that day, working on a story about cat cruelty – instead of the human variety to be found in Notting Hill – and so had been out of the loop that day, otherwise he would surely have been on to the murder more quickly. The evening editions of the newspapers were reporting it as a botched abortion, but the information his police contact, a reliable source, gave him made Procter follow up the story, using his contacts to full effect. As Procter wrote, 'An hour later I phoned the *Daily Mail* with the greatest crime scoop of the year. I had the full, and the first, story of the most sadistic murder of the century. I dictated.' The night editor on the *Daily Mail* was not convinced of the accuracy of Procter's story, saying that the rest of Fleet Street and the Press Association were still calling it a failed abortion. It was with some trepidation that Procter's story was allowed through, after he had fought for it to be accepted. Within days, he was the toast of Fleet Street.

At this stage Procter had no idea that Heath was in any way involved or had been staying so close to where he lived. It might be remembered that Procter had arranged to meet Heath the following day, Saturday, at their mutual friend's house in Stanmore, Middlesex. Procter went there as arranged, and unsurprisingly Heath did not turn up. When the friend said that he would telephone Heath, and that he was staying in Notting Hill near where Procter lived, the reporter apparently made the connection. All of the newspapers were following up, sensing a big story, and it was now widely known as a murder, thanks to Procter's scoop. Procter called the police, who interviewed him and his friend in Stanmore. They gave the police everything they knew about Neville Heath, including a detailed physical description.

The next day, 23 June, the *Sunday Pictorial* national tabloid carried a piece on the hunt for Margery Gardner's murderer on the second page. Headlined 'YARD IN SEARCH OF "SQUARE-FACE"', a reference to Heath's prominent square jaw, it gave his correct full name but his age as twenty-seven, two years younger than he was. He was physically described as '5ft 11in tall, fresh complexion, fair hair, blue eyes and square face'. The police had decided not to release a photograph of Heath to the press, as it was thought it could prejudice any future trial. There would be criticism of this decision as events developed. It also stated that he had a 'military walk' and was 'known to frequent good-class hotels'. Heath was described as being a member of the Caterpillar Club, a select group of pilots who had saved their own lives by parachute jumps, which indeed Heath had. It was also reported that he had taken money from 'a passenger' – actually the *Daily Mail* journalist to whom Procter had lent most of the money – to fly him to Copenhagen and that the home of Heath's parents in Wimbledon was under police observation.

Regarding Margery Gardner, the *Pictorial* said that her mother, aged seventy, was looking after the victim's two-year-old child in Sheffield, and that her estranged husband had visited Notting Hill police station the previous day. The paper had interviewed a 'close friend' of Margery Gardner: 'Margery was living on her own, but was on friendly terms with her husband. She told me the day before she died that she had no money in the world. She said she particularly wanted some because she was to meet a man later and they were going to a party.' Also interviewed was Mrs Eva Cole, the landlady of the Nag's Head in Kinnerton Street, Westminster, where Gardner had been a regular and where Harry Procter had been drinking with Heath the previous Wednesday evening when Heath took the call from Gardner arranging the date that would end in her death. Mrs Cole said of Margery Gardner, 'She had one of the sweetest natures I have ever known.'

Divisional Detective Inspector Reginald Spooner was soon leading the murder hunt for Heath. He was no ordinary policeman, having just left MI5, in which he had served during the war. Spooner had brought back William Joyce, known as Lord Haw-Haw, from Germany the previous year. The American-born Joyce had been hanged just over six months earlier on 3 January 1946 at Wandsworth Prison, for treason. He had worked for the Germans throughout the war, broadcasting pro-Nazi and anti-Allied propaganda.

Superintendent Barratt, who was in charge of the district, assisted Spooner in the murder investigation. Identifying Heath had been automatic, as uncharacteristically he had used his own name to sign in at the Pembridge, perhaps an indication that there was no premeditation. DI Spooner and his team soon accumulated details about Neville Heath and his actions over the previous few days. They also built a picture of his criminal past, and his fraud convictions on file at Scotland Yard's Criminal Records Office helped that task. As the police discovered more about Neville Heath, their certainty that he was the killer only increased.

Heath may have only previously been a petty criminal and fraudster with a spell in borstal and no recorded acts of violence, but there was something in the impulsiveness and cunning he had always displayed that interested the police. The injuries inflicted on Margery Gardner were horrific, and the worst that any of the officers had seen – out of character for a fraud merchant, surely? But there was an increasing realisation that Heath was a Jekyll and Hyde character, an insight that the newspapers were soon to latch on to.

Spooner and his team began interviewing witnesses, building up a picture of Margery Gardner and Neville Heath that night. First they spoke to Alice Wyatt at the Pembridge Court Hotel and asked her if anyone had heard any screaming or cries for help during the night. She said that nobody had, even though there were three rooms close to Heath's. However, a door had been heard slamming at about 1.30 a.m. Could this have been Heath leaving? But if it was, where was he all night? The occupants of those rooms confirmed her answer. The fact that Margery Gardner had been gagged obviously accounted for no cries being heard, but the actual violence must have made some noise too.

A civil servant, Iris Humphrey, who had known Margery Gardner for eight years, was interviewed next. Mrs Humphrey had seen Margery on the night she was murdered, Thursday 20 June, in the Panama Club, South Kensington, sitting with a very good-looking man who fitted Heath's description. Further interviews at the Panama Club confirmed Heath's identity. He was described as tall and heavily built with piercing blue eyes, an infectious smile which showed perfect white teeth and a jutting square jaw and well-defined chin. For a confidence man, and now also killer, it was Heath's bad fortune to be so recognisable: the looks that had entranced women were now working against him. The police began to build a picture of his sexual history, discovering that he had had numerous conquests, often making promises of marriage to get what he wanted, and that he had been ejected from a hotel for caning a screaming young woman just weeks earlier. The jigsaw was piecing together. Spooner became even more firmly convinced that this cad was their killer.

Another witness the police spoke to was the taxi driver who had dropped Heath and Gardner near the Pembridge Court Hotel, who said that the last he had seen of them Heath had had his arm around Gardner's waist, and they were walking towards the hotel, very drunk.

The detectives knew that they had to pick up Heath quickly, as he was obviously a sadist who would murder to satisfy his cravings. Every unassigned police officer in London was employed in the search, so deep was the fear that he would strike again. Within a week it was estimated that 50,000 police all over the country were searching for Heath. They had no idea where he was – in London, elsewhere in the country, or if he had got hold of a plane and flown to the continent – but they had to get him.

CHAPTER
5

Neville Heath left the Pembridge Court Hotel on Friday morning, leaving the lifeless and mutilated body of Margery Gardner in room 4. He took his suitcase with him, which contained items connected with her murder, and went to Victoria railway station, later saying that he had a cup of coffee – he explained that it was too early for breakfast! – at the Grosvenor Hotel, also in Victoria. From there he took a train to Brighton and then went on to Worthing, a little further along the Sussex coast. There could only be one reason for Heath to go there: to see Yvonne Symonds, who had spent the night with him in room 4 a few days earlier.

Heath was running low on money. In his memoirs Harry Procter said that Heath telephoned him at the *Daily Mail* offices from Surrey while he was on the run, begging for a loan of fifty pounds, and they agreed to meet. Procter said that he immediately told Scotland Yard about the rendezvous, and then went to keep it in his car. According to Procter, when he arrived two plain-clothes policemen arrested him, as he was of a similar build and looked a little like Heath. If this is true, perhaps Procter got Surrey mixed up with Sussex, as there is no record of Heath being in Surrey while on the run.

When he arrived in Worthing, Heath checked into the Ocean Hotel. The newspapers, prompted largely by Harry Procter's piece in the Daily Mail on Saturday, would splash on the murder that Sunday, but Margery Gardner still lay undiscovered when Heath arrived at the Ocean. Heath then telephoned Symonds and invited her to lunch at the hotel. She later said that he had seemed very 'normal' and relaxed that afternoon.

They met again the next morning. Having seen Procter's story in the Daily Mail, Heath told Symonds that he was 'indirectly' connected with the murder but gave no indication that he knew Procter. He told Symonds that the woman's body had been found in the very room they had shared on their first night together on 16 June and that he would fill her in more about this 'connection' later, but first he had to meet her parents. He charmed them, as he charmed everyone he met. That evening Heath and Symonds had dinner and danced at the Blue Peter Club in nearby Angmering.

It was there that Yvonne Symonds pressed Heath on what he knew about the murder. The story that he gave her absolved him of all blame for the crime and concealed the fact that he had been with another woman. He told her in his ingratiating way that a man had approached him and asked if he could borrow the room to entertain a woman (Gardner), and that he had given the man the key. In a later version, which he gave to the police, Heath said that he had given the key to Margery Gardner for her to make some money by entertaining a male friend. Also, that the agreement was that if he returned in the early hours Heath himself could spend the rest of the night with her. Of course Yvonne Symonds would not have liked the second version, but in any event neither of them was true and there were witnesses (at the Panama Club and the taxi driver) to what actually happened.

Heath went further. He told her that 'Inspector Barratt of Scotland Yard' (in fact a superintendent) had been in touch with him about the matter, and that Barratt had taken him to see the victim's body, which Heath described as 'a gruesome sight'. He added that it must have been the work of 'a sexual maniac' – a glimpse of self-awareness. Heath then said that a poker had been thrust up inside the woman, and that he knew that this was the cause of death. 'Inspector' Barratt, on the other hand, Heath said, was of the view that the woman had been suffocated. Only the police, the pathologist Dr Keith Simpson and the killer himself knew these facts. Heath was the latter, and what he said to Symonds would later add to the evidence against him. However, it is a mark of his plausible manner that Symonds swallowed this story that evening.

But the next morning, Sunday, the murder was all over the newspapers and, as we have seen, the *Sunday Pictorial* was one of the papers that named Heath and gave his description, appealing for information as to his whereabouts. Yvonne Symonds saw the papers and spoke to her parents, and they were of course very concerned. She then telephoned Heath at the Ocean Hotel, explaining that her parents were very worried about his name being connected with a murder.

Heath told her that he was taking a car to London in order to sort it all out with the police and would telephone her later that evening to tell her what had happened. Yvonne Symonds never spoke to Neville Heath again, and the next time she saw him was in court.

Heath knew now that he could not stay in Worthing, as Yvonne's parents would eventually tell the police of his whereabouts. But before he left, Heath wrote a letter to Superintendent Barratt at Scotland Yard, this time giving him the rank of chief inspector.

Sir,

I feel it to be my duty to inform you of certain facts in connection with the death of Mrs Gardner at Notting Hill Gate. I booked in at the hotel last Sunday, but not with Mrs Gardner, whom I met for the first time during the week. I had drinks with her on Friday evening, and while I was with her she met an acquaintance with whom she was obliged to sleep. The reasons, as I understand them, were mainly financial. It was then that Mrs Gardner asked if she could use my hotel room until two o'clock and intimated that if I returned after that, I might spend the remainder of the night with her. I gave her my keys and told her to leave the hotel door open. It must have been almost 3 a.m. when I returned to the hotel and found her in the condition of which you are aware. I realised that I was in an invidious position, and rather than notify the police, I packed my belongings and left. Since then I have been in several minds whether to come forward or not, but in view of the circumstances I have been afraid to. I can give you a description of the man. He was aged approx. 30, dark hair (black), with small moustache. Height about 5' 9" slim build. His name was Jack and I gathered he was a friend of Mrs Gardner of some long standing. I have the instrument with which Mrs Gardner was beaten and am forwarding this to you to-day. You will find my fingerprints on it, but you should also find others as well.

N. G. C. Heath

Heath never did send anything to the police, and this was probably because there were no other fingerprints on the 'instrument', which was still in his suitcase. We also know that Heath had not first met Margery Gardner the previous week, but two months earlier, in April. The invention of the mystery man Jack and the detailed physical description show the creative imagination which had enabled Heath to carry out his many impersonations.

When he left Worthing, Heath headed by train to Bournemouth, further west on the south coast of England. There seems no special reason why he chose that place, but he may have thought it would be easier for him to blend in and avoid detection in a busy seaside town in early summer. When he arrived at Bournemouth West station on that Sunday evening, 23 June 1946, he deposited the suitcase containing the murder items at the cloakroom and was given a left-luggage ticket. He then checked in at the Tollard Royal Hotel, on the West Cliff overlooking the sea, another classy hotel. He chose as his new persona Group Captain Rupert Brooke, inspired by the First World War poet who had died young, a romantic flourish typical of Heath. He was given room 71, but four days later, on 27 June, he asked to be moved as his room did not have a gas fire and was relocated to room 81 on the second floor. Heath would later say that he wanted a gas fire as he was considering committing suicide, but there is no firm evidence of this.

Heath only had the clothes that he stood up in, it seems. He apparently wore the same grey flannel trousers, brown sports jacket and shirt for his entire thirteen-day stay there. He was low on money by now, and it is unlikely that he would ever have been able to pay for his room, but of course Heath was used to ducking and diving out of hotels and situations – his whole adult life had consisted of it – and this was no different, except that he was for the first time on the run for a hanging offence.

The newspapers continued to report on the hunt for him, but the police had still not released a picture to the press, the thinking being that it could jeopardise any conviction in a trial. So Heath managed to stay free, although he was scarcely inconspicuous. He was chatty with the other guests, often being seen drinking in the hotel bars (his drinks almost always went on his bill) and going out to dances. He even struck up a friendship with the hotel night porter. Heath was irrepressible and showed no signs of strain during this time, probably because he was a psychopath.

It was on Wednesday 3 July, ten days after Margery Gardner's murder, that Heath met an ex-Wren called Doreen Marshall on the promenade. He later said in a police statement that he had met Marshall and her friend (whom he had spoken to at a dance) out walking that morning and that after her friend had left, he invited Doreen Marshall to tea that afternoon at the Tollard Royal. He saw her on the promenade again at 2.45 p.m. and they walked back to his hotel together for tea at 3.45. After enjoying each other's company, he invited her back to the Tollard Royal for dinner with him that evening. She accepted.

Doreen Marshall was in Bournemouth recovering from a nasty bout of flu. Like Yvonne Symonds, she was nineteen years old, ten years younger than Heath, and 5 feet 9 inches tall, and photographs show that she was a real beauty, with dark wavy fashionably styled hair and very attractive features. She was from Pinner, Middlesex. As arranged, she returned to the Tollard Royal that evening, Heath saying in his police statement that he saw her arrive on foot – although in fact she had taken a taxi from her own hotel, the Norfolk – and they had dinner together at 8.15 p.m. Marshall was wearing a yellow camel hair coat, a black dress and an imitation pearl necklace, and she was carrying a handbag. After dinner they sat talking in the hotel lounge, going into the 'writing-room' at about 10 p.m., where the night porter (Heath's new friend) served them with drinks. As on the night of Margery Gardner's murder, Heath drank heavily.

In his police statement, which of course must be read with caution, Heath said that during their conversation Doreen Marshall told him that 'she was considering cutting short her holiday in Bournemouth and returning home on Friday instead of Monday'. He also said that she mentioned two

American men, one of whom she had met in Bournemouth
and taken her out, but that she had gone off him, and another
called Pat, to whom she had been 'unofficially engaged' some
time before. He added, 'At 11 p.m. Miss Marshall suggested
going away, but I persuaded her to stay a little longer. At
about 11.30 p.m. the weather was clear, and we left the hotel
and sat on a seat near the hotel overlooking the sea.' In a
characteristic disarming tactic, Heath told the police when
giving his statement that all times were approximate as he
didn't have a watch.

This was not how the night porter remembered that
evening. He told the police that Doreen Marshall looked pale
and somewhat distressed when he served them drinks in the
writing-room. Did Heath proposition her, pressuring her to
spend the night in his room? Did Doreen detect something
strange about Heath, or even suspect that he could be the
man wanted by the police? This will never be known. It is
known that Doreen Marshall pulled another hotel guest aside
and asked them to get her a taxi, but Heath told the guest
not to bother, as he would walk her back to the Norfolk.

A little after midnight they left the Tollard Royal Hotel,
walking into the night. On their way out Heath turned to
the night porter, saying, 'I'll be back in half an hour,' to
which Doreen Marshall said, 'No, in quarter of an hour.'

Thursday, 4 July 1946. 4.30 a.m.

The night porter of the Tollard Royal Hotel is confused, as
Group Captain Rupert Brooke has apparently still not
returned. He decides to check on him. He goes up to the

second floor and along to room 81. After a quiet knock, he turns the door handle and peers into the room. There is Brooke, sleeping soundly in his bed. The night porter notices that Brooke's shoes, which have not been put outside to be cleaned and are just inside the door of the room, are heavily covered in sand. He closes the door, wondering how the group captain managed to get back into his room without him noticing.

Later that morning, when Rupert Brooke appears downstairs, he shares the fun of his practical joke on the night porter with other hotel staff. He reveals that he got in by using a builder's ladder outside the hotel to reach the first floor, and then pulled it up after him to reach his room on the second floor. Brooke doesn't tell the night porter himself until that evening. How they laugh. Brooke is as relaxed and charming as ever, but there are two key differences about him this evening. He is wearing a scarf (a pilot's silk escape scarf with a map of Germany on the inner lining in case of being shot down) tightly around his neck. Also, he surprises the barman by paying for his drinks in cash.

On Saturday, 6 July Mr Relf, manager of the Tollard Royal Hotel received a telephone call from his opposite number at the Norfolk Hotel. The latter had also called the police, saying that one of his guests had not been seen for three days. The manager of the Norfolk asked Mr Relf if he knew anything about a Doreen Marshall from Pinner, as she was believed to have dined with one of the Tollard Royal's guests that Wednesday evening. It wasn't long before Mr Relf was informed that Group Captain Rupert Brooke had indeed dined with a female companion that evening. When Relf asked Heath if his guest had been a Doreen Marshall from Pinner, he laughed. 'Oh no. I've known that lady for a long while, and she certainly doesn't come from Pinner!'

Relf accepted this but told Heath that he should make contact with the Bournemouth police to rule himself out of their investigation into Doreen Marshall's disappearance. Heath agreed to do so, and indeed soon telephoned the police station, but when he asked to speak to the officer in charge of the case, was informed that the officer was out of the station just then. Heath agreed to call back, and telephoned at 3.30 p.m. that afternoon, speaking to Detective Constable Souter, in charge of the case. DC Souter asked him to come into the station to take a look at the photograph he had of Doreen Marshall, just to make doubly sure. Heath arrived at Bournemouth police station at 5.30 p.m.

Heath looked at the photograph and agreed that it was of the young woman he had had dinner with at his hotel, knowing that many witnesses there, especially the night porter, could confirm this. Heath said that Doreen Marshall had told him she was going to go away with an American boyfriend, a GI, a story he would contradict very soon. DC Souter accepted this and thanked Group Captain Rupert Brooke for his cooperation. Heath was just about to leave the station when something very spooky happened. Into the station walked an older man with none other than Doreen Marshall. Or so Heath thought.

DC Souter did not fail to notice that the blood drained from Heath's face when he saw the pair. The woman was in fact Doreen Marshall's sister and almost her spitting image, and the man their father, coming to see how the inquiry was going. Heath swiftly regained control of himself and was introduced to them both. He was back to his relaxed self, so relaxed that he loosened his scarf. DC Souter immediately saw two scratch marks on his neck, the reason he had taken to wearing it. This aroused Souter's suspicions, and while Heath and the Marshalls exchanged pleasantries, he flicked through the 'wanted' photographs and descriptions issued to all police stations. Souter realised that Rupert Brooke bore a marked resemblance to Neville Heath and asked him if he was Heath, to which the group captain replied calmly that he was not.

But DC Souter was now almost certain that Brooke was Heath, and managed to keep him at the station completing a statement about Doreen Marshall's dinner with him until a senior officer, Detective Inspector George Gates, got back just after 6.30 p.m. DI Gates spoke to Brooke/Heath in an interview room. When he was searched, four pounds and ten shillings were found in his pockets, the remains of the proceeds of pawning Doreen Marshall's crystal fob watch for three pounds and her ring for five pounds the previous day, it would later be revealed. Heath was then told that he was to be detained for further questioning. He was only wearing his shirt and flannel trousers, and as the evening was setting in said that he was getting cold and asked if he could go and get his sports jacket from the Tollard Royal. DI Gates went to get the mustard-brown jacket himself. When he returned, and the jacket was searched, it was immediately obvious why Heath wanted to get his hands on it. There was the return part of a Bournemouth–London railway ticket, later proved to be Doreen Marshall's, as well as one artificial pearl from the necklace she was wearing on the night she disappeared. Also in a pocket was Heath's 23 June left-luggage ticket from Bournemouth railway station. The contents of the slightly battered hard leather suitcase told the terrible story of the murder of Margery Gardner. There was a leather riding whip with a criss-cross weave and a plaited thong, the weapon that had left the seventeen deep lash marks. The leather had worn away at the end of the switch and wires were exposed. There was still some dried blood on the switch, although there had been some attempt to clean it. There were also items of clothing: a navy-blue scarf made of wool, which was bloodstained, as was a blue neckerchief. The scarf also had hairs on it which were later found to belong to Margery Gardner. Finally, there was a hat, a mackintosh and a few other pieces of clothing, all marked with the name Heath. No wonder Group Captain Rupert Brooke had been anxious to dispose of the left-luggage ticket.

It was not until a quarter to ten that DI Gates told Heath he knew his true identity and that Metropolitan Police officers were on their way from London to interview him. Heath, now tired and apparently resigned to his predicament, remained calm. 'Oh, all right,' he said. Police officers were now also searching room 81 of the Tollard Royal Hotel. Yet more evidence was gathered from there, this time relating to Doreen Marshall. In a dressing-table drawer a dirty, blood-stained handkerchief was found with a tight knot in it. There were several hairs enmeshed in that knot that belonged to Marshall. The inference was that she had been murdered, just like Margery Gardner. But where was her body?

Although Divisional Inspector Reg Spooner and members of his team had not yet arrived from London, Heath must have known that the game was up, although he would still deny the murder of Margery Gardner and that he had 'done' anything to Doreen Marshall. At 11.30 p.m. he began to write out a statement, which would take him until 2.45 a.m. the following morning. It started, 'I, Neville George Clevely Heath, lately residing at the Tollard Royal Hotel, Bournemouth, hereby state . . .' In it he related how he had met Doreen Marshall and the story of her two American friends, already mentioned. He wrote that, after they had sat talking on a bench, 'I left her at the pier and watched her cross the road and enter the gardens.' He was clever, inventing a reason for her disappearance, saying that he had asked if he could see her the following day (Thursday 4 July), but she had said she would be busy and would call him on the Sunday (7 July). Then he wrote something very cunning, but also despicable: he 'thought' he had seen Doreen Marshall walking into a shop, Bobby's Ltd, on Thursday morning. This was the morning after they had left the Tollard Royal together just after midnight.

Meanwhile, DI Spooner had arrived from London. The Bournemouth police briefed him on the developments in the Margery Gardner case (the suitcase) and about the Doreen Marshall disappearance inquiry, including the bloody hand-kerchief found in Heath's room. Spooner knew it didn't look good for Doreen Marshall and he was probably now looking at a double murderer in Neville Heath. The newspapers were also aware of Heath's detention, and on Sunday, 7 July the *Sunday Pictorial* ran the small headline 'HEATH: NEW YARD MOVE' over a piece stating he was in custody in Bournemouth.

Spooner did not come face to face with Heath until 5.20 a.m. on Monday, 8 July. Heath admitted his real identity and said that he had been at the Pembridge Court Hotel but had not murdered Margery Gardner and that the whip in the suitcase was the one he was going to send to Superintendent Barratt. He then said that he was tired. 'I'll make a statement after I've had some sleep.' Heath was taken by car to London later that morning, and that evening DI Spooner of F Division charged him with the murder of Margery Gardner. 'I have nothing to say at the moment,' Heath said.

Monday, 8 July 1946, Branksome Chine, Bournemouth

Just west of Bournemouth town centre, near the West Pier, the gardens in the small river valley (known locally as a chine) are beginning to fill with holidaymakers and dog-walkers. A young woman, Miss Evans, is walking her black spaniel, as she does here most mornings. It is going to be another warm day, and the dispersing fluffy clouds are giving way to blue sky. It is about a mile from the Tollard Royal Hotel, which lies to the east. Miss Evans takes her usual route with her dog, up a winding path. But then she sees something unusual. On the other side of the landscaped path she sees a large swarm of flies excitedly circling some rhododendron bushes. After watching the flies for over a minute she shrugs and continues her walk.

But later that day Miss Evans reads a newspaper account about the disappearance of Doreen Marshall, aged nineteen. She has dinner with her father that evening and tells him what she has seen. Mr Evans asks his daughter to take him to the spot on Branksome Chine, which she does, and they arrive back at the bushes just after eight o'clock. The flies are still swarming on the light summer evening. Mr Evans goes into the bushes to investigate, and what he sees confirms his worst fears but also unsettles him a great deal. They leave the spot and immediately alert the police, who arrive at about 8.30 p.m.

It was the body of Doreen Marshall, completely naked except for her left shoe, although her black dress, underwear and yellow camel hair coat are draped over her, and some boughs complete the makeshift camouflage. When the police removed the clothing and bag it up as evidence, they saw the extent of her injuries, and a pathologist later detailed them.

There was a red mark on her left collarbone, which was likely caused by her killer kneeling on her. Her back was ripped in places and there was a large bruise on her right shoulder. Several of her ribs were fractured and one had entered her left lung. Outwardly, there was extensive bruising to her chest and arm on the left side. One nipple had been completely bitten off. Random slashes ran from her vagina up to her chest to join a deep diagonal cut from each nipple, the wounds making a rough Y shape. Internally, her vagina and anus had both been scratched and cut. She also had two very deep knife cuts across her throat.

Self-defence wounds were evident. Her wrists were very bruised; the killer's fingernails had dug into them, and there were marks to show that her wrists had been tied. The fronts of her fingers had numerous cuts. It was certain that Doreen

Marshall had fought hard for her life. It was ascertained that some of the injuries had been inflicted before she died, and the cause of death was the two knife wounds across her throat. The cuts on her breasts, the slashes from the vagina to the chest and the removal of the nipple were almost certainly done post-mortem.

There was a great deal of blood, now dried on the surrounding undergrowth, but it was obvious she had been moved. There were bloodstains twenty feet away and Doreen Marshall's broken necklace was found too – twenty-seven artificial pearls were scattered around. With the one in Heath's jacket pocket, the necklace was complete. Her blue powder compact was found much further away. The struggle may have covered some distance, or Heath could have dropped it there.

So how did Heath carry out Doreen Marshall's murder? There were no bloodstains on his clothes – remembering he only had one set – so it is probable he stripped off completely after temporarily incapacitating her in some way. After he finished his sadistic and inhuman mutilations and hid her body in the bushes, he probably gathered his clothes, walked down to the nearby sea and walked into it, washing off the blood. Getting dressed, he then walked back up the beach, which explains why his shoes were covered in sand (there was no sand on the path to his hotel or in the chine). But he couldn't get rid of the two scratch marks on his neck which made DC Souter suspicious.

Now the police had him, and for the sake of Margery Gardner and Doreen Marshall, they had to convict him. A conviction for murder could only mean death in 1946. Neville

Heath was a sadist, a monster; and just like Jack the Ripper, another mutilating sadist, his sadism was increasing with each kill. To have him in custody undoubtedly saved other women from the same or even worse tortures. Serial killers do not stop. They sometimes pause or take a break, but the only way the cycle truly ends is by capture or suicide. Neville Heath might have asked for a gas fire in his hotel room, but there is no evidence that he was at all the suicidal type.

The following day Heath was included in an identity parade, from which he was picked out by the taxi driver who had driven him and Margery Gardner to the Pembridge Court Hotel and the receptionist from the Panama Club. The police now began to prepare all their evidence relating to the two murders. In early August Heath appeared at the West London Police Court within the jurisdiction of F Division. Yvonne Symonds was present, and other women were flocking to see him. He appeared three times in all, always pleading not guilty. Mr J. L. Pratt heard the case; H. A. K. Morgan represented the director of public prosecutions, and Heath was represented by Anthony Jessel, who would also help defend him at the Old Bailey.

On Sunday, 4 August the *Sunday Pictorial* published a photograph of Heath in the back of a police car, flanked by DI Symes and Sergeant Swarbrick, on the way back to Brixton Prison after a court appearance. Heath looks dreamy, very handsome, a little like a fuller-faced version of Bing Crosby. Wearing a stylish sports jacket – actually supplied by the police – white shirt and a tie, with immaculately styled hair, a large pipe hangs nonchalantly from his lips. Heath is the picture of calm and sophistication, and it is easy to see why he was so popular with the ladies.

At his third police court appearance Heath was committed for trial at the Central Criminal Court, the Old Bailey. This would not begin for another seven weeks, and in the meantime the prosecution prepared its case. It was decided at an early stage to prosecute on the murder of Margery Gardner and not that of Doreen Marshall, as it was felt that going for both might confuse matters. But of course if Heath were found guilty he would hang anyway – unless he was found to be insane, in which case he would never be released from Broadmoor. An insanity plea was an obvious option for the defence, but Heath was having none of it, maintaining he was just not guilty.

While Heath was held at Brixton Prison waiting for his trial to start, like any prisoner on remand he was allowed special privileges. He ordered expensive meals from outside when appearing in court, although he was on a special diet in Brixton Prison hospital, where he was being psychologically assessed. But he was allowed to wear his own clothes, and in letters he pestered friends to send him magazines, novels – especially British mysteries, as he found American mysteries too lurid! – and cigarettes. Meanwhile the press was continuing to feature stories about him, and he was rapidly becoming a household name. The tabloid *Sunday Pictorial*, which would later pay Heath for his exclusive story, would carry something about him every Sunday for weeks to come.

On Sunday, 11 August it published a photograph of Heath taken earlier that year at the opening of a cocktail bar at the

Falstaff in Fleet Street. Heath had been drinking in the
Falstaff's Dive Bar on the day he murdered Margery Gardner.
He is pictured looking dapper wearing his uniform and pilot's
wings, smiling among a group of men. The headline read
'BEHIND THE SCENES IN THE HEATH CASE', and the piece went
on to say that Heath was 'annoyed' with the Brixton Prison
authorities, as they had refused to allow a particular (unnamed)
mystery novel to be sent to him. There was also a photograph
of one of Heath's letters to a friend, asking for South African
newspapers to be sent to him. The report described his last
appearance in the police court, where 'a gallery of goggle-
eyed women in West London's tiny courthouse had seen him
stand, hand in pocket, to plead not guilty'.

The article described him as a 'handsome young giant with
an appetite to match his bulk', and listed the food he had
ordered for his court appearances – for his second chicken
and for the last two portions of stewed steak and suet
pudding. It also revealed that Heath had ordered an off-the-
peg 'grey check suit, preferably with a red stripe' to wear at
the Old Bailey, for which he had paid with 'his new coupons
like the rest of us'. It went on to say that he got on well
with the 'ordinary blokes' on the prison staff and called the
governor 'the Boss'. His days were spent reading and smoking
and making notes for his defence, with some exercise in the
yard. The 'Pictorial Reporter' had got inside to see him at
the West London Police Court and said that he really was
handsome, and that outside the court there had been 'a flock
of not-so-young women' struggling to get in, although there
were only thirteen seats in the court gallery. The article ended
by saying that one of his friends had offered Heath a

sweepstake ticket on the Cambridgeshire Cup horse race, to be run on 16 October.

This is the flavour of the tabloid media coverage. Not yet convicted of two sadistic murders, he is portrayed as jocular and jovial, and a little jaunty, which the Dr Jekyll side of him certainly was. His charm and good looks sold newspapers and attracted women. Heath was perfect for the post-war media age, a good-looking bad boy, ex-borstal. Although he was believed to have tortured and mutilated two innocent young women, the newspapers chose the side of him that they wanted – and airbrushed Mr Hyde.

On 18 August the *Sunday Pictorial* carried the page 4 headline 'HEATH CAN'T GET HIS STEAK NOW'. He was not allowed outside food now that his court appearances had ended, and he was reading novels and chain-smoking. Heath claimed to a friend in a letter that he would smoke 200 cigarettes (apparently supplied by a Bond Street tobacconist) and half a pound of pipe tobacco that week. The following Sunday it was reported 'HEATH SEES NEUROLOGIST' – a leading brain specialist had gone to see him, hired by his defence. Apparently Heath was constantly 'cracking jokes' with other prisoners in the hospital wing. On Sunday, 15 September it was revealed that Heath had placed a one pound each-way bet on White Jacket in the St Leger. The horse had finished tenth out of a field of eleven. The following Sunday, two days before his trial opened, it transpired that Heath would not be letting his parents attend his trial; he had refused visits from them in prison despite repeated requests. He did not want to upset them.

★   ★   ★

The trial of Neville George Clevely Heath for the murder of Margery Gardner opened on Tuesday, 24 September 1946 before Mr Justice Morris. Mr Anthony Hawke and Mr Henry Elam appeared for the Crown, while the eminent Mr J. D. Casswell KC, Mr Anthony Jessel and Mr J. MacGillivray Asher appeared for Heath. The trial would take just three days.

Heath was very willing to give evidence in his own defence but Casswell instructed him not to do so. Casswell felt that his calm detachment would appear callous when set against the gruesome details of the murder of Margery Gardner. There was also the fact that although Heath was only being tried for this crime, it was almost impossible for the jury not to have read about the murder of Doreen Marshall. Heath was already seen as a charmer and confidence man who also had an extremely dark side to his personality that emerged through sexual depravity. Under the modern definition, Heath was undoubtedly a psychopath. This is shown by his lack of emotion and steely calmness in the wake of extreme sadism. J. D. Casswell had to show that Heath did not know what he was doing was wrong at the time of Margery Gardner's murder to claim insanity for him under the M'Naghten Rules on insanity. But Heath had fled the murder scene and tried to cover his tracks by telling provable lies. Moreover, he did not think he was insane and had no wish to rot away in Broadmoor.

Heath remained calm in court throughout, wearing the suit he had ordered from prison, his hair immaculate and fingernails well manicured. There were again many women in the public gallery, watching him intently, something that Heath was well aware of. He looked the ace flier, the handsome and charming man about town.

Despite Heath's insistence that he was sane, Casswell tried to show that he had a long history of mental instability over his criminal career, stretching back a decade, and cross-examined DI Spooner sharply on Heath's criminal record to make this point. Casswell tried to press home to the jury that Heath was 'morally defective' and 'morally insane'. But this is in itself a contradiction, as insanity can only be clinical, as we now know. It is true that there seemed no premeditation for Margery Gardner's murder: signing into the Pembridge Court Hotel under his own name and again at the Ocean Hotel in the aftermath. He had openly connected himself to the murder during talks with Yvonne Symonds. He had also written the letter to the police and behaved as if nothing had happened, all signs of abnormality. But was he insane? Casswell stated in court that Heath might have known what he was doing, but did not know what he was doing was wrong. For this reason, Casswell argued, Heath came within the remit of the M'Naghten Rules and should be found guilty but insane.

However, the defence made a serious mistake when they called an expert psychiatric witness. Casswell did not know that Dr W. H. de Bargue Hubert was a morphine addict. The witness arrived late and sweating, and had to inject himself in court. Hubert was supposed to strengthen the guilty-but-insane argument, but Anthony Hawke ran rings around him in cross-examination, tripping him up on numerous key points. Hubert committed suicide a year later. Matters were made worse for Casswell when two witnesses for the Crown, prison psychiatrists, told the court that in their opinion Heath was not insane although he had behaved in an abnormal way. It also came out for the first time that as a schoolboy Heath had sexually assaulted a girl, and another attack had been discovered in South Africa, although these incidents were not remotely comparable to what had happened in June–July 1946.

As Gordon Honeycombe points out in *The Murders of the Black Museum*, no women were called as character witnesses. This was an oversight. Yvonne Symonds told the police that Heath had treated her with respect and gentleness. Why did he flip out and turn into a murderous sadist when he was with Margery Gardner? It is true that they were having sado-masochistic sex by mutual consent for the second time. But Doreen Marshall had no such taste, although of course he was not on trial for her murder. What made Neville Heath turn? Could it have been an early sexual experience which he had kept back from the doctors? We will never know.

On Thursday, 27 September Justice Morris made his summing-up speech, calling the murder of Margery Gardner 'a terrible crime'. The jury retired at just after 3.30 p.m. They were out for about an hour. When they returned at 4.45 p.m. they brought in a verdict of guilty. Justice Morris then donned the traditional black cap and passed sentence of death on Heath. When asked if he had anything to say, Heath replied, 'Nothing.'

At the end of his trial Heath was approached by the *Sunday Pictorial* for his full story, and he agreed to tell all for a large sum. There is now a law against criminals profiting from their crimes, but in 1946 Fleet Street's Murder Gang, including such luminaries as Jock Rae of the *News of the*

World and Harry Procter, then of the *Daily Mail* and later of the *Sunday Pictorial*, were authorised by their editors to go after the inside stories of notorious killers and to secure them at all costs.

As we have seen, Procter had been the first to splash on the murder of Margery Gardner. However, it was the *Sunday Pictorial* got the full inside story on Heath, from his own mouth, his letters and accounts he wrote of his life and the nights of the murders while in prison. It is impossible to know exactly how much the paper paid for Heath's story – the payments were confidential and no records exist – but it was likely to have been in the region of three to five thousand pounds, the rumoured rate for such a story then. 'HEATH'S OWN STORY: EXCLUSIVE: BEGINS TODAY', as it was trumpeted across the front page of the *Sunday Pictorial* on 29 September, just days after Heath was sentenced to death, would run for the next three Sundays. Neville Heath was a confidence man and never confessed to the murders, or even showed real remorse, so his version of events must be read with caution. However, his inside view is useful in building a picture of this extraordinary but very dangerous man.

On that first Sunday in large print on the front page was a quote from Heath: 'I cannot believe I am responsible for these atrocities.' This was in marked contrast to the rest of the front page, which featured a large photograph of a newborn baby, mouth wide open, illustrating a story on the post-war British 'baby boom'. Heath's quote showed that he was still in denial, whether wilfully or because he could not take in the horror of what he had done, although he had just been sentenced to death and the evidence against him

was enormous. Over a double spread on pages 5 and 6, a
similar quote appeared: 'I cannot believe I did it.' As Heath
was now a convicted murderer awaiting sentence, the tone
of the tabloid's treatment of him had changed markedly. 'We
are able to reveal here the incredible life story of the most
murderous sadistic monster of modern times.' However, the
'Pictorial Reporter' could not help but include jaunty details
about Heath including little eccentricities, as the Jekyll and
Hyde aspects of his personality played so well with readers
looking for shocks and thrills on a Sunday. This mixture of
the human and inhuman is what tabloids thrived on then,
and still do today.

Under a 'NEW FACTS' heading it was revealed that:

- Heath had written a novel about a captured 'flyer' who
  became a spy for Britain!
- He wrote a short story, 'a love tale', based on his own
  life!
- He wrote a poem about the RAF!
- He wrote a powerful plea for 'one last chance to make
  good'!
- He wrote an account of his last days of freedom!

Heath's view of himself was suffused with self-denial:
nothing is ever his fault. He speaks and writes romantically
of his flying days, and we can assume that he had used some
of these lines – his near-death experiences and bravery – on
young women. We know that Heath forged his flight logbook,
but he was still claiming to have flown 2,300 hours. A typical
quote apropos his flying days is: 'I have done things which

I am ashamed of, but never in the air.' It is also interesting how Heath's looks – now that he is a convicted sadistic killer – have changed. Whereas the week before he was described as handsome, now: 'The dropping line of his mouth is cruel. His upper lip is thin. His blue eyes seem unnaturally penetrating.' The *Pic*'s reporter knew exactly how to create a mood for his readers, mirroring what they would be feeling about Heath now.

There were details of Heath's address and telephone book. 'It reads like the stock-in-trade of a confidence trickster.' There were 356 names and telephone numbers in his book, including 'a prince, a peer, several titled people, the editors of six London newspapers, some show folk and the Russian Embassy'. Heath then went on to describe his childhood and military service, always making himself a maverick pilot, doomed by fate despite his repeated and intrepid attempts to make good and his parents proud. In reality, his criminal record sheet spoke for itself.

In a foretaste of coming details, at the close Heath was quoted about his last two weeks of freedom before Margery Gardner's murder: 'I just drifted around for a fortnight or so, becoming a frequent visitor to night haunts. I went from club to club in London, drinking mostly and doing very little eating.'

In the following week's *Sunday Pictorial*, again flagged on the front page with a double spread inside, the headline was '177 WOMEN NAMED IN HEATH'S ADDRESS BOOK'. In the book many of the women were identified next to their telephone numbers by only their first names: 'Sue or Pat or Maxine'. The *Pictorial* had called some of these women, asking if they knew Heath, getting a mixed response. Some said that they could not remember meeting him, others that they may have met him at a cocktail party. A few said, 'Of course I knew Jimmy! He was always very pleasant.' The books which Heath had been banned from receiving in prison were also revealed as pulp novels entitled *Bring the Bride a Shroud* and *Call the Lady Indiscreet*.

We also get the first mentions of Heath's supposed blackouts, which he would say happened on the night of both murders. In a box titled 'HEATH SAYS . . .' he is quoted: 'Even in my wilder moments I never did nay harm to anyone else. The only person who suffered was myself.' Also: 'I must have lived with many women – but there has never been any suggestion of sexual mania.' It was all geared to absolve him of responsibility, but strangely also to deny that there was anything wrong with his mental health, which many murderers would have jumped on as an excuse.

In addition, a letter that Heath had received while awaiting trial in Brixton Prison is mentioned, reportedly from his 'wife' in Coventry – a woman he had never heard of – who wrote that she had 'witnessed' his death. In a letter written by Heath himself on the evening he was sentenced to death, he is quoted regarding Judge Morris's summing-up speech: 'In the light of Morris's summing-up, the jury could have brought in no other. After hearing his address I made the odds 30–1 on.'

Sunday 13 October saw the last part of 'Heath's Own Story' in the *Sunday Pictorial*, just three days before he was to be hanged. A headline read 'ONLY A HOME OFFICE REPRIEVE CAN SAVE HIM'. This was what readers had been waiting for, the salacious details of the nights of the two murders, and the headline quote from Heath, 'I FOUND BLOOD ON MY HANDS', did not disappoint. It was revealed that Heath had decided that he would rather be hanged than spend the rest of his life in Broadmoor: 'In my opinion the possible alternative may well prove worse than the present situation.' This was in contrast to what he had written just a few days earlier: 'If anything is going to be done for me it will have to be quick – I am going to be strung up on the sixteenth.'

Heath described the night of Margery Gardner's murder after they had returned to the Pembridge Court Hotel. He said he remembered getting into bed, but his next memory was of waking up, as if he had had a blackout. 'Of what had happened in that period I had no recollection. But I saw the result. There was the body of a woman on my bed.' He went on: 'I had no idea what to do. There were stains of blood on me so I bathed in the bathroom on the next floor, going back to the bedroom to shave and dress. I was confused in mind, but it would be wrong to say that I was panicky. I noticed particularly how steady my hand was when I was holding the razor.' On his flight: 'My instinct then was to go away, anywhere . . . Everything seemed like a dream or nightmare. I wanted to get away to where things were light and bright and different. So I went to Brighton.'

About changing his room at the Tollard Royal Hotel in Bournemouth to one with a gas fire, Heath claimed, 'I had quite made up my mind to kill myself, so I asked for the room to be changed for one with a gas fire, using a bleak and windy day as excuse.' On his last walk with Doreen Marshall: 'I have absolutely no recollection of going anywhere near

Branksome Chine. The next thing I recall is lighting a cigarette. As I was flicking the match away I saw blood on my
hands.' He then went on to admit that he washed the blood
from his hands in the sea but not to account for the fact that
there were no bloodstains on his clothes, and the next day
pawned Doreen Marshall's ring and watch because 'I had no
money'.

As ever, Heath refused to take any responsibility for two
of the most sadistic murders in the history of crime, or spare
a thought for the two young women he had killed.

Albert Pierrepoint hanged Neville Heath at Pentonville
Prison on Wednesday, 16 October 1946, ironically the day
on which the Cambridgeshire Cup was run, for which a
friend had offered to buy Heath a sweepstake ticket.
Pierrepoint used a 'special strap' on Heath, which he used
several times in his long career and reserved for executions
of 'special interest'. Heath was calm as he was taken through
to stand in front of the trapdoor.

The governor of Pentonville had earlier asked him if he
had any last request. Heath asked for a whisky. Then he
corrected himself: 'You might make that a double.'

On Sunday, 20 October the *Sunday Pictorial* published
Heath's last letter, which was written to a friend the day
before he was hanged and signed with one of his
pseudonyms.

> Just a line to say cheerio. I don't know what licensing
> hours they have where I'm off to, but I'll be there
> at opening time. I hope the beer is better than it is

here. To my mind, this is just a one-way 'op', but if there is anything in this reincarnation business, please break your morning egg very gently for the next couple of months because it may be me. I have written to my Father, but in spite of your very convincing argument I still would rather see nobody. I, more than anyone, appreciate their loyalty but – no visitors.

I'll be looking for you some time or other.

Ever yours,

Jimmy

CHAPTER
6

Summer 1947

Last winter was a bitter one, but it is pleasant now. John George Haigh has moved into room 404 of the sumptuous Onslow Court Hotel in Queen's Gate, using the proceeds gained from the disappearance of the McSwan family and other scams to pay for his keep. This is the life for Haigh. The Onslow Court is a large hotel in a street of Regency houses, magnificent in design and size in the heart of leafy and affluent South Kensington. There are signs of the war still around, but the residents of this hotel have been much less affected than most Londoners. You won't find powdered egg here. Never a man to keep a low profile, Haigh is already well known. He chats with the other guests, despite the fact that most of them are at least twenty years older than he is. Haigh is thirty-nine years old and particularly popular with elderly ladies. The attractive blonde receptionist at the Onslow Court, Mrs Lansley Gera, who speaks to Haigh daily, will later comment on how he was only 'interested in platonic relationships' with women.

The fashionable women outside on the streets are wearing the New Look, inspired by Christian Dior's Corolle line released in April. Skirts are full and reach the middle of shapely calves; drawn-in waists are all the rage, as is padding around hips and breasts, and batwing sleeves complete the look. Some go further with a glimpse of petticoat – to the delight of most men – but Haigh has no interest in that. Inside his elegant room he plays his favourite music, Tchaikovsky's *Swan Lake*, again and again on his gramophone until the stylus or the record wears out. His guests comment on this.

Haigh followed the hunt, capture and hanging of Neville Heath with interest in the previous year. They knew each other, frequenting some of the same pubs and clubs. According to the journalist Gerald Byrne, who will write a book about Haigh, they went to the same club near Gatwick, not far from the workshop that Haigh has been renting from his old boss at Hurstlea Products in Crawley. Haigh mixes in the same social circles in Kensington and Chelsea that Heath's first victim, Margery Gardner, inhabited the periphery of, a set that Gerald Byrne will say had 'strange practices'. But Haigh has a low opinion of Heath, thinking him 'insignificant', and will later call him a 'hopeless blunderer'. Haigh sees himself as in a far higher league than Heath and his 'successes', murderous or otherwise, as vastly superior.

Haigh's smugness and urbane manner show his inner arrogance. This is the life he was born to live. But soon he will need to replenish his funds yet again. Style does not come cheap.

Autumn 1947

Haigh met Dr Archibald Henderson and his wife Rosalie a few weeks ago. A wealthy couple, they were engaged in a property deal, selling a property in Ladbroke Square which Haigh expressed interest in buying. He was not able to come up with the money, but Haigh made sure that he kept up his acquaintance with them. Haigh is beginning to cultivate them, although his financial need is not desperate yet. He has his fingers in several fraudulent pies, and is just embarking on a car fraud scam in Stockport near Manchester. He genuinely likes the Hendersons. Archie is forty-nine years old; Rose is thirty-nine, less than a year older than Haigh. They were the kind of people that Haigh liked to befriend.

Archie, like the McSwans a Scot, was born in 1898 and attended Glasgow Grammar School. From there he went on to Glasgow University, where he studied medicine, graduating in 1928 as Dr A. Henderson, MB, CH.B. In his university days he was something of a dandy, an affectation popular in the 1920s, and wanting the good things in life would stay with him throughout his life – but also help end it. He was gregarious, a friendly and personable man, never the quiet one at a party. In 1930, when he was thirty-two, Archie married Dorothy Orr, a young woman who had inherited £50,000, a massive sum in those days. They set up home in Chester, where Archie worked at the Royal Infirmary as the senior house surgeon.

For a while the marriage was a happy one, but then it went stale and Archie began to drink heavily, a habit that would stay with him on and off. They moved to London, where Archie took another medical post, but the change of scene did not mend the marriage, and within a couple of years Archie began an affair with Rose. Rosalie Burlin was born in Manchester in 1908. Her father was A. L. Burlin, a noted scientist and chemist. She also had a brother, Arnold, who will reappear in this story. In the spring of 1937 Archie's wife Dorothy caught pneumonia, and she died on 22 April – coincidentally in the splendour of Bailey's Hotel, almost opposite where Haigh would dispose of the entire McSwan family in acid in his basement workshop at 79 Gloucester Road seven and eight years later.

Dorothy left Archie the remainder of her inheritance in her will, around £20,000. Rose was married to a German scientist, Rudolf Arnold Erran, and the affair now intensified. The adultery became obvious to Rudolf, and he initiated divorce proceedings. The divorce came through on 29 July 1937, with Archie cited as co-respondent. He and Rose wasted little time and were married on 6 October 1938 at Caxton Hall, Westminster. Archie was forty, Rose thirty.

Archie and Rose Henderson invested in some property, but they were also very extravagant with their money, spending as if it was last year's fashion and had to be used up – particularly Archie, who liked a drink and a flutter on the horses, just like Haigh. Archie was sometimes short of funds, occasionally almost having to pawn his favourite gold cigarette case and gold watch and chain. He dressed well, as did Rose. She was very beautiful, with a fine-featured face, a flawless complexion and dark brown eyes. Archie had a face of character but was also handsome, his small moustache and slightly jug ears giving him a resemblance to the older Clark Gable.

February 1948

Haigh and the Hendersons are staying at the Metropole Hotel in Brighton for a short holiday. They have left the London winter behind, with its scars of war, the smell of burning rubbish mixed with the smoke of deadly coal fires. Brighton has a bracing sea breeze. It is also not too far from Haigh's workshop at Crawley.

Haigh is in need of funds now. The car scam in Stockport didn't work out. He is behind with his rent, and the Onslow Court Hotel management is beginning to put on the pressure. He likes the Hendersons, likes them a lot, but he knows that this life doesn't really matter anyway. Plymouth Brethren teachings are still ingrained in him. That's why he has engineered this holiday at the seaside. The sale of the Ladbroke Square property to another vendor has come through, and Haigh knows that Archie has several hundred pounds on him in cash. He also knows that there is plenty more in cash and assets elsewhere. Haigh does like to be beside the seaside, beside the sea . . .

It isn't difficult to persuade Archie to visit his workshop in Crawley. Haigh has interested Archie in a business venture, and there are samples of the new product in his workshop, where there are also two drums and a large quantity of acid, which Mr Davies, an acquaintance of Haigh's and a welding engineer, has recently delivered from London. Haigh knows it will be too difficult to get Archie and Rose to come together, so he takes Archie there first. Where the husband goes, the wife will shortly follow. It is perhaps Thursday, 12 February, as Haigh will make a significant mark in his 1948 diary this evening. However, he will also say later that it was on Friday, 13 February – Friday the thirteenth.

Haigh and Archie chat excitedly as they drive into Crawley, a small town. They turn off Leopold Road and into Giles Yard, a small run-down area of little workshops and car lock-ups. The yard is sporadically overgrown, and rubble is strewn around with an old car axle and a couple of old tyres tangled in weeds. It is deserted, just how Haigh wants it. Archie doesn't notice the rough state of the yard, as he's too focused on the business proposition John has been talking up on the way down, which is going to make them both a lot of money as partners. Haigh turns the padlock key and opens the workshop door.

Haigh doesn't hang about. He takes a stolen revolver out of his pocket and shoots Archie in the back of the head as soon as the door is closed behind them. Archie goes down. Haigh doesn't bother catching him. Haigh then removes Archie's blue Glasgow University blazer, his gold cigarette case, watch and chain, and his wallet containing a large wad of notes, just as he expected. Then Archie is trussed up, before being placed in a drum. The effort it takes to get him in makes Haigh sweat a little.

Next Haigh gets changed into his acid bath kit. His method has improved. He puts on rubber boots, a rubber mac, a rubber apron and gloves. This outfit is topped off with a war-issue gas mask in the interests of health and safety due to the acrid fumes about to be released in the workshop. Haigh still has his own health and safety on his mind as he begins to fill the drum with acid by means of a stirrup pump, slowly covering Archie. It takes a while, but soon his friend is submerged. Off with the kit. No time for a cup of tea; there's more work to do. Carefully padlocking the workshop door, Heath walks back through Giles Yard and gets into his car. He's soon on the road to Brighton.

When he arrives at the Hotel Metropole, he goes straight to Archie and Rose's room. He finds Rose there and tells her that Archie's been taken ill. 'You're not to worry, dear, but I think it's best that you come now,' says Haigh. Rose is worried and agrees to come. She remains concerned for her husband all the way to Crawley, but John constantly reassures her. Haigh parks the car and they go into the workshop. Like her husband of almost ten years, Rose is shot in the head from behind. Just a little murmur this time. Haigh undresses Rose, as her clothes can be sold or given away. He removes her engagement and wedding rings and other jewellery. Then he follows exactly the same process again as with Archie, until both husband and wife are well on the way to dissolving.

After taking off his murder outfit again, Haigh straightens his hair and takes a last look at the drums standing side by side. Everything is going to plan. He's pleased with the refinements. His method has improved since the McSwans. He locks up the workshop and drives back to Brighton, staying at the Hotel Metropole that night. In the morning he drives back up to Crawley, to see how the Hendersons are coming on. Not quite gone yet. He drives to Horsham and walks into Bull's the jewellers. There he sells Rose's rings and jewellery and Archie's gold watch and chain and cigarette case. In total Haigh gets just over £300 for the lot, to be added to the cash from Archie's wallet, but he knows that the real money is in the Hendersons' assets.

Haigh stays at the Hotel Metropole in Brighton until 16 February. He settles his own bill and that of the Hendersons until that date, a total of twenty pounds, four shillings and one penny. The previous day the job was complete, Archie and Rose Henderson having vanished. Haigh simply poured the sludge of their remains into the weeds, stones and debris of Giles Yard. He then drives all the way to Edinburgh.

September 1948

The music coming out of room 404 is yet again *Swan Lake*, and a red setter is lying at the foot of the bed, quiet for once. It is evening, and John George Haigh is writing a letter. He has a lot of tracks to cover, as his friends Archie and Rose Henderson have a life to live. Arnold, Rose's brother in Manchester, is particularly inquisitive about his sister and brother-in-law's whereabouts. Little does Arnold know that Haigh has already forged a power of attorney, gaining access to the Hendersons' assets, their property and their car, which he recently sold. He also sold some clothes belonging to the Hendersons at Jennings of Bell Street, Paddington, including Archie's navy-blue Glasgow University blazer. The proprietor removed the metal buttons, as they made the jacket less saleable, but Haigh then returned and bought the blazer back, as he decided he wanted it for himself. In total, the disposal of the Hendersons has netted him just over £8,000, a very large sum. Haigh has been paying his hotel rent in advance for a while now, but he is also spending a lot on the horses.

The dog is called Pat and belonged to the Hendersons too.

At first Haigh likes looking after him and the elderly ladies in the hotel fawn over him, but recently Haigh has begun to find him a burden. Soon Pat will be taken to the kennels.

Haigh, ever meticulous, keeps carbon copies of every letter he writes. There is a later one to Archie dated 28 August, which Haigh wrote on Onslow Court notepaper and showed to Arnold when he met him in London recently. Just as he did with the McSwans, Haigh has also been busy travelling up and down posting letters to himself from the Hendersons. The first was from Edinburgh on 17 February, the day after he checked out of the Hotel Metropole in Brighton. 'Dear John,' it begins. It is a typed letter, as they all are – minimises the risk – but this one is forged with Rose's signature, and Arnold accepted this. Another is a typed note asking Haigh to look after their affairs in their absence signed with Archie's forged signature. Then a postcard postmarked 27 February, signed 'Archie Henderson'. Haigh had gone to Birmingham to post that one. Six days later, on 5 March, another postcard arrives, postmarked Rugby in Warwickshire, this time signed by Rose. Just over two weeks later, a typed letter comes from Glasgow, ending, 'Yours Very Sincerely, Rose Henderson'.

Then there are no more letters for a while: Haigh has put it about that the Hendersons are in South Africa. There is a carbon copy of a letter from Rose to her housekeeper, saying that she and her husband are in South Africa. But on 30 July 1948 a letter comes from Archie on notepaper from the Hotel Beau Rivage, Geneva, one of the most luxurious hotels in Switzerland. Haigh has taken a nice break there, paid for posthumously by the Hendersons.

Haigh gets up and places the stylus at the beginning of

the record again. Pat the dog fidgets a little, but he knows *Swan Lake* so well now that it sends him to sleep. Haigh sits back down at his desk, picking up his fountain pen again, before checking something in his diary. It is open at the month of September, but if he flicked back a few months, something strange could be seen in the space for 12 February. It is blank except for two sets of initials: A.H. and R.H. Just to the right of the initials of the Hendersons Haigh has drawn a small cross. You can take the boy out of the Plymouth Brethren, but you cannot take the Plymouth Brethren doctrine out of the boy.

Haigh has never entered any victims in his diary before. But then he was very fond of the Hendersons.

CHAPTER
7

The household in St Marks Road on the Ladbroke Grove side of Notting Hill was a crowded one but organised and kept spotlessly clean. Mrs Thomasina Probert, her husband Penry and two daughters had been happy to take their son and brother Timothy's new wife Beryl into the fold. They liked her from the start. Twenty-two-year-old Timothy John Evans and eighteen-year-old Beryl Susanna Thorley had married not very far away at Kensington Register Office just a few months before on 20 September 1947.

Early in 1948 Beryl discovered that she was pregnant with their first child, and Tim was thrilled. He was going to be a father, and it somehow made some sense of his life. The house in St Marks Road was too small for another child, and with limited funds it wouldn't be easy for Timothy and Beryl to find somewhere to live. Tim's pay as a delivery driver for Lancaster Foods would be stretched, and his joy was tempered with the realisation that he would now have more responsibility. Little did he know how much their lives would change. But finding a marital home for themselves and the baby became a priority.

It was Tim's sister Eileen who saw the sign. From a train window, going towards Ladbroke Grove, there it was: 'FLAT TO LET.' Instead of walking straight home, Eileen got off the train, walked round to 10 Rillington Place and jotted down the name of the letting agents, Martin East of Gerrard Street in Soho. If only Eileen had known that there were two women buried in the back garden . . . She gave the information to Tim and Beryl, and they arranged with the agent to take a look at the flat.

24 March 1948

The sound of a nearby train rumbles past the north side of Rillington Place W11 – in the Royal Borough of Kensington, as the street sign says. Little more than a boy, Tim Evans looks personable if a little spivvy in his grey chalk-striped double-breasted suit and striped tie, making the most of his height of five feet five and a half inches. His dark wavy hair fashionably swept back from his high forehead, he looks like any other young man starting out, a bundle of nervous energy. There's no outward sign of the troubles he's had, and when he smiles he makes an impression. His collar is done up today, tie tightly knotted, different to how he usually has it – slightly loose, top button of his shirt undone. Today the impression he makes is very important. Landlords make decisions on first appearances.

Beryl is a credit to him. She is strikingly attractive, her

dark good looks and finely boned face giving her a fragility, her youth increasing that impression. Tim is her protector, so proud to call her his wife, and sometimes, although he would never admit it to her, he can't believe his luck that he won her. It makes him taller, standing next to her, pride adding an inch or two, and the coming child only adds to the power he feels. Those years when it seemed that nothing good would ever happen are now behind him, he knows. Fortune smiles on the brave, they say, and now Tim's inclined to believe it.

Built in the late 1860s, a period that saw huge development in Notting Hill, Rillington Place took its name from a village in West Yorkshire near where the owner of the land, Colonel St Quintin, had his family seat. The colonel being prone to mental illness, his wife had signed over control of his estate ten years earlier. The houses, sold on long leases, including number 10 at the end of the terraced row, had been occupied by comfortable middle-class families at first, but by the start of the twentieth century working-class people, some poorer than others, lived in Rillington Place. As time went on, the houses were split, with multiple tenants in each. Now John and Ethel Christie live in the ground-floor flat of number 10; the elderly almost-blind Charles Kitchener is on the first floor, and the top-floor flat which Tim and Beryl Evans have come to look at was vacated by a Henry Williams almost three weeks ago on 9 March.

The Christies' flat is bigger than the top one, which only has a bedroom facing the street and a small kitchen overlooking the back garden, where Ruth Fuerst and Muriel Eady are buried. Everyone shares the outside toilet and wash house. Rillington Place is dank and bleak on the outside, and the top flat is very run-down and in need of redecoration, especially with a new baby coming.

Not that Beryl is showing much yet. It's almost Easter and the baby's not due until the autumn. But Tim and Beryl tell everyone they meet about their coming baby, including the landlord. It's a family area, he tells them despite the smashed windows and drabness of the street, which make Rillington Place look little better than a slum. The landlord won't disturb Mr Kitchener, but he knows that the Christies are in downstairs. A nice couple, approaching late middle age. He takes Tim and Beryl down and knocks on the door of the ground-floor flat. It's John who opens the door. Tall and thin, shirt neatly tucked into his trousers, which are secured high up his waist by a belt. He looks at them through his wire-rimmed glasses, eyes peering through the lenses, thin lips breaking into a faint smile, bald pate dominating his face, making his forehead seem to go on for ever.

Tim and Beryl like the idea of having an older couple downstairs. It's somehow reassuring. Although Tim's mother Mrs Probert and sister Eileen don't live very far away, Mr and Mrs Christie look like good neighbours to have, especially with a baby coming. When Tim tells them Beryl is expecting a baby, Mrs Christie lights up, her maternal urges still strong despite her age and never having any children of her own. Ethel is stout and matronly, her hair parted in the centre and curled at the sides, her large features more attractive when she smiles. Neither Tim nor Beryl Evans notice that Mr Christie spends most of the time looking at Beryl, nor that Mrs Christie is completely in thrall to her husband of almost twenty-eight years. On the other hand, the Christies do not notice how limited Tim's vocabulary is, and know nothing of the struggles he has had, making his courtship and marriage to Beryl, a woman 'above his station', a minor miracle.

A Scorpio, Tim Evans displayed many of the characteristics of that astrological sign – to those who believe in astrology. Impulsive, hating detail and routine, forever seeking stimulation, the circumstances of his upbringing were stacked against him from the start, making him one of life's natural outsiders. Born on 20 November 1924 in the mining village of Merthyr Vale in south Wales, the street where he was brought up fatherless until the age of five was called Mount Pleasant in cruel – or ironic – contradiction to its surroundings. Overcrowded and claustrophobic, with families living in each other's threadbare pockets, Mount Pleasant and its neighbours must have been a dispiriting place. 'Knowing your place' was one way to cope with life, dreaming of escape another. For most men the pub was the mecca at the end of the day; for women the constant pressure of making ends meet and keeping a household going was alleviated slightly by the sisterhood of hardship.

Daniel Evans was a coal haulier, a tough and dirty job, and he and Thomasina already had a little girl named Eileen, aged three, when Daniel walked out just before Tim was born. Timothy Evans would never know his true father. It was a struggle for Thomasina, bringing up two young children alone, and this would continue until 1929, just before the Great Depression. Families such as the Evanses survived on bread and dripping, and whatever they could scavenge. In that year, as the Wall Street Crash occurred on the other side of the Atlantic, and New York bankers jumped from the tottering citadels of finance, Thomasina met and married another coalman, Penry Probert. Eileen was now eight and Tim five years old. But the boy would never take the name Probert, unlike his mother, remaining Timothy Evans.

Tim was a very slow developer – it was only at the age of five that he started to speak normally – and it is difficult to know now how much the lack of a father contributed to this. Starting school, Tim was soon found to have serious learning problems, making his progress far slower than other children his age. In those days there was nothing in the way of remedial classes in Merthyr Vale, and Tim had to press on in a class of children with normal learning abilities. As if this were not enough, an accident when he was almost eight stunted his mental development still further. Swimming one day in the nearby River Taff, Tim stepped on some glass shards on the riverbed. This should have been dealt with by a doctor, but before the welfare state doctors had to be paid, and the deep cut was cleaned at home then covered with a dirty handkerchief. Infection set in, caused by tuberculosis bacteria, and Tim developed a tubercular verruca on his left foot that would plague him for years, meaning lengthy periods of hospital treatment and missed school.

Already a lonely boy because of his slow development, this misfortune pushed Tim behind his contemporaries even more. Even worse, he was now also physically impaired, and the one area in which he had been equal was taken from him, as he could no longer take part in sports and games with the other boys. Being slow either mentally or physically can be ostracising for a child, but to have both impairments is truly stifling. In the tough world of the Welsh valleys, where physical strength and vitality was the measure of a boy and young man, with rugby and mining being key activities, Tim was at a distinct disadvantage. The fact that he also lacked a quick mind – although this would improve somewhat later – and articulacy set him apart even more.

Like many children who do not fit in, Tim Evans began to cultivate a rich interior life, making him a dreamer, a characteristic that would dominate his life. This was the defence mechanism that allowed Tim to survive. But when he was almost eleven there was a change in his life that could have meant a fresh start and a chance to be happier.

The Depression had led to many miners losing their jobs, the coal industry suffering particularly badly. Small mining villages like Merthyr Vale and men such as Penry Probert were hit accordingly, and Mr Probert was soon out of a job. Like many men he had no choice but to look further afield, but unlike a lot he was lucky and managed to find a job in London as a painter and decorator, in Notting Hill. With prospects very bleak in south Wales, the Proberts moved to London in 1935, a city they knew nothing about other than what they had seen on Pathé newsreels and read in books and newspapers. It was a world away from Merthyr Vale with its tiny population and everybody knowing your business. London's anonymity can be a tonic for some new arrivals, meaning they feel less different, but this was not the case for Tim Evans, who found the sea of strange faces he saw every day disconcerting to say the least.

Moreover some negative aspects of his old life continued to trouble Tim. His mother Thomasina was a devout Roman Catholic, so it was only natural that he began to attend a Roman Catholic school, St Francis'. However, within weeks of Tim starting at school, and before he had settled in, his tubercular verruca flared up again and he was hospitalised. It was soon obvious that his foot was in a very bad way, and this was not to be a short hospital stay. Once he had been there for a while, Tim got used to the routine, which became his life. Missing school was putting him more and more behind, but the primary concern was to get his foot better and to stop the tuberculosis spreading to the rest of his body, which could prove fatal. Tim would stay there for nine months, which must have seemed a lifetime for a boy of his age. He would have remained longer if a measles virus had not hit his ward. The hospital asked his mother to take him home, as a measles infection would only have worsened his condition, attacking his underdeveloped body from a second angle.

The fact that he fought his mother to stay in hospital shows how much Tim had become accustomed to life there, indeed institutionalised. He resisted for a week, every day risking catching measles, until Mrs Probert finally got him home. It was humiliating for eleven-year-old Tim to be taken home from hospital in a pram, having to face the outside world again, which had never been kind to him. It proved no more welcoming than before, and his foot intermittently worsened and got better, meaning more visits to the hospital. On at least one occasion his leg blew up like a balloon, confining him to bed. This was all very disruptive to both his

education and making friends, and on both scores Tim
needed all the help he could get, not being a natural mixer.
His stepfather Penry and sister Eileen offered him all the
support they could but Thomasina continued to be very
worried about him.

The future seemed bleak to Tim, trapped in a strange
world where he knew few people, the thousands of strangers
in the streets offering no warmth. The boy who had struggled
in the valleys of south Wales felt overwhelmed in London, his
foot infection hindering what progress he could have made.
His mother knew that Tim was depressed, but did not know
what to do. It was when he was twelve that Tim himself
offered her a possible solution, asking his mother if he could
return to Wales. He had not been happy there, but the grass
of the valleys seemed greener to him than the concrete of
the metropolis. Thomasina and Penry agonised but eventually decided that it was worth a go, Thomasina asking her
mother if Tim could stay with her.

Tim's grandmother agreed, so he was packed off to
Merthyr Vale by train in 1937, by now accustomed to change,
the constant quest for acceptance growing in him. Tim was
a sensitive boy, although becoming increasingly tough and
savvy through experience and necessity. This mixture of acute
self-awareness, the desire to be accepted and the survival
instinct that his unstable life had brought about would stay
with Tim into adulthood. But his foot still stopped him from
returning to school immediately, and he had to bide his time
until it allowed him to do so. On going back, he found
schoolwork very difficult – his lengthy spell in hospital in
London had set him back enormously – but one aspect of

his personality had changed since going to London, and that was the ability to impress others.

The need to make an impression on other boys led him to make his rich inner world of imagination external. He saw many of the same boys again, most of whom had not accepted him before, but this time Tim told them anecdotes about his London life, the vast majority untrue, as of course he had spent most of his time there in hospital. However, in 1937 to children in the Welsh valleys London was another world, if not another planet. Tim was now worldly and had done things they could only dream of, even if most of those things had only been dreamt up by Tim himself. His London escapades gave him some status, and for the first time he achieved some acceptance even if he knew he would never really be one of the lads. This reaction would make him into the voluble crowd- and bar-pleasing Welshman he would become as a man.

Although he lived with his grandmother, he also spent time with an uncle, Mr Lynch, who will return later in Tim's story. Mr Lynch saw Tim as a solitary boy at this time, an outsider, later saying that Tim's favourite pastime was looking for rats in a coal bunker. When Tim left school, he did not return to London but took a job as a miner in Merthyr Vale's pit, although this tough job was never a realistic option for him, as his foot again proved when it swelled up yet again, sending him back to hospital. He was there for a few weeks before Thomasina decided to bring him to Cornwall Road in Notting Hill, where the Proberts now lived. It was 1940, and while many children were being evacuated out of London to avoid the Blitz, Tim Evans, almost sixteen, made the opposite journey. His foot was now stable, and although it would remain malformed due to the infection, it would no longer plague and disrupt his life, as it had for much of his childhood, which was just as well as he now had to go out to work.

Tim was now in fact growing into quite a handsome young man, although he had a very slight physique and a slight limp. He must have been conscious of this, but at least life seemed more stable now. He did apply for active service in the military once he was sixteen, but unsurprisingly he failed the medical examination. Tim also became very close to his elder sister Eileen, who was protective and maternal towards him. He looked up to her, never wanting to disappoint her. As well as Eileen, Tim's half-sister Maureen (known as Mary) was now also living with the Proberts too. Although his mind would later be characterised as slower than it was, his ability to survive and adapt to changing situations, developed in his challenging childhood, had given him the ability to shield his deficiencies from all but those who really knew him well.

Tim's lack of education, particularly his near-illiteracy, and poor mental dexterity ruled out a desk job. So Tim was only able to do physical jobs, which were often transient and irregular in nature, but at least his foot now let him do them. The fact that he was now earning a wage, although small, liberated him, giving him some spending money after he had paid his keep to his mother, for which Thomasina was no doubt very grateful with a busy household to run. Financial independence brought alcohol into Tim's life, and he began to spend time in pubs when he wasn't working. This would be a defining image of Tim for the rest of his life. Standing in the bars of local pubs, telling tall tales to other regulars, a magnet for those with time to kill, Tim became a sort of Dylan Thomas with a limited vocabulary, but legendary among just a few locally rather than internationally, as Thomas would be within a decade. Interestingly, Dylan Thomas was spending much of his time in pubs a few miles to the east, in Fitzrovia and Soho, having arrived from south Wales in the mid-1930s. Now in his late teenage years, Tim was also developing a slightly bohemian lifestyle. Although living at Cornwall Road, he often disappeared for a few days at a time, pubs undoubtedly his home from home.

There are no records of Tim having proper girlfriends at this time, but he may have had casual ones. It is known that he visited prostitutes, at least later and before he was married, but this was not uncommon at a time when sex was very difficult to find outside marriage. His mother Thomasina almost definitely had no knowledge of this, and as a strict Catholic would have found it difficult to accept.

In 1946 Tim and his mother began work at the same toy factory. Tim was now in his early twenties, and his pattern of visiting local pubs in the evenings was now entrenched. It would remain so for the rest of his life.

Late 1946, Kensington Palace Hotel, Ladbroke Grove, London

Tim Evans, now twenty-two, is in his favourite bar, which he always calls the KPH. 'I'm off down the KPH,' he says often, but sometimes he also goes to the nearby Elgin too. At the bar a few regulars hang on his every word. His voice has that Welsh lilt suited to telling stories, although it is not as melodic as Dylan Thomas's. That other loquacious Welshman has recently published his seminal collection of poetry *Deaths and Entrances*, the former event being much closer to Tim Evans than he could possibly imagine, even though he has had more than enough experience of the randomness and tragedies of life. This evening the beer is flowing, and Tim stands here, his double-breasted suit under his dark trench coat filling out his slight frame. He is ready to face the winter chill outside, but just not yet. Always after the next story, which if good enough might get him a free drink.

Recently he told this same audience that his brother – who does not exist – is a successful businessman who owns expensive cars that ferry around wealthy people for a fee. But tonight's story is even better. With his limited vocabulary Tim manages to set the scene of his story well, drawing in his increasingly sozzled audience. 'My father's an Italian count, see, and he was born in a castle. We moved to Wales when I was a boy. But the castle's still there, high on a mountain, looking down on all beneath it.'

Those listening smile, knowing deep down that Tim is no more blue-blooded than any of them, but it doesn't matter. It's the entertainment that counts, and Tim is always worth a free drink or two. With rationing in force and bombsites everywhere, any amusement is worth its weight in gold, or at least the best china. 'How big is the castle, Tim?' 'Does it have a drawbridge?' 'Does your father wear a cape like Count Dracula?' They know Tim has as much chance of knowing Dracula as having an Italian count for a father.

'Oh, it's big . . . Towers over everything it does. Fills the sky it does.'

No count, no castle, and his real father was a coal haulier, but Tim's never met him, and he's certainly not Italian with a name like Evans. Tim looks a little aristocratic himself, his swept-back dark hair giving him an intelligent look, personable and impecuniously debonair. His words are simple, but his tales fluent, and that's all anyone cares about in the KPH.

Soon Tim will go on a double date with a friend to the cinema. They take out two attractive young women, little more than girls. Tim is immediately attracted to Beryl Thorley, eighteen years old and a real stunner. She lives in nearby Cambridge Garden, very close to where Tim and the Proberts have moved to on St Marks Road. For her part, Beryl is taken with Tim's charm and warmth. His limited education isn't obvious to her; he's the life and soul when he wants to be. Beryl works at the Grosvenor House Hotel in Mayfair as a switchboard operator. Mayfair! From the poverty of Merthyr Vale and his troubled childhood to courting a beautiful young woman who works in one of London's richest districts. Tim takes Beryl to visit his mother and sister most evenings. They like Beryl and are so pleased for Tim. After they get married next September Beryl will move into St Marks Road, but after she gets pregnant they will move into 10 Rillington Place just before the Easter of 1948.

John and Ethel Christie have lived at number 10 since 1938, and two young women have been buried in the back garden for almost half that time, unknown to Ethel. The final chapter of the short tragic lives of Tim and Beryl Evans – and that of their baby – is about to begin.

Early 1949, Rillington Place

It's a cold, cold winter, and hatted and coated people rush down nearby Lancaster Road towards the refuge of their homes, like a moving L. S. Lowry painting. Mr Girardot is sitting at his window, snug as a bug, watching the world go by outside. The cul-de-sac is quiet at this time in the evening, but then it's never like Piccadilly Circus. He hasn't seen the Christies all day, but that's no surprise, as they often stay indoors. He looks at the flat directly opposite, the one on the top floor of number 10. The Evanses, a young couple, moved in there last year, and he sometimes swaps pleasantries with them in the street, Mrs Evans usually holding their baby, who must be a few months old now. But this evening, through the slightly misted-up window of their flat, he doesn't see Mrs Evans but Mr Evans sitting with the baby on his lap, cooing and playing with his little girl, before putting her in her high chair.

He can make out a smile on the face of Tim Evans, and knows that he is devoted to the little newcomer. But Mr Girardot has seen Tim through that window several times before when there was no smile on his face. In fact he can sometimes hear the cries of anger and recrimination that come from across the road. Mr Girardot often wonders how noisy it is for old Mr Kitchener directly under their squabbles and the Christies below him. He expects Mr Christie does not like it; he is such a quiet man and so officious. Mr Girardot remembers when Mr Christie was a special reserve constable in the war, and how particular he was about his duties, watching the neighbourhood like a hawk, beady eyes noting all. No, not much escaped Mr Christie.

Mr Girardot doesn't know the causes of the rows between Mr and Mrs Evans, but he can guess – young couple, early married life, cramped in that tiny flat, not enough money to go round, Mr Evans out all day or down the KPH. Then the added stress of a little baby, crying and demanding the attention of two tired young parents. Mrs Evans is particularly young, and so beautiful. One time he heard a muffled argument between them, which Mr Evans had finished, getting the last word. 'You can get on with it then!' he had shouted so loudly, his words travelling clearly across the narrow street. Yes, that top-floor flat is a real pressure cooker, but young couples have to live somewhere, and such difficulties are the price they have to pay for a degree of so-called freedom. But who is really free? Mr Girardot has no idea. We're all slaves in one way or another, time has taught him.

When Tim and Beryl Evans moved into 10 Rillington Place, they spent some time redecorating their flat. It was in a bad state, mouldy and musty, but they did their best to paint over and brighten the place up, especially with a baby coming. It was their first home, and it meant a lot to them, even though it was very cramped and privacy was limited by the shared facilities. Tim was working long hours as a delivery driver for Lancaster Foods, usually making around eight pounds a week driving long distances. He left at around 6.30 in the morning and came home at around six in the evening, so Beryl needed help with the decorating. This help duly came from Tim's older sister Eileen, whom he was very close to. Eileen unselfishly helped Beryl as much as she could, and with Tim's mother and stepfather Thomasina and Penry standing as guarantors, they acquired furniture on hire purchase. Not that they could afford the new House Proud No. 390 Refrigerator that Beryl had cooed over when she saw it in an old copy of *Woman's Journal*. But by Easter their flat was ready for habitation.

Tim, Beryl and Eileen did not see very much of Ethel Christie. She was reserved and sweet, almost mouse-like, especially with her husband. It was obvious John Christie was the dominant partner in their marriage. But they all liked Ethel, who was unassuming and gentle. John appeared that way too, but there was a steely air about him, an inner confidence. His whispering voice and reserved, considered manner hid his neurotic side, the controlling aspect of his personality which could not cope when events were out of his control, but this showed itself in his domination of his wife. John did the talking when they were together, while Ethel smiled meekly and nodded. But Tim and Beryl liked the Christies and would soon feel they could confide in John. The older couple offered security.

However, Eileen felt differently. While she was helping with redecoration, she began to feel jumpy around Christie. She found him sneaky and almost insipid, a judgement which proved accurate. He would appear next to her as if from nowhere, making no noise as he moved around the house, up and down the stairs, which were bare boards, with no carpets to soften his footsteps. After a few days Eileen didn't like to be in the same room as him, and she would look over her shoulder to check he wasn't too close to her. Eileen also disliked Ethel's subservience to him, and would later say that in her opinion he intimidated her. If Ethel really was afraid of him how right she was, although she had no idea about Ruth Fuerst and Muriel Eady buried out the back.

Tim and Beryl must have settled well into their new flat, for just a few weeks after they moved in Tim's mother saw another flat advertised, and told them about it. That one had a toilet and garden space to itself, but the newly married couple did not want to move. Beryl especially was very content to stay. They had the flat just as they wanted it, and with the baby coming any disruption was the last thing Beryl needed. By the time Beryl went into hospital to have the baby in October 1948, they had been in the top-floor flat for almost six months. The new arrival was a little girl, and they named her Geraldine. Eileen, Tim's half-sister Mary and Tim's mother fussed and fretted over Geraldine. Coincidentally, Thomasina Probert, Eileen and Mary all worked at the Osram factory, where Ethel Christie had worked during the war.

There is a photograph, probably taken in early 1949, in the small, low-walled back garden of number 10, not far from the spot where Fuerst and Eady were buried, that attests to all this. Tim is on the left, arms by his side, looking at the camera and displaying the smile and excitement of a proud first-time father. Next to him, Mary is holding and looking adoringly down at Geraldine, who is facing the camera with a bemused expression. On the other side of Geraldine is her mother Beryl, just nineteen years old and smiling with pride too, looking quite beautiful. The only thing that ruins this happy image is the fact that it was almost definitely taken by John Reginald Halliday Christie.

The long hours that Tim worked were tiring, but to meet the considerable costs of a newborn baby and pay the rent and housekeeping, a combined weekly sum of five pounds, ten shillings, he had little choice. With Tim's mother (he would do jobs for her on Sunday mornings), Eileen or Mary looking after Geraldine, the new parents were able to go to the 'flicks' sometimes, and Tim continued to frequent the KPH and less often the Elgin when he could, especially on Saturdays. The stories he spun in the pub must have been a welcome relief from his routine, the drink letting him escape, as it had done before he met Beryl, and Tim could certainly sink a few beers. Any young couple with a new baby facing financial pressures and living in a tiny space would feel the stress, and Tim and Beryl were no different.

However, even before Geraldine was born there had been tensions. Beryl was little more than a girl and not domestically inclined. Her previous job as a switchboard operator had given her a measure of independence, and the death of her mother when she was young had not helped prepare her for the role of wife and mother in the late 1940s. Beryl could not cook very well and made little effort to learn, and when Tim came home from a long day delivering in his van, there was often no meal ready for him. Beryl was not a good homemaker, so the newly decorated flat was usually in some disarray, and when Tim's mother or Eileen visited, they would sometimes tidy up for Beryl. It can be imagined how the disagreements developed – to begin with, Tim trying to ignore it, then comments and protestations; Tim prodded by his family to get his wife to do her duty, and finally the inevitable rows.

The birth of Geraldine worsened the situation. Beryl loved her daughter but was not a natural mother or efficient carer.

Eileen soon started to take Geraldine round to St Marks Road for a thorough wash and a change of clothes on Saturday mornings, and she must have told her mother and brother Tim that the baby was not kept as clean as she might have been. This was not wilful neglect on Beryl's part, but this was little consolation to Tim. With his financial worries – rent, furniture payments and day-to-day expenses – it is little wonder that tempers began to flare. Debt is a cause of argument in many young families, and there is evidence that Tim was falling behind.

While Beryl was an incompetent household manager, Tim was no saint. He spent any spare money he had down the pub on beer, and as the pressures grew so did his consumption. Able to hold a good amount of alcohol, there is no evidence that he was an alcoholic, but a binge was a serious problem when there was no money left. As Ludovic Kennedy pointed out in *Ten Rillington Place*, 'On one occasion Beryl threw a jar at Evans's head, and he had to go round to his mother's to get the wound dressed. Another time they were seen exchanging blows in front of the window.' It is likely that Mr Girardot witnessed the latter scene. There is no evidence that Tim was physically abusive to Beryl, but they would tussle when arguing: Beryl was feisty, and gave as good as she got.

The Christies heard the fights too – it would have been impossible for them not to. They probably secretly pleased Christie, although he would whisper soothing words to Beryl on the stairs and in the hallway until some trust built up between them while moaning to Ethel about the noise. In the cramped confines of the house, contact with Christie and to a lesser extent his wife was inevitable, especially as John Christie would ensure that he ran into Beryl – a beautiful young woman, right there and closer than on his doorstep – whenever possible.

Christie squints his penetrating eyes behind the strong lenses of his glasses, his ear pressed against the inside of the kitchen door of his flat. Ethel is shopping, and he has eavesdropping time. He knows the sound of each tenant's footsteps. Tim's are springy, heavy and bounding, but he's at work anyway, and won't be back for some time yet. Mr Kitchener is slow and with a broken rhythm, as he tackles the stairs like an assault course with his increasingly failing eyes. Then there's Beryl's, soft and swift. That's what he hears coming down now, the footfalls ever nearer.

Christie knows exactly how hard he can lean against his door without making a sound. He's also acutely aware when he needs to open the door to catch his prey in the hallway. And abruptly won't do. Soft is the key here, as if he's popping out to the lavatory himself, or perhaps checking on the clothes drying in the wash house. He hears it now, that step on the stairs which creaks more than the others, even under Beryl's light weight, the creak that he has to avoid when he goes up the stairs himself in his old plimsolls. He waits for two more of Beryl's soft steps. Now is the time to strike.

He opens the door gently. Just as planned, Beryl is right outside the door.

'Oh, Mr Christie, you gave me a fright!'

'I am sorry, my dear,' says Christie. His Yorkshire accent is just discernible, so soothing to the ear. Christie tells people that he has some medical knowledge, but in reality his only qualification is his voice, which would improve many a doctor's bedside manner. 'How are things with Timothy?' says Christie. 'Calmer, are they?'

He knows he has her. It's just not the right time to go in for the kill, although he would like nothing more. Control is important here, he knows. The release will come later, and all the better for the wait. As Beryl keeps talking, his eyes undress her. It won't be too long now . . .

It was in the August of 1949 that the tensions between Tim and Beryl came to a climax. Geraldine was now almost ten months old when Beryl invited her friend Lucy Endecott, two years younger than her at seventeen, blonde and attractive, to come and stay. Beryl and Lucy shared the bed, while Tim, after a hard day's driving and delivering, found himself on the cold floor of the small kitchen. After another row, Tim must have gone round to his mother's in St Marks Road and poured out his heart, needing a release. This prompted Thomasina Probert, who had helped her son through his many troubles, to go round to 10 Rillington Place and inform Lucy that she would have to leave. This led to blows, and for some reason Beryl struck Lucy, who lashed out at Thomasina. Tim lunged at Beryl, who picked up a sharp knife to protect herself, and Tim threatened to push her out of the window. Incredibly, a short time later Tim, who was attracted to Lucy, left with her, telling Beryl he would not return.

Tim stayed somewhere with Lucy for one night, but they too fell out. Tim went back to Rillington Place and found a note that Beryl had left for him, obviously knowing he would return. The note, which Tim had to ask a friend to read, told him that she did not want any more contact with him. Tim was distraught, but Beryl backed down when he apologised, and he was soon back living with his wife and baby.

It was not too long after these events that perhaps the worst thing that could have happened in the circumstances did. Beryl found herself pregnant again. With their finances already stretched to the limit and tensions still close to the surface, the timing was awful. Beryl, who worked part time now and was already struggling with Geraldine, could not face the struggle that would come from a second baby. After taking pills several times to induce a miscarriage, each occasion unsuccessfully, she told Tim she intended to have an abortion. Tim was very unhappy about this, partly because he did not want a child of his terminated, partly because of the risk to Beryl (considerable in 1949) and partly because it was illegal. But Beryl was adamant.

Tim had been brought up as a Roman Catholic, and his mother and sister would have been vehemently against any abortion. Thomasina Probert lived by a religion that considered abortion nothing short of murder. Tim was probably less steadfast, but initially it just was not an option for him. However, Beryl was the one carrying the baby, and would be most affected by its birth. On Beryl's side there were no family constraints to consider. Her mother had passed away years before, and the relationship that she had with her father, who lived in Brighton, was less than close.

Backstreet terminations were common and abortion would remain illegal in Britain until the late 1960s. Although the

National Health Service had been established just the year before in 1948, there was nobody to talk to about an unwanted baby and Beryl knew that she would have to act soon. Through a friend, Beryl learned that there was a doctor on the Edgware Road in central London who carried out abortions for a fee of one pound, but she knew there were serious risks in such procedures for the mother. Nevertheless she was firmly against having the baby, and Tim was coming round to the idea that an abortion was the only option but that it had to be kept secret. Little did they know at this stage that a possible solution lay very close to home, with a man whom they trusted but in reality was already a double murderer.

Beginning of November, 1949

Two builders, Mr Jones and Mr Willis, have been repairing the roof outside the Christies' flat. Tim Evans walks through the front door of 10 Rillington Place, gladly shutting it on the drizzly evening outside. After a long day's driving and delivering, he is hungry and hopes that Beryl has prepared something hot. But as he turns to go up the stairs, Mr Christie comes silently out of his flat, greeting him in the hallway. Christie knows about Beryl's unwanted pregnancy and her attempts to miscarry, both she and Tim having confided in the homely and avuncular older couple downstairs. As usual speaking in little more than a whisper, the last voice heard by Ruth Fuerst and Muriel Eady, Christie brings up the subject of Beryl's dilemma and invites Tim into his living room.

Christie is reassuring and measured as he always is,

particularly because he has been thinking about what he will say all day and the night before. Why didn't you ask me to help? he asks. I had no idea that you could, says Tim. Didn't you know that I started training to be a doctor before the war? No, I had no idea, says Tim, taking off his wet overcoat. Why did you stop training? Oh, I had an accident and was forced to stop, says Christie. Tim is still not convinced. I've performed such a procedure several times successfully already, says Christie. Tim looks more impressed, and Christie, the shrewd watcher, takes his chance to take out his 'medical textbook', which he has placed conveniently to hand. The illiterate Tim looks at the thin book, which is actually a first aid manual produced by the St John's Ambulance service. Tim sees some diagrams. It certainly is a medical book, but he does not know that Christie got the manual when he was a special reserve constable and that he has no medical training at all.

Tim asks Christie how he did 'the procedure'. Oh, it's too technical, and only medical men understand it, says Christie, although he does add that it can be dangerous, and that one in ten women die during or as a result of it. Tim thanks him but says that they don't need his help, thank you, and picking up his overcoat leaves Christie and makes his way upstairs to his flat. But Tim doesn't know that Christie has already planted the seed of a possible solution to her problem in Beryl's mind when talking to her earlier (Christie is off work with a doctor's note because of 'nervous diarrhoea'), and that the increasingly desperate Beryl is taking Mr Christie's kind offer seriously.

Up in the flat, where Geraldine has 'just gone down', Beryl

asks quietly if kind Mr Christie has spoken to him. Tim tells her all Christie said and that he told their neighbour that they are not interested. But Beryl tells him that she *is* interested, that she is the one who should make the choice, as it's her body, and that kind Mr Christie is her best option. They go to bed that night with the matter unresolved, but Beryl has already made up her own mind. Downstairs, Mr Christie waits for his seed to bear fruit, the prize being intimate contact with Beryl, who still has not noticed that her prospective abortionist licks his lips and undresses her with his eyes.

Domestic life did not improve for Tim and Beryl over the next few days, with the question of the abortion hanging in the air. Added to this were the usual financial worries, Beryl having mismanaged the household budget. The builders did not help, as when Beryl was not at work she was stuck in the tiny flat with the constant sound of banging coming from outside. Tim came home and went to work, but another serious argument on Sunday about money, worsened by underlying tension over the developing baby, took a heavy toll, with Tim threatening to leave, and Beryl telling him that it was fine with her if he did. Storming out, Tim spent the rest of the day sinking drinks at the KPH, punctuated by a trip to the flicks on his own, drowning his worries until tomorrow.

On getting up for work the next morning, as wind and rain lashed against the rattling window panes, Tim and Beryl had another sarcastic interchange. He tried to block out her anxious cajoling about the abortion, which saturated her waking thoughts. When Tim looked in on little Geraldine before he set off for work, Beryl told him that she was going to go down to her father's in Brighton with the baby. Assuming this was an empty threat, Tim told his nineteen-year-old wife that it would make his life easier.

At some point that day, while Tim was eating up the miles in his van, Beryl either went down to speak to Mr Christie or he came up to see her in the flat. Christie again reassured her that he could carry out the procedure with no trouble. This was exactly what Beryl needed to hear and she agreed. They arranged for the abortion to take place the following morning, a Tuesday, on Beryl's own bed. It is not known whether Ethel Christie had any knowledge of this plan. When Tim came home that Monday evening, he asked his wife why she was not in Brighton with her father, picking up the conversation where they had left it that morning. She told Tim that she had no intention of making his life any easier and that Mr Christie was going to do 'it' early the next day. Somehow not saying the word was easier. An abortion was an ending to a life not yet lived, and an ending that could not be restarted.

Tim could hardly believe it, but Beryl had made up her mind. Tim would later say that another argument took place later that evening, which ended with him threatening, 'I'd slap her face'. At this Beryl grabbed an empty milk bottle to throw at him. Tim wrestled the proposed missile from her, pushed her into the chair in the tiny kitchen and then went down to the KPH, his refuge from reality.

At six o'clock the next morning, Tuesday, 8 November 1949, just twelve days before his twenty-fifth birthday, Tim

Evans got up for work, and Beryl unusually got up with him. As he drank his usual cup of strong tea and enjoyed his first cigarette of the day, Beryl told him to tell Mr Christie on his way out that 'everything is all right'. This meant that she was ready for Christie to 'do' it, and if Tim didn't tell Christie this, she would just go downstairs and tell him herself. Now sure that Beryl was serious, he did what he was told. Christie's machinations had worked, and he was finally going to get what he had dreamed about for months. But as Tim went to work that morning, leaving the house a few minutes after 6.30, he did not know that he would never see Beryl alive again. That is what Timothy Evans later said, anyway.

CHAPTER
8

The self-satisfied smirk on the face of John George Haigh does not give away the envy he feels of the man who breezes past wearing a I Zingari club blazer in the Tudor Lounge of the Onslow Court Hotel. Haigh knows that it is superior to the one he is wearing, inherited from his friend Dr Archie Henderson. The passing man's blazer is hardly of the January 1949 moment but was de rigueur for an earlier generation in the West End clubs. The man's advanced age reflects this, but thirty-nine-year-old Haigh knows that he could have one whenever he wants, if he should be so inclined. He has the power to get what he wants, as well as the power of life and death. As he sits with his usual upright posture in the finely carved Georgian easy chair, Haigh does not know (or need to know) that clothes rationing will end in two months. But then nobody else knows either, including the sixty-nine-year-old widow sitting opposite him in the twin of his own chair. Quickly looking back at his friend Mrs Durand-Deacon, he gives her one of his attentive smiles, showing no teeth, as he has had dentistry problems recently. Olive Durand-Deacon smiles back, flashing teeth that she was not born with and in fact acquired not so long ago.

Haigh is avuncular and safe, calling a man he met through business a 'good egg', a phrase he knows that women of Mrs Durand-Deacon's age feel at home with. Haigh usually tries to steer the conversation around to his 'business' when talking to the widow, it being firmly in his interests to do so. Mrs Durand-Deacon has taken to him, and has been his acquaintance for some time, since Haigh arrived at the hotel, but recently they have seen much more of each other, sharing a dining table and sitting in the lounge when Haigh is not out dealing with business. Haigh attends literary luncheons arranged by Foyles bookshop on the Charing Cross Road in the West End, and patronises classical concerts and the ballet, satisfying the musical passion that has stayed with him since his days as a choirboy at Wakefield Cathedral. He often goes to these concerts with a female friend. Barbara Stephens is much younger than Haigh, almost half his age at twenty, and attractive, and they enjoy each other's company, but there is no sexual side to their relationship. Haigh hasn't had a sex life since his wife divorced him after having their child years ago. He met Barbara in 1944, when he worked in Crawley, where she is from, when she was just fifteen years old.

Mrs Durand-Deacon is well dressed, as always, her large black hat resembling a bicorne of the kind once worn by Lord Nelson, and her hair is well dyed a dark brown, helping to make her look younger than her years. In fact, a member of the hotel staff will later say that she could pass as fifty-five, fourteen years younger than her actual age.

She is tall at five feet nine inches and plump, the latter being evident by the way she fills her chair. The pearl necklace around her neck, her other jewellery and the expensive dress she wears show that she is an elderly lady of some means, her late husband having left her very well provided for. None of this has of course been lost on Haigh, nor the fact that she doesn't mention family much, although she has a sister who also lives in Kensington, in Ashburn Gardens. She also has several good friends, especially Mrs Lane, another woman of her age who also resides at the hotel.

Olive Henrietta Helen Olivia Robarts Durand-Deacon has lived at the Onslow Court Hotel for a little over six years, moving there in the middle of the war. Her husband was a military man, a colonel in the Gloucestershire Regiment, but he died in 1938, and Olive has never stopped missing him. She is very well bred, a stickler for manners and something of a snob, although she knows that Haigh is not of good family, his slight Yorkshire accent and too-ostentatious dress telling her that. But he is impeccably mannered and courteous, what she calls a 'gentleman', and the glint in his eye makes him interesting. Little does she know that five other people who have seen that glint are all dead, and not just that, but vanished – they have ceased to exist. Almost painfully polite herself, she does not suffer fools gladly, as they say. A fellow guest will later say that if somebody did not meet her standards, 'she would more than likely get up from her seat and move away'. Her life at the hotel is comfortable and predictable. Mrs Durand-Deacon likes routine and

loathes confusion, and she is shrewd. Each evening she wears
a different gown for dinner, and sometimes she wears the
equivalent of five hundred pounds' worth of jewellery at
one time.

Haigh also knows that Mrs Durand-Deacon's room at the
hotel is far superior to his and so costs much more. In fact,
Olive Durand-Deacon pays twelve pounds and twelve shillings a week for her double room, number 115 on the first
floor, a very considerable sum, around one and a half times
the average working man's weekly wage. Haigh's single
room, 404, costs him less than half that, five pounds, fifteen
shillings and six pence a week, not forgetting 10 per cent
extra for services, also a significant rent. But while Mrs
Durand-Deacon pays her rent in advance without undue
calculation (like royalty she doesn't carry much cash, paying
for almost everything by cheque), Haigh is already a week
behind with his, is overdrawn at the bank, with no wage
coming in and no large sum on the horizon. Incredibly, he
has already squandered the huge sum he gained from the
murder and disposal of his friends Archie and Rose Henderson,
who in fact had sat in these very same chairs with him in
the hotel lounge just over a year before.

The fact that Haigh is once again on his uppers is very
telling. The thousands of pounds he got from the Hendersons
in cash and assets through forgery is more money than most
people will ever have at one time, but Haigh lives big, and
his expensive meals in restaurants and frequenting of clubs,
some of which the late Neville Heath also went to, is only
half the story. Haigh now has a serious gambling problem.
As they say in America, he's in love with the gee-gees, and

horse and greyhound races have accounted for much of the life-changing sum the Hendersons unwillingly bequeathed him. He loses far more than he wins, and for Haigh, who needs to be in control, this is very frustrating, but he cannot stop, and like most people with an addiction does not know he has one. This is what has led him to begin again, and he has big plans for the elderly widow smiling sweetly in front of him.

When the manageress of the Onslow Court walks through the lounge, greeting them as always, Haigh feels a twinge of unease, but he covers it well. The manageress had words with him yesterday, taking him aside quietly to discuss his rent. Haigh was charm personified, explaining that he was waiting for a cheque to clear, so sorry for the inconvenience, and how embarrassing that she had personally to bring it to his attention. However, Haigh knows that even his old-fashioned easy charm will not hold the manageress off for ever. In hotels such as this regular residents are never late with their bills. They live there because they can afford to do so. All is far from lost, however. Ever the schemer, Haigh glances at Mrs Durand-Deacon, noting that the necklace she wears would pay his rent for some weeks. The same thin-lipped smile crosses his face as he pours her another cup of well-strained tea into the finest china this side of Buckingham Palace, just as she likes it.

The opportunity that Haigh had been waiting for came several weeks later, rather cruelly on St Valentine's Day, 14 February. It was a Monday, and as on every Monday Mrs Durand-Deacon had lunch with her friend Mrs Gwendoline

Birin, who was the assistant secretary of the Francis Bacon Society. As they were chatting about everyday subjects, having spoken about the original Francis Bacon (the subsequently internationally famous twentieth-century artist was probably battling away in his studio across town or drinking in one pub or another), Mr Haigh came over to their table. Not sitting down until he was invited, it was soon clear to him that Mrs Durand-Deacon had a reason for allowing him to interrupt her lunch with Mrs Birin. She took a small box out of the pocket of her expensive Persian lamb coat and gave it to Haigh. He opened it and saw that it contained artificial fingernails made of plastic. Mrs Durand-Deacon told Haigh that such fingernails were now very popular, and they agreed to meet in the lounge later to discuss the matter further, Haigh saying that he did not wish to impose on them any longer and apologising to Mrs Birin. As the dapper Haigh walked away, the two ladies commented on what a nice man he was.

Haigh was now seriously in debt. His bank overdraft stood at eighty-three pounds, and he had not paid his rent since early January. No longer able to write cheques without them bouncing, the increasingly firm reminders he was receiving from the Onslow Court manageress were becoming trouble-some, as he now owed around fifty pounds, once service charges and meals were added. When Mrs Durand-Deacon showed him those fingernails, he inferred that she was suggesting a possible business proposition, as she knew him as a businessman and engineer, and he was extremely inter-ested. Not that the beauty product excited him – the profit, if any, from such a business venture would take far too long to come in. No, he already secretly had a better business proposition, and the product was Mrs-Durand Deacon herself. She would of course be a silent and unknowing partner, having no idea of his intentions until a split second before she fell to the ground.

When he met Mrs Durand-Deacon later that day the 'in' that he needed was indeed presented to him. Haigh listened attentively, his characteristic smile indicating his excitement. She told him of a new kind of artificial fingernail that she wished to produce, offering out her outstretched hands to show him some paper nails glued to her own fingernails that she had made. He nodded his approval. She asked him if he could make and market them. Haigh said that it was a good idea and that he would come back with an answer for her very soon. Of course, he knew the answer, and it was yes.

Haigh wasted no time, a sign of his increasing arrogance. He had disposed of the McSwans and the Hendersons with no comeback, and two more people he would claim to have killed, although those two were probably fantasy. His desperate need for cash also perhaps made him move more quickly than he usually did. The very next day he began to put his next macabre project in motion.

Haigh drove down to his Giles Yard workshop in Crawley, where he had disposed of the Hendersons almost exactly a year before, in his Alvis. Then he went and saw a welding engineer he knew, Mr Davies, who had obtained some sulphuric acid for him a year earlier, not knowing of course that it was to make two people vanish. Haigh asked Davies to perform the same task again for him, which Davies agreed to do. The operation involved Haigh ordering a carboy (ten gallons) of acid from White's of London EC1 under his own name and Davies collecting it and taking it to Giles Yard, where a further two carboys already sat. Haigh's next task was to visit his former boss Mr Jones at Hurstlea Products, from whom he rented the workshop. Haigh, needing ready cash, asked Jones for a short-term loan of fifty pounds, to which Jones agreed, with Haigh promising to pay it back by the end of the week.

The money was not to put his plan into action, one beauty of which was its cheapness. He would have to speculate very little to accumulate a great deal from Mrs Durand-Deacon. He paid off his hotel bill, much to the relief of the manageress, and this left him with the princely sum of four shillings, eleven pence, but he knew that he had much more coming very soon. To that end, he approached Mrs Durand-Deacon at breakfast on Wednesday morning, telling her that he liked her artificial fingernail idea, and inviting her down to his 'factory' in Crawley. She agreed to go with him on Friday. Haigh would later say in a police statement, 'She was inveigled into going to Crawley by me in view of her interest in artificial fingernails.' Also that Wednesday afternoon, Haigh drove over to Barking in east London and bought a forty-five-gallon acid-resistant green tank, which he took down to the workshop.

The day of their outing, Haigh breakfasted with Mrs Durand-Deacon in the Onslow Court dining room, arranging to meet her in the Tudor Lounge at lunchtime. Haigh was to make two trips to Crawley that day, both in his Alvis, as that morning he drove down to check that the acid was prepared. While he was there, he helped his former boss Mr

Jones to remove some materials from Giles Yard and take them round to the Hurstlea Products building on nearby West Street. He was back at the Onslow Court at lunchtime as arranged. Mrs Durand-Deacon had already had lunch, so they decided to leave immediately. Haigh had yet to eat, something he would rectify later, but now he had pressing work to do.

Friday, 18 February 1949

The drive down to Crawley in Haigh's Alvis is going smoothly. Olive Durand-Deacon sits beside him. She is wearing stud pearl earrings and a pearl necklace, and on her fingers are several rings, a dress ring on her right hand set with a pale-green emerald surrounded by small diamonds; on the other a blue sapphire ring with two diamonds and two further half-hoop diamond rings. She also has a ruby and diamond wristwatch and a gold cruciform brooch on her Persian lamb coat, underneath which she wears an expensive royal-blue dress. As always, her outfit is topped with a large black hat, and she has a handbag, of course. She and Haigh chat about their business idea, him telling her that he would like her to look at some special paper he feels could be used to manu-facture the fingernails. She doesn't notice that Haigh, in his fawn overcoat, occasionally stares at her jewellery.

As they come into Crawley, Haigh pulls into the George Hotel. They want to use the toilets. It is now 4.15 p.m. – hotel staff will later verify the time. After they leave, Haigh drives directly to Leopold Road, turning into Giles Yard. They walk through the untidy yard and, as Haigh unlocks the workshop door, Mrs Durand-Deacon doubtless thinks to herself that this is a very modest factory. What happens next is almost a carbon copy of the method used on the Hendersons. Haigh wastes no time. He takes Mrs Durand-Deacon over to the table where he has laid out some paper, which she begins to examine for its suitability for fingernails. The shot comes from behind into the back of her head, and Mrs Durand-Deacon is taken completely unaware. Once she is laid out on the floor, Haigh goes out to his Alvis and brings in a drinking glass. Haigh's statements must always be read with caution, but he later told the police that he 'made an incision, I think with a penknife, in the side of the throat. I collected a glass of blood, which I then drank.'

Haigh removes Mrs Durand-Deacon's coat, the rings, earrings, necklace, cruciform brooch and watch, but leaves her clothed in her dress. It takes quite an effort to lift her into the green tank. Mrs Durand-Deacon is heavy. He picks up her handbag and removes around thirty shillings in cash and a good fountain pen, and then throws the rest of the contents and the bag itself into the tank on top of the body. Haigh then decides to take a break from his labours, the hard work now done. Locking up the workshop, he goes round to West Street and tells Mr Jones that the visitor he had said he was expecting when he saw him that morning has not come after all. It is now about 4.50 p.m.

Having covered his tracks in this regard, Haigh goes back to the workshop. At around ten past six a man who usually leaves his van overnight in Giles Yard sees Haigh going backwards and forwards between the workshop and his car. At about 6.45 p.m. Haigh walks into the nearby Ancient Prior's restaurant. There he has a chat with the owner, Mr Outram, whom he knows quite well, and who later says that Haigh was no different to normal. He orders and consumes a cup of tea and poached egg on toast. After his very late lunch, Haigh returns to the workshop. It is now a little after seven o'clock.

Again using his stirrup pump, he fills the tank with sulphuric acid. It is a slow process, but not as slow as waiting for it to react. Haigh puts his revolver back inside the hatbox in the workshop from which he had taken it earlier. At about 9 p.m. he enters the George Hotel, where he and the late Olive Durand-Deacon had dropped in less than five hours earlier. Haigh, now knowing that new funds are imminent, enjoys a three-course dinner with all the trimmings. After that he drives to London and is back at the Onslow Court Hotel in South Kensington by just after 10.30. Mrs Durand-Deacon's jewellery and coat are now in his possession, and Haigh is proud of his day's work.

It was at breakfast on Saturday morning that questions began to be asked. Mrs Durand-Deacon had not turned up for dinner the previous evening, and a waitress, Mary, who knew her well, asked Haigh if he knew if she was well. He said that he did not know and immediately went over to Mrs Constance Lane's table. She was Mrs Durand-Deacon's best friend at the Onslow Court and had lived there for about nine years. Mrs Lane knew everybody although Haigh only in passing. It was characteristic of Haigh to be proactive in building his story, a way for him to gain control over the situation. He asked Mrs Lane if she knew whether Mrs Durand-Deacon had been taken ill, and Mrs Lane replied that she had not spoken to Olive but had noticed that she had not been at dinner the night before too.

Mrs Lane then said something that made Haigh realise this was not going to be as easy as the vanishing of the McSwans and the Hendersons. She said that Olive had told her that she had arranged to meet Mr Haigh the previous day and to drive with him down to Sussex. Haigh's reply was fast, and may or may not have been thought out. He told Mrs Lane that he had arranged to meet Mrs Durand-Deacon outside the Army & Navy Stores in Victoria Street, SW1. When he came to meet her at the hotel, he said, he had not had lunch, and so she had gone shopping and asked him to collect her outside the department store later. However, Mrs Durand-Deacon had not kept the appointment. It was typical of Haigh to mix fact with fiction (he had not had lunch), and this account tallied with what he had told Mr Jones in Crawley – that his visitor had not come after all. Mrs Lane was worried now, and asked hotel staff and residents if they had seen Mrs Durand-Deacon, even getting a maid to check her room, which had not been slept in.

This turn of events did not stop Haigh from continuing with his plans. He had committed the murder, and now was the time to collect. He expected to make a killing. If questions continued to be asked, it would make it more difficult and risky to get his hands on Mrs Durand-Deacon's assets by forgery, but he still had the items he had taken from her body. That Saturday morning he got back into his Alvis and drove to Putney in south-west London, on the way to Crawley. In Putney High Street Haigh used a fictitious name and address to sell Mrs Durand-Deacon's expensive wristwatch for ten pounds. Then he continued to Crawley, went back to the Giles Yard workshop but saw that the elderly widow was not yet dissolved. Driving to Horsham, he went to Bull's, where he had sold some of the Hendersons' possessions the year before, for a valuation of his victim's jewellery. But the proprietor was not there, so Haigh went on to Reigate in Surrey on his way back to London, where he left Mrs Durand-Deacon's coat at Cottage Cleaners to be dry-cleaned.

The next morning, as the Onslow Court Hotel residents and guests were enjoying a leisurely Sunday breakfast in the dining room, Haigh, playing the concerned fellow friend, went over to Mrs Lane to ask if she had heard anything of Mrs Durand-Deacon. Mrs Lane said that she had not heard anything and commented on how strange it was, as Olive was such a woman of routine. She added that she was going to report Olive missing at nearby Chelsea police station. This must have sent a chill through Haigh, if he had any normal reactions at all. He left her, needing time to think, but a short while later approached Mrs Lane again, this time in the Tudor Lounge, saying that he would go to the police station with her. This was a bold move by Haigh, as he would have to use his real name and had a long criminal record for fraud, if not for violence. But again it was his way of attempting to get some purchase on a situation rapidly spinning out of his control.

It was at about a quarter past two on that Sunday afternoon, 20 February 1949, that Haigh opened the front passenger door of his Alvis and courteously waited for Mrs Lane to be seated before getting into the driver's seat himself.

One wonders if it ever crossed Haigh's mind to do to Mrs Lane what he had done to her friend to silence her, but that would have made him a prime suspect in two disappearances. However, if Mrs Lane had known what nice Mr Haigh – whom remember she did not know well – had done to poor Olive, she would certainly not have got into that car alone with him, just as Olive had done almost exactly two days earlier.

When they got to Chelsea police station, they spoke to a policewoman, Sergeant Lambourne, who would later say that she instantly distrusted the smug and spivvy Haigh. Mrs Lane reported Olive Durand-Deacon missing and gave a description of her, while Haigh repeated his cover story: that she had not kept their appointment outside the Army & Navy Stores. That same afternoon Sergeant Lambourne went to the Onslow Court Hotel herself and began making preliminary inquiries, building up a picture of the missing woman, and what the hotel's manageress told her about Mr Haigh often being late with his rent deepened the policewoman's unease about him.

However, Haigh had no knowledge of this, and the next morning he drove down to Crawley again to check on Mrs Durand-Deacon's progress. He found dissolution still not complete and siphoned off some sludge containing fat and bone by using a bucket, and then poured this residue into Giles Yard. Putting on his gas mask and rubber outfit, he stirrup-pumped more acid into the green tank to dissolve the rest of the body. Having removed his killing clothes, he got back in his car and went to Horsham again, calling at Bull's. The owner was in this time. Haigh presented Mrs

Durand-Deacon's jewellery and asked for a probate valuation. Mr Bull quoted him a little over £130 for the lot. Back in Crawley, he called in on Mr Jones at Hurstlea Products on West Street, telling him that he would pay back the loan of fifty pounds the following day.

Ever cool and collected, or probably psychopathic or at least sociopathic, Haigh betrayed no shock and was unflustered when he was greeted by Detective Inspector Symes and Detective Inspector Webb back at the Onslow Court Hotel that evening. DI Symes informed Haigh that he was making inquiries into Mrs Durand-Deacon's disappearance, and Haigh responded that he had been expecting this, as he had reported her missing with Mrs Lane. DI Webb wrote down Haigh's words as he repeated once again the failed meeting at the Army & Navy and how he and Mrs Lane had been very concerned about Mrs Durand-Deacon's welfare.

Haigh had no idea that the presence of these senior officers was largely due to Sergeant Lambourne, who had felt uneasy about Haigh the previous day. That very morning, while Haigh was checking on progress in Crawley, Sergeant Lambourne had telephoned Scotland Yard and asked if they had a John George Haigh on their files. They had reported back to her that Haigh had a lengthy criminal record and had been to prison for fraud three times. This was too much of a coincidence for the police to ignore, especially coupled with the fact that Haigh was sometimes very late paying his hotel bill. The police were sniffing around him now and would continue to do so.

Haigh ploughed on regardless. He drove back to Horsham the next day, and Mr Bull the jeweller bought Mrs

Durand-Deacon's pieces for one hundred pounds, giving Haigh sixty pounds there and then, asking him to come back for the other forty the following day. Just as he had done when selling the wristwatch in Putney, Haigh gave a fictitious name and address. Then he motored on to Crawley and paid back thirty-six of the fifty pounds he owed Mr Jones, saying he would come back the next day with the remainder. At the workshop the dissolution of Mrs Durand-Deacon was complete (or so Haigh thought), and he poured the rest of the sludge into Giles Yard. But her handbag had hardly dissolved at all – it was made of plastic – although the handle and bottom had broken apart. Careless or arrogant, Haigh hid it behind the yard fence under some loose bricks. As Haigh got back into his Alvis he must have been thinking once again, as he had since the beginning of his murderous career, corpus delicti: no body, no conviction.

The next day was Wednesday, and Haigh was back at Bull's in Horsham, collecting his forty pounds. After stopping at his bank in Crawley to deposit five pounds in his account, Haigh went to see Mr Jones on West Street to pay back the other fourteen pounds he owed. Jones was not happy to see him, saying that the police had visited, asking questions. Haigh laughed this off, but Jones said that he would rather that Haigh left and did not come back, which Haigh did, without paying the fourteen pounds.

Any normal person would have been unsettled by the fact that the police had linked them to an old employer whose premises were very close to where a missing woman was supposed to have been on the last day she was seen. But Haigh was not remotely normal, and did not react accordingly. Another killer would have fled, but Haigh continued as usual. The following day the police were back at the Onslow Court asking more questions, and he again repeated his cover story, adding more colour this time. The police would later comment on how eager to help Haigh had seemed, but they were very suspicious of him now. Unknown to him, he was their chief suspect, and the West Sussex Police were cooperating with their colleagues in London to investigate Haigh, leaving no stone, and eventually sludge, unturned.

That Saturday was the turning point in the investigation. Haigh's former boss Mr Jones, who owned the Giles Yard workshop, took West Sussex Detective Sergeant Heslin to the modest shed that Haigh had called his factory when inviting the late Mrs Durand-Deacon there. The door was locked, and the policeman had to force his way in. Inside were the three carboys, and a search revealed Haigh's killing apparatus: the rubber clothing, stirrup pump and gas mask. There was also a briefcase, which contained a key that was found to fit a leather hatbox. When the hatbox was opened, a .38 Enfield revolver and some ammunition were revealed, along with a receipt from Cottage Cleaners of Reigate for one Persian lamb coat. The evidence against Haigh was building fast. Over the next two days DI Symes visited the workshop from London and picked up Mrs Durand-Deacon's coat from Cottage Cleaners. Mrs Lane and others swiftly identified this as their missing friend's coat.

In his book *Villain's Paradise* Donald Thomas recounts how at some point around this time a journalist called Conrad

Phillips spied Haigh in a tea room in Kensington and tried to get him to talk about Mrs Durand-Deacon's disappearance. This shows that some in the press were well aware of the suspicions about Haigh held by the police and is not surprising as the Murder Gang had many inside contacts. Unsurprisingly, Phillips could get nothing out of him, but as Haigh's afternoon tea arrived at the table, the reporter asked him how he could sit there calmly with all that was going on. 'They put real butter on the scones,' said Haigh.

In his memoirs Harry Procter wrote that it was on that Sunday evening that he went to room 404 of the Onslow Court Hotel and knocked on the door. He also wrote that there was 'an army of crime reporters' waiting for Haigh outside the hotel who had no idea that he was in his room – another illustration of the special contacts and knowledge of the elite Murder Gang. Procter heard Haigh call 'Come in!' from inside his room. When Procter opened the door, Haigh came towards him, asking how he could have known he was there. But this was the sort of tenacity that got Procter his scoops, now for the *Sunday Pictorial*. A Yorkshireman like Haigh – although Haigh was actually born in Lincolnshire – Procter reminisced about life in the north, relaxing Haigh, a technique he often employed on his targets. Soon Haigh was talking about the police, Procter quoting him as saying, 'The police are a lot of imbeciles. They couldn't catch colds. They have nothing on me, but even if they had they'd never prove it. To an intelligent man like me these coppers are like children.'

But then Procter went in for the kill, having done some research himself. He told Haigh that he could not have parked his car in the car park in Victoria Street when he went to meet Mrs Durand-Deacon at the Army & Navy Stores, as he had told the police. Procter had visited the car park and spoken to the elderly man in charge of it, who charged each motorist a shilling to park there, giving out a ticket and keeping a record of every car. The reporter had looked at the man's log, and there was no note of the registration of Haigh's Alvis on that day. Procter wrote that when he said this Haigh 'went white'. Harry Procter then noted that he told the police about this and that Haigh was arrested two days later. He may well have told the police, but this evidence was hardly enough to make an arrest. That evidence was being gathered at the Crawley workshop.

Moreover, although Harry Procter would write Haigh's story for his paper, he got his information from secondary sources, as did many others, and it was Norman 'Jock' Rae of the *News of the World* who would get the story from Haigh's mouth with details not even given to the police. In his 1950 book *Crime Man* Fleet Street reporter Stanley Firmin, a fellow member of the Murder Gang with Rae and Procter, wrote, 'Norman is one of the best-known crime reporters at the Yard. He is also well known to judges and counsel at Assize courts throughout the country.' This veteran and his paper, which had the biggest circulation of any British newspaper at the time, would get one of the juiciest crime scoops of the century with Haigh.

In fact, on the very day Procter said he knocked on the door of Haigh's room at the Onslow Court Hotel, Sunday, 27 February 1949, the *News of the World* ran its first report on the disappearance of Mrs Olive Durand-Deacon, putting it on the front page. There was no mention of Haigh, as he had not been arrested or charged with anything, and gossip among reporters was, legally speaking, hearsay. Under the headline 'MISSING WIDOW: MURDER FEAR – YARD MIDNIGHT APPEAL: HAVE YOU SEEN HER?' there was a photograph of Mrs Durand-Deacon, a large black hat setting off her black outfit, her face solemn, and an expensive necklace around her neck, undoubtedly one of those that Haigh had salivated over. There was also a subtitle – 'THE LADY VANISHES' – perhaps an allusion to Alfred Hitchcock's popular 1938 thriller of the same name, the last film he made in Britain before going to America.

Police operations in Crawley and Horsham as well as London were mentioned, and also the fact that an anony-mous member of the public had called the police claiming to have seen Mrs Durand-Deacon when, as subsequently became clear, she had been dead for nine days. The report stated that no cheques had been cashed on Mrs Durand-Deacon's bank account since her disappearance, something that Haigh would have eventually rectified with forgeries if the furore had not erupted. The piece ended with a quote from Mrs Durand-Deacon's sister, Miss Fargus: 'I've no idea of any reason for my sister's disappearance. It is a complete mystery.' The reason was money, and she had been killed by what would later be called a serial killer, a man she had trusted and chatted with almost daily.

It was the next day, Monday, 28 February, that Haigh was finally brought in by the police. Detective Inspector Webb called at the Onslow Court to ask Haigh to accompany him to Chelsea police station and, as ever, Haigh was the epitome of cooperation. That was at about quarter past four in the afternoon, but Detective Inspector Symes and his superior Superintendent Barratt would not interview Haigh until over three hours later. Haigh remained unruffled and accommodating.

DI Symes started with Mrs Durand-Deacon's Persian lamb coat, which had been retrieved from Cottage Cleaners in Reigate. Haigh offered no explanation for the receipt found in the hatbox at his Crawley workshop. Next, the focus was on Horsham, where Haigh had sold his victim's jewellery. Haigh said that while at one time he had gone to Horsham frequently, lately he had only been there on one or two occasions in the evening, to go to the cinema. Symes confronted Haigh with the fact that the police knew he had been to the town four times recently, always in the morning. This caused Haigh to open up a little and he confessed that he had sold Mrs Durand-Deacon's jewellery at Bull's. Then DI Symes returned to the coat. He showed Haigh the cleaning receipt, asked him how he had got it, and quickly followed up with a question regarding the whereabouts of Mrs Durand-Deacon.

After thinking for a few moments, Haigh said it was a case of blackmail and if he told them what he knew other people would be dragged into the investigation. At that moment and apparently on the verge of a breakthrough – which of course would all be lies – DI Symes and Superintendent Barratt left the room, and DI Webb was left alone with Haigh. After a short while Haigh turned to Webb and voiced a question that an innocent man would never have asked: 'Tell me, frankly, what are the chances of anyone being released from

Broadmoor?' What was then called an asylum for the criminally insane, Broadmoor would only have been Haigh's
destination if he were found guilty but insane. Haigh realised
that the police had him; he was clearly weighing up his
options and the best way to proceed. DI Webb did not give
him an answer.

Then Haigh made a startling statement: 'If I told you the
truth, you wouldn't believe me. It sounds too fantastic for
belief.' When Webb reminded him that everything he said
would be taken down in evidence, Haigh said, 'I understand
that, and I'll tell you all about it. Mrs Durand-Deacon no
longer exists. She's disappeared completely, and no trace of
her can ever be found again.' Webb asked what had happened
to the elderly widow, and Haigh came clean: 'I've destroyed
her with acid. You'll find the sludge that remains at Leopold
Road. Every trace has gone. How can you prove murder if
there's no body?'

But Haigh was wrong on two points. First, murder can be
proved without a body. In fact just the previous year, in 1948,
a man called James Camb had been sentenced to life for
murder after pushing a young starlet called Gay Gibson
through the porthole of the *Queen Mary* after raping her.
Gibson was never found. Camb only escaped the noose
because for a brief period in early 1948 death sentences were
not handed down while capital punishment was being
reviewed. In 1934 Thomas Davidson had been convicted of
the murder of his eight-year-old son by drowning. The boy's
body was also never found. Corpus delicti does not apply in
modern courts if other evidence of murder can be ascertained. Second, traces of Mrs Durand-Deacon still existed.

DI Symes and Superintendent Barratt were called back into the interview room, and DI Webb filled them in on what Haigh had said – to their considerable surprise. Haigh then said he would tell them the whole story, but it would take a long time. DI Symes said he was willing to listen. Haigh then went on to tell his story, which took two and a half hours. He started with Mrs Durand-Deacon and continued with the incredible story of his whole murderous career, beginning with the killing and disposal of the three members of the McSwan family in 1944–5 and his friends the Hendersons in 1948. After all of the murders Heath claimed to have drunk his victims' blood. He had confessed to six murders, and of course the police detained him while they searched his room at the Onslow Court Hotel, finding many incriminating items. But the most damning evidence against Haigh would come from the yard outside his Crawley workshop, where he had thought no evidence of Mrs Durand-Deacon's existence could be found.

Just as for Neville Heath's first murder, the police called in the leading Home Office pathologist, Dr Keith Simpson. As Dr Simpson related in his memoirs, Detective Chief Inspector Guy Mahon now took charge of the investigation, but DI Symes remained on the case under his command. Simpson remembered arriving at the Giles Yard workshop, which he called a storeroom: 'The ground outside the storeroom was rough, with many small pebbles lying on the earth . . . I picked one up and examined it through a lens. It was about the size of a cherry and looked very much like the other stones, except that it had polished facets.' This 'pebble' turned out to be a gallstone, a common complaint among women of Mrs Durand-Deacon's age. Soon after, Simpson found some pieces of burned bone in the sludge, which, examined and X-rayed, made up a large part of a human left foot. This was later found to fit a shoe taken from Mrs Durand-Deacon's hotel room.

Simpson asked DCI Mahon to get his men to box up the sludge and surrounding earth so that it could be examined in his laboratory. They did this, crating up 475 pounds of material. A further two gallstones were identified, along with twenty-eight pounds of animal fat, eighteen pieces of bone and a set of false teeth identified by her dentist as having been made for Mrs Durand-Deacon in September 1947. The full reconstruction proved that the remains were of Olive Durand-Deacon. When the workshop was forensically examined, tiny splatters of blood were found on the wall above the table where Mrs Durand-Deacon had been standing when Haigh shot her from behind, while, in the bottom of the green tank used to dissolve her body, her hatpin was discovered. As Simpson wrote, 'Haigh's labours had been in vain. The remains of Mrs Durand-Deacon were identified as surely as if her body had never been in an acid bath.'

Haigh was charged with the murder of Olive Durand-Deacon on 2 March 1949 at Horsham police station, and then remanded in Lewes Prison, also in Sussex, as the murder had been committed in this jurisdiction. But on 4 March Haigh asked to speak to DI Webb once again, and the London policeman travelled down to Lewes Prison to see him. Haigh claimed in a new statement that he had killed (not by shooting but by hitting them over the head) and dissolved another three people, and also drunk their blood. The first was an unnamed woman he had picked up in Hammersmith in February 1945 between the McSwan murders. Then there was Max, a man in his thirties whom Haigh had met in the Goat pub in Kensington High Street, the same pub from which he and William McSwan had walked to his 79 Gloucester Road workshop on the night of the latter's murder. Finally, there was Mary, a Welsh woman he met in Eastbourne, Sussex in the summer of 1948, between killing the Hendersons and Mrs Durand-Deacon. The police were not able to find any missing persons who matched these three people, and it is highly likely that these murders were inventions devised by Haigh to support an insanity plea. No proof was also ever found that Haigh had drunk the blood of any of his victims, a lurid claim that if believed might well have caused doubts about his sanity. However, the police did find a penknife with specks of dried blood on it in Haigh's Alvis . . .

The media response to Haigh's arrest was immediate. On Sunday, 6 March 1949 the *News of the World* had Haigh splashed all over their front page. A large photograph showed him looking dapper in suit and tie, hair slicked back as ever, small neat moustache and his usual intense expression, a posed portrait he had obviously had taken, affecting to look like matinee idol Ronald Colman, whom he thought he resembled. Haigh was now in the hospital wing of Lewes Prison, where Barbara Stephens, his twenty-year-old platonic friend, had been his only visitor. Like Neville Heath, Haigh had reportedly requested books from the prison library. He was also reading the papers and 'eats heartily, but has given up smoking for the moment'. Finally, the report stated, 'At Haigh's first appearance at Horsham, hundreds of people tried to rush the doors, but police reinforcements held them off.' This was the beginning of a tabloid feeding frenzy which would delight the arrogant and egotistical Haigh. On pages 4 and 5 of the paper there was also a double spread entitled 'FIVE PEOPLE VANISH AND NOBODY KNOWS HOW', which detailed the mysterious disappearance of the McSwans and Hendersons.

Haigh's early appearances at Horsham town hall, where a special court had been convened for the initial hearings, greatly excited the public gathered outside, especially the women present. Not as good-looking as Neville Heath, he was however smartly turned out in an Austin Reed suit and usually a red tie. As Haigh left after one hearing, members of the public rushed the police vehicle driving him back to Lewes Prison, an event which the newspapers fully reported.

Haigh patently enjoyed all the attention. The photographs that show him arriving and leaving the hearings show him smirking and self-satisfied, lapping it up, as well as the large crowds. True, the impact of such sensational events was always going to be more pronounced in small-town Horsham than it would be in London outside the Old Bailey, but the public response was still nothing short of phenomenal. Haigh wrote a letter to his devout Plymouth Brethren parents from prison that included the boast 'It isn't everybody who can create more sensation than a film star. Only Princess Margaret or Mr Churchill could command such interest.'

One newspaper was already publishing leaks from Haigh's

police statements. The *Daily Mirror* was giving the story front-page headlines, calling the murderer 'The Vampire Killer' and referring to 'acid cremations', details that should not yet have been in the public domain. Although the paper was careful not to name Haigh, everybody knew it was him. The editor of the *Daily Mirror*, Silvester Bolam, was charged with contempt of court, the case being heard by three judges, including the lord chief justice, who also summoned the newspaper's owners to court. They were told, 'Let the directors beware that if they, for the purpose of increasing the circulation of their paper, should ever again venture to publish such matter as this, the directors themselves may find that the arm of this court is long enough to reach them individually.' The *Mirror* was fined £10,000 plus costs, an enormous sum and probably more than the *News of the World* would pay for Haigh's complete story, personally written by Jock Rae. Silvester Bolam was sentenced to three months in Brixton Prison. Ironically, Haigh spent some of his time on remand in Brixton too.

CHAPTER
9

A letter that Haigh wrote to his young friend Barbara Stephens from Lewes Prison on 4 March 1949, two days after he had been charged with the murder of Mrs Durand-Deacon, shows his frame of mind. He wrote that he was 'very badly shaken' by her visit, as she had seemed so sad, and went on to say that he had loved her 'intensely' for the past five years although, as we have seen, it was a platonic relationship. He called her foolish for asking why he had not murdered her too, writing that he could never harm her. William McSwan and Archie and Rose Henderson had also been his friends, but perhaps this was different – she may have been the only person apart from his parents (and himself) that he truly loved. He signed off the letter with his 'undying love'. She continued to write to him and he to her. Interestingly, in this letter Haigh also said that he had killed his victims for their blood and not their money. Could this have been true? It must be remembered that Haigh knew that the authorities would read his letters, and, as we have also seen, revelations such as this could have been useful in a possible insanity plea. Or did he want to appear less mercenary to someone he seemed genuinely to care for? Or did he really have bloodlust?

On 13 March the *News of the World* carried a photograph of Haigh's former wife Beatrice, taken before they were married years before, the caption underneath reporting that at the time of her marriage she 'had been regarded as one of the most beautiful girls in Cheshire'. She is indeed striking, but it was unfair and irrelevant to publish her picture, as they had divorced long before Haigh started killing. On page 5 Haigh's last appearance at Horsham town hall was documented. Around 200 people were waiting outside the town hall. The paper reported that 'about a dozen women with babies in perambulators, and others with young children, led a stampede down the narrow side street to which the police car had been driven, and Haigh smiled towards the crowd as he walked quickly up the steps with his escort'. Haigh was described as continuing to smile in court, where 150 people watched from the gallery, where 'women predominated by about three to one'. He was 'well-groomed and sleek, he had carefully trimmed his small moustache'. At this hearing Haigh was ordered to serve his remand in Brixton Prison, to be closer to his counsel Mr J. L. Eager.

While Haigh was undergoing psychiatric observation, the results of which would emerge at his trial, the *News of the World* reported on its front page on Sunday, 3 April, 'ATTORNEY-GENERAL TO LEAD AGAINST HAIGH'. It also stated that the trial would take place at the Old Bailey in London in mid-May,

although in fact it would eventually be held at Lewes Assize
Court in Sussex, two months later, under Justice Travers
Humphreys. Humphreys was eighty-two years old and the
most senior judge on the circuit. The jurisdiction covering
Mrs Durand-Deacon's murder had won out over the most
celebrated criminal court in the country. However, the fact
that Attorney General Sir Hartley Shawcross KC, MP was to
prosecute showed the enormity of Haigh's case and its legal
significance. Shawcross had made his international reputation
prosecuting Nazi war criminals at the Nuremberg Trials,
several years earlier. Haigh's counsel was announced as the
respected G. R. F. Morris, but in reality, although Morris
would be part of the defence team, the eminent Sir David
Maxwell Fyfe KC would be Haigh's main counsel. Maxwell
Fyfe was also a Member of Parliament. Sir Hartley Shawcross
had once been Maxwell Fyfe's pupil, and the latter had also
appeared at Nuremberg. The hiring of Sir David Maxwell
Fyfe was due to the deal that Haigh had made with Jock Rae
of the *News of the World*, who had visited him in prison. Rae
had secured Haigh's full inside story, to be written by him
– although as with anything Haigh said, it was not all true.
In return, the *News of the World* agreed to pay a very large
sum, likely to have been between five and ten thousand
pounds, although no records are available. The newspaper
would also pay Haigh's legal costs.

The trial of John George Haigh for the murder of Mrs
Olive Durand-Deacon began on the morning of Monday, 18
July 1949. The day before, the *News of the World* splashed on
its front page with 'JOHN HAIGH DRIVEN BY SECRET ROUTE TO
LEWES FOR HIS TRIAL' and reported on a 'WEEK-END OF

Excitement in Sussex Town'. On the Monday morning three trumpeters played a fanfare as Mr Justice Humphreys entered court, dressed in his scarlet robes, faced by the black-gowned prosecution and defence counsels, Sir Hartley Shawcross for the Crown and Sir David Maxwell Fyfe for Haigh. Haigh had written in a letter from prison about Maxwell Fyfe, 'I'm very glad to see that we've got old Maxy. He's no fool.'

Haigh pleaded not guilty when he stood for arraignment, and given that he had already confessed to all the murders, and added more, it could only mean that an insanity defence was coming. The fact that Haigh had asked DI Webb at the police station about the likelihood of release from Broadmoor shows that this had probably been Haigh's plan for some time, bloodlust and three unsubstantiated further murders later embellishments. Haigh was certainly meticulous and calculating enough.

In all, the prosecution would call thirty-three witnesses to the witness box. After Shawcross had made his opening speech, the first three were called: Mr Outram, the owner of the Ancient Prior's restaurant in Crawley where Haigh had gone for a bite to eat before immersing Mrs Durand-Deacon in acid, and then DI Symes and DI Webb. When defence counsel questioned them, it was clear they were trying to prove that Haigh was insane. Mr Outram was prompted to tell the court that Haigh had been 'jocular' when he came into his restaurant, although he had just killed Mrs Durand-Deacon. The defence cross-examination of DI Symes focused on Haigh's statement and his claim to have drunk the blood of his victims. However, there was no mention of him having done so with Mrs Durand-Deacon,

only with the McSwans and the Hendersons, although he
was actually only being tried for the murder of Mrs Durand-
Deacon. This was a strange omission by the defence, unless
they had an ulterior motive. DI Webb was asked about the
three untraceable victims that Haigh had later confessed to
and then asked to confirm that a bloodstained penknife had
been found in Haigh's car. Webb did so. The defence needed
to establish the truth of Haigh's self-proclaimed bloodlust,
as without it the murders appeared entirely calculated and
mercenary.

When DCI Mahon was called, Sir Hartley Shawcross went
on the attack, in an attempt to demonstrate that Haigh had
profited from the murders. Of course in the case of Mrs
Durand-Deacon, Haigh had not had the time or the opportunity to get his hands on her real wealth, making less than
£200, although murders have been committed for much
less. However, in the cases of the McSwans and the
Hendersons, Haigh had received thousands of pounds
through forgery, small fortunes at the time. But when
Shawcross asked DCI Mahon to reveal the scale of Haigh's
gains from the McSwans and the Hendersons, Mr Justice
Humphreys interceded, saying that this had no relevance
to the charge that he was facing.

The prosecution nevertheless managed to establish that
Haigh had killed Mrs Durand-Deacon, using the forensic
evidence unearthed by Dr Keith Simpson, the receipt for
the Persian lamb coat, the revolver in the hatbox and the
sale of the jewellery, as well as other circumstantial evidence.
It was obvious Haigh had done it, and done it on purpose,
and the defence had no way to deny this. Haigh, who had

always prided himself on his ingenuity, thinking himself superior to Neville Heath, not least in the vanishing of his victims, had left a long trail with his final murder. He did operate as a murderer for four and a half years, whereas Heath only lasted for weeks, but in the end Haigh slipped up badly with Mrs Durand-Deacon, not disposing of her body carefully and choosing a victim who would be immediately missed, his need for cash and the arrogance of invincibility bringing him down.

The only weapon the defence had at its disposal was that Haigh was insane and so not in control of his actions when he killed Mrs Durand-Deacon. To do so, his counsel had to prove that he was mad under the M'Naghten Rules. If Haigh was in control of his mind and actions when he pulled the trigger of the .38 Enfield and shot Mrs Durand-Deacon from behind, then he was not insane under the Rules, but if he was not in control of his mind and actions, he was 'McNaghten mad'. The difference was the hangman's noose or life in Broadmoor. But in law sanity is presumed until proven otherwise.

While Haigh was in the prison hospitals at Lewes and Brixton he had been observed by no less than nine different psychiatrists – for over a solid day when the sessions are added up – eight of them deciding that he was sane and had been in control of his actions. But as Haigh sat in the dock at his trial, doodling and writing (perhaps his life story for the *News of the World*), sometimes doing a crossword, occasionally looking up and smiling, it did seem as if he might be insane, although only one psychiatrist had reached this conclusion. Dr Henry Yellowlees was a highly respected practitioner (his son would become chief medical officer of England twenty-five years later) and had concluded that Haigh had a paranoid constitution which could have led to paranoid actions. Yellowlees said, 'The absolute callous, cheerful, bland and almost friendly indifference of the accused to the crimes, which he freely admits having committed, is unique in my experience.' Yellowlees also thought Haigh's unusual and insular Plymouth Brethren childhood could have been a major cause of his paranoia.

However, the prosecution was ready for Yellowlees, Sir Hartley Shawcross forcing him to admit that Haigh knew what he was doing was wrong, in law, if not morally.

Shawcross: 'I am asking you to look at the facts and tell the jury whether there is any doubt that he must have known that, according to English law, he was preparing to do and subsequently had done something which was wrong?'

Yellowlees: 'I will say yes to that if you say "punishable by law" instead of "wrong".'

Shawcross: 'Punishable by law and therefore wrong by the law of this country?'

Yellowlees: 'Yes, I think he knew that.'

Dr Yellowlees may or may not have been right in saying that Haigh did not know that killing people was morally wrong, but Haigh was not on trial for his morals but whether he had broken English law by committing murder, the sentence for which was death. He had obviously known what he was doing was wrong in law, as he had tried to cover his tracks, perhaps more than any other (caught) murderer in history, by devising a way to make his unfortunate victims vanish.

That was effectively the end of the defence. There was little chance of a guilty but insane verdict from the jury now. Haigh had the opportunity to speak in his own defence the following day, but he did not do so, and this was almost definitely the decision of his defence team. It was unlikely Haigh would have missed a chance to play to the gallery, but his slick and self-satisfied demeanour would surely have done him no good in the context of the clinical brutality and horror of his multiple murders.

The jury retired at just after 4.20 p.m. on Tuesday, 19 July 1949. They were out for just seventeen minutes, returning with a firm 'Guilty'. When Haigh was asked, like all those convicted, if he had anything to say, he simply said, 'Nothing at all.' But he would go on to say a great deal in the *News of the World*. Mr Justice Humphreys then passed sentence of death on John George Haigh, a man considered by the law bad but not mad.

In a letter to his solicitor, Mr J. L. Eager, from Wandsworth Prison, where he awaited execution, Haigh wrote that he had been bored by the trial and had been glad to have a crossword with him. There were signs of megalomania and a messiah complex in the letter: madness is 'a label which has been applied to all men of distinction', and all men who have thought differently have faced that accusation. Haigh also referred to Christ and Pilate, writing that his spirit would return to earth in another body and 'build a greater church'. He then asked a rhetorical question – 'Was I not burned at the stake as a Wharlock in Salem?' – and closed the letter by saying that he laughed at death and would come back to continue his 'spiritual sacrifices'. These could have been the

words of his father thirty years earlier, teaching his son the
ways of the Plymouth Brethren.

Two days earlier, on Sunday, 24 July, the *News of the World*
had featured a close-up photograph of Haigh's intense eyes
on its front page, the headline informing readers that Haigh
was celebrating his fortieth birthday that day in the condemned
cell at Wandsworth Prison. It went on to trail his 'AMAZING
AND EXCLUSIVE MEMOIRS', as told to Jock Rae, which would
start the following Sunday.

As promised, on Sunday, 31 July 1949 the *News of the World*
began its serialisation of Haigh's memoirs. The front page
was dominated by the banner headline 'HAIGH'S SENSATIONAL
CONFESSION: WRITTEN EXCLUSIVELY FOR THE "NEWS OF THE
WORLD"'. Underneath was a facsimile of a numbered murder
list that Haigh had written and signed in his Wandsworth
cell, naming his six certain victims and also the unsubstantiated three he had belatedly revealed to DI Webb for a tally
of nine in total.

The report continued on pages 5 and 6, the traditional
murder pages in the *News of the World*, where every exclusive
that Jock Rae acquired was printed after being heralded on
the front page. It would be read by seven million people.
Unlike Harry Procter at the *Daily Mail* and then the *Sunday
Pictorial*, Rae was rarely mentioned in his pieces. But he didn't
need to be named, as everybody knew that the large, bald,
gruff Scot was the *News of the World*'s 'murder whiz'. In fact,
the paper held Rae in such high esteem that he now had his
own car and driver.

'It all began with a dream, and I am led to the young

McSwan' was the excerpted quote from Haigh on that double
spread, referring to his first murder, that of his 'pal' Mac in
the autumn of 1944 – Haigh's 'confession' was pervaded by
a spiritual tone. Based on his story as given to the police,
there was more colour and detail, and it had been obviously
embellished, Haigh's ego having its final say. The *News of the
World* memoirs gave free rein to the messiah complex that
was also present in Haigh's letters from prison. He talked of
having 'a calling', something which several serial killers,
including Yorkshire Ripper Peter Sutcliffe, murderously active
in the 1970s, have claimed since. Haigh wrote, 'I believed I
was being cared for by some supreme force.'

In that first instalment of his memoirs Haigh wrote of the
dreams he had had, starting with the one when he was a
choirboy at Wakefield Cathedral and the image of Christ on
the Cross had come to him. He went on to recall how he
had dreamed that he had built a 'huge telescopic ladder, by
means of which I reached the moon' and continued, 'Always,
in some way or another, my dreams were associated with
blood, and they played a terrible and fascinating part in my
life.' Visits to a slaughterhouse when he was at school are
mentioned, and other childhood incidents involving blood.
This of course chimed in with his professed bloodlust, even
though he had clinically fleeced all of his victims of money
and assets, using the skills of an expert forger. But Rae knew
his readers were more interested in vampire revelations than
financial motives. Two photographs of Haigh's basement
workshop at 79 Gloucester Road, where he had killed and
dissolved three members of the McSwan family, played up
to this. The first showed an outside view of the workshop,

captioned 'The Way In', and the second, a close-up of the large drain inside down which the remains of the McSwans were washed, was labelled 'The Way Out'.

Letters which Haigh wrote on 1 August 1949 from Wandsworth Prison, five days before he was executed, illustrate how strongly Haigh ascribed his actions to some sort of 'calling' within him, but was this truly how he felt or a convenient way of denying what he had done, either consciously or unconsciously? These included three short letters to his solicitor Mr Eager, his counsel Sir David Maxwell Fyfe, and the psychiatrist Dr Yellowlees who had given evidence on his behalf. His solicitor and counsel Haigh thanked for their efforts on his behalf, but it is the letter to the psychiatrist that is most enlightening. Haigh puts himself in the same bracket as Confucius, Jesus, Julius Caesar, Napoleon, 'and even Hitler'. Like himself, he infers, these men thought and therefore acted differently from others, and Haigh goes on to mention that his former headmistress and later headmaster had 'reported' that he was not a 'normal' boy. But there is no mention of the Plymouth Brethren or his parents. Finally, he praises Dr Yellowlees for his 'greater perception' than others in recognising that he was indeed different. The letter that Haigh wrote on the same day to his parents where they were now living in Leeds continued in the same vein. England had not 'got past the days of beheading heretics' and 'religious freedom is not yet complete'. He concluded the letter by saying that he would go down in history as a martyr 'as great as [Thomas] Cranmer or any other'.

On Sunday, 7 August the *News of the World* continued

Haigh's memoirs with the story of his murder of Dr Archie and Rose Henderson in February 1948. It also stated that Haigh was still being examined by psychiatrists and that his only hope was a last-minute reprieve. Sentence of death was due to be carried out three days later, and only the Home Secretary could grant such a reprieve. It would only be given if it was proved that Haigh was insane.

Albert Pierrepoint hanged John George Haigh on the morning of Wednesday, 10 August 1949, a large crowd gathering outside Wandsworth Prison. Pierrepoint used the same leather strap that he used for Neville Heath, which he reserved for special executions. Haigh walked the final fifteen paces to his death calmly and seemed at peace. Death in this life, including his own, had no meaning to him at all.

On Sunday, 14 August 1949 the *News of the World* published the final part of Haigh's memoirs, which dealt with the murder of Mrs Olive Durand-Deacon almost six months earlier. The headline on the front page was 'To MADAME TUSSAUD'S – MY GREEN SUIT AND RED TIE', referring to the fact that Haigh had bequeathed these items to the famous waxwork museum. It had been Haigh's last hurrah before being executed four days earlier. Ironically, in Madame Tussauds he would stand next to Neville Heath, whom he had known and felt superior to in life. Just in front of him was Dr Buck Ruxton, who had murdered and dismembered his wife and maid twenty-three years earlier. The inside story of Dr Ruxton had been Jock Rae's breakthrough murder scoop.

Meanwhile, Haigh's parents, whom he had loved deeply,

were left with the large sum of money brokered by Rae and paid by the *News of the World* to cushion their old age. But of course to them John George was not dead; he had gone on to another life, the one that really mattered.

CHAPTER
10

Wednesday, 9 November 1949, Ladbroke Grove, London

The local cinema is doing great business showing *The Third Man* starring Orson Welles and Joseph Cotten, but the flicks is the last thing on Tim Evans' mind. He walks briskly this chilly evening, his head down, preoccupied, towards his mother's house on St Marks Road. When he arrives, as always Thomasina Probert is pleased to see her only son. How are Beryl and Geraldine? she asks, emphasising her granddaughter's name. Beryl's taken little Geraldine to stay with her father, Mr Thorley, in Brighton, says Tim. This surprises Thomasina, as Beryl's father is hardly a hands-on grandfather. Why is he suddenly showing such an interest? she asks. Tim shrugs. After leaving St Marks Road, Tim pops into the KPH and sinks a couple of beers, transporting himself to a better place for a short while. On returning to 10 Rillington Place, John and Ethel Christie come out of their flat and ask Tim where Beryl and Geraldine are. Tim tells them that they have gone to stay in Bristol for a while, the city having changed in just over an hour.

In fact, Geraldine is up in the flat, alone but snug in her cot. There's no sign of Beryl anywhere. Tim feeds her and they both go to sleep. It is early on Thursday morning, 10 November, when Tim gets up and packs Geraldine's clothes and baby things into a small suitcase and kisses his daughter passionately, tears in his eyes. Then he goes downstairs and knocks on the Christies' door. John Christie comes out alone, as if he has been awake for some time. Ethel is asleep in their bedroom. Tim hands the suitcase to Christie, entrusts him with Geraldine's pram and highchair, and they speak. Christie is reassuring. Tim sets off for work. It is just after half past six.

Later that morning Mr Jones and Mr Willis, the builders who have been working on the house, arrive at 10 Rillington Place. They are now dealing with damp patches in the plaster in the outside washroom. Neither of them hears a baby crying. Actually, the whole house is very quiet, only the Christies being in. Mr Kitchener is in hospital having an operation on his eyes, and the two women buried in the back garden are silent as usual. Mr Christie slinks around in his plimsolls, master of the house. He does well to mask his neuroses, the fact that he doesn't sleep well and his worsening medical problems, both real and imagined – he is a hypochondriac. Christie has recently been to see Dr Odess about a serious attack of fibrositis in his back, and has also complained of having diarrhoea, probably caused by his nerves.

During the day Beryl's friend Joan Vincent calls in. She

had been round recently, and Beryl (at least she assumed it was Beryl) had been behind the kitchen door of the top-floor flat and stopped her opening it. Now she wants to confront Beryl and ask her why. The front door of the house is open to let the workmen in and out, and Joan is about to go upstairs to Beryl's flat when Mr Christie appears from his ground-floor living room and tells her that she's out of luck: Beryl and the baby have gone to Bristol.

'But Beryl wouldn't leave London without telling me,' says Joan.

'I'm afraid that's just what she's done,' says Christie. Just then Joan spots Geraldine's highchair and pram just inside the door of the Christies' living room, the door of which is still ajar.

'Why have you got Geraldine's things?' asks Joan.

'Oh, those. I'm just taking care of them. I'll be sending them off to Bristol shortly,' says Christie.

'Why didn't Beryl take them with her? She'll need them,' says Joan.

'Look, I think it would be better if you didn't come round here any more. Beryl doesn't want to see you, and she doesn't appreciate you coming here showing off your posh frocks,' says Christie.

Shocked at Mr Christie's nastiness, Joan Vincent leaves immediately, confused and upset.

Meanwhile, Tim's day is not going well. He asks his boss at Lancaster Foods for yet another advance on his wages to send to Beryl. It is the final straw. Tim has been less than a model employee, taking liberties that the other van drivers do not dare to. He lies and makes excuses about delivery times and is generally considered less than trustworthy. His boss fires him with immediate effect. When he gets back to 10 Rillington Place, having stopped off at the KPH and the Elgin to fortify himself and tell one or two acquaintances that he has left his job of his own accord, Tim is still very angry. He has never been one to hide his emotions.

Tim tells Mr Christie about losing his job and Christie quickly suggests that he go away for a while. Perhaps he could sell his furniture to put him in funds? Tim agrees to think it over, even though selling the furniture will be illegal, as it is not actually his, the hire-purchase payments still far from finished.

The next day was Friday, 11 November 1949. Tim had made up his mind, and that morning he walked down to nearby Portobello Road market and went into a second-hand furniture dealership. The proprietor, Robert Hookway, agreed to come to 10 Rillington Place and give Tim a valuation on his furniture after the weekend. Back at Rillington Place Mr Jones and Mr Willis continued their work in the wash house. On his return, Evans also had to walk past a carpenter, Robert Anderson, who was replacing rotten floorboards in the hall outside the Christies' flat. The workmen finished their work that day and before leaving cleared up the outside wash house.

That weekend Tim went to the KPH and the Elgin, again telling anyone that would listen at the bar that he had left his job by his own choice. One or two people asked Tim for money that he owed them. He also went to the cinema. On Sunday afternoon he ate with John and Ethel Christie in their flat, Ethel preparing a traditional roast dinner.

On Monday morning Tim got up at six o'clock and cut up all of the bedding and Beryl's clothes, which a rag-and-bone man took away in two bags later. In the afternoon Robert Hookway arrived in his van, had a look and was impressed. He offered Tim the sizeable sum of forty pounds – the equivalent of more than five weeks' wages for Tim when he had a job – for all the furniture and the linoleum, which Beryl had picked out. Tim accepted, and Hookway wasted no time in loading it all into the back of his van, giving Tim the cash. Everything else in the flat, which Beryl had been so proud of when they had moved in and redecorated, went to the kindly Christies.

When Hookway had gone, Tim spoke to Christie, who told the much younger man that he should call in on Joan Vincent, whom Tim had never liked and would never usually go and see, and in fact did not trust him. Christie told Tim to tell Joan that Beryl and Geraldine had gone to Bristol but that Beryl would be in touch by letter. Tim agreed, but before going to see Vincent went shopping, spending fourteen pounds on a brand new camel hair coat. When Joan saw his new coat, she was taken aback at how expensive it looked, and when he told her how much he had paid for it, her surprise intensified.

After telling Ethel Christie he was going to Bristol, Tim packed the rest of his meagre belongings into one suitcase and left 10 Rillington Place. He went straight to Paddington station, which could take him to either Bristol or Wales. Tim left his suitcase at left luggage, to be collected later, and visited a couple of his favourite pubs, ending the day by going to the cinema again to kill time. At half past midnight

Tim Evans took the last train to Cardiff, after collecting his suitcase. He arrived in Cardiff before it was light and took a train to Merthyr Vale, the village of his birth in south Wales. Tim reached Merthyr Vale at just after 6.30 a.m. on Tuesday, 15 November, five days before his twenty-fifth birthday.

Tim went back to the street where it all began for him, knocking on the door of Mr and Mrs Lynch, his uncle and aunt, at 93 Mount Pleasant. He had not warned them he was coming, and they were surprised to see him. Tim told his relatives that Beryl and Geraldine had gone to Brighton, the same story he had told his mother, as they would no doubt be in contact with each other. But he neglected to tell his aunt and uncle that he had lost his job, instead saying that he was in Wales because he and his boss were on a reconnaissance mission around the mid-west of England. Apparently, their car had broken down in Cardiff and getting it fixed would take some time. It was a typical Tim lie, but it was accepted at face value. The next day Tim went to Cardiff and bought himself some more clothes, which along with his expensive coat made him look very sophisticated in the cobbled streets of Merthyr Vale. He went to the pub and told stories about his life in London, again mostly lies or highly embellished truth. But when he was speaking about fourteen-month-old Geraldine, it was obvious how much he doted on the little girl. He came back from Merthyr Tydfil one day with a cuddly toy for her.

Tim celebrated his birthday in Merthyr Vale on Sunday, 20 November 1949. The next day he went back to London by train, probably spending the two days following this in pubs and the pictures, perhaps staying in a boarding house. It was not until Wednesday, 23 November that Tim turned up back at 10 Rillington Place. Christie seemed slightly startled to see him. Tim did not go in, and they talked at the front door. Later that evening Tim took another train back to Merthyr Vale. He had not visited his mother or sisters in London. Some time during the next few days his aunt wrote to her sister-in-law, Tim's mother, telling her that Tim was in Merthyr Vale with them.

It was on Tuesday, 29 November that Thomasina Probert gave in to her concerns and frustrations and sent a telegram to Beryl's father, Mr Thorley, in Brighton, asking after Beryl. Mr Thorley sent one back saying that he had seen nothing of his daughter. Tim's sister Eileen then went to 10 Rillington Place to ask after Beryl and Geraldine. Eileen spoke to Ethel Christie, who told her that Beryl and the baby had left on 8 November. When Tim's half-sister Mary went round, Ethel told her the same. But then John Christie came out and got involved.

Christie seemed angry and snapped at Mary, refusing to let her past the front door of the house, saying that Tim had gone to Bristol and Beryl to Brighton, and that Tim had sold all their furniture before going. As Ludovic Kennedy recounted in *Ten Rillington Place*, Mary said, 'Well, one of you is telling lies.' Ethel was now silent, as she usually was when her husband was around, but nevertheless Christie told her to shut up, to stop her saying anything more. Christie then said he had always thought that Tim was bad news, ever since he knew of him when he was a special constable. This was long before Tim and Beryl Evans moved into 10

Rillington Place, and Mary called Christie a liar, adding that if they had not heard from Tim or Beryl by Friday, her mother would inform the police. John Christie was in a real rage now, and Mary later said that she thought he was going to hit her. His voice raised above a whisper for once, Christie told Mary that he knew more about Tim and Beryl's situation, and that her brother would not be grateful to them if they went to the police.

All this prompted Thomasina to act. That same day she wrote an anguished letter to Mrs Lynch at 93 Mount Pleasant. It read, 'I don't know what lies Tim has told you down there, I know nothing about him and I have not seen him for 3 weeks . . . his name stinks up here everywhere I go people asking for him for money he owes them. I am ashamed to say he is my son.' The letter arrived at 93 Mount Pleasant the following morning, and Mrs Lynch read it out to Tim. He wasn't angry but was missing Geraldine intensely, unable to sleep, a bundle of nerves. His mother's comments were the final straw. At ten past three that afternoon, Wednesday, 30 November 1949, Tim Evans walked into Merthyr Vale police station.

'I want to give myself up. I have disposed of my wife,' says Tim Evans.

The policeman on duty at Merthyr Vale police station, Detective Constable Gwynfryn Evans, is somewhat taken aback by this unusual statement from a man who has walked in off the street.

'What do you mean by that, sir?'

'I put her down the drain,' says Tim.

'I must warn you that you should be careful about what you're saying,' says DC Evans.

'I know what I'm saying. I can't sleep and I want to get it off my chest.'

Tim is told to wait, and soon he is taken to CID at Merthyr Tydfil, where he is put into an interview room. He is cautioned and begins to unburden himself. His first statement is written down as he speaks, and the key information is then sent in a telegram to the Metropolitan Police in London. The telegram reads:

A man named Timothy John Evans has come to this station this afternoon and stated that on 8-11-49 at 10, Rillington Place, W11, his wife had a miscarriage at that address, after which she apparently drank some liquid which he obtained from a lorry driver some time previous at a cafe between Chelmsford and Ipswich. During the night of 9-11-49 between 1 a.m. and 2 a.m. he disposed of his wife's body down a manhole or drain outside that address. He handed his 14-month-old child to a man named Reginald Christie at the same address, who stated he could have the child taken care of. He also sold the furniture and left the address. Will you please cause enquiries to be made. A written statement has been taken from Evans.

The telegram is called an action copy, and the Metropolitan Police do take action while Tim sits in an interview room in Merthyr Tydfil hundreds of miles away, his camel hair coat neatly folded over the back of a chair. A car arrives at

10 Rillington Place from Notting Hill police station, with three policemen inside. They find the manhole outside the house, in front of the Christies' living room. It takes all three of them to get the cover off. Nothing suspicious is in the drain. When this information is relayed to Merthyr Tydfil, Tim Evans is visibly shaken, and he asks to make a second statement. In this he refutes his first, saying 'I said that to protect a man named Christie. It's not true about the man in the cafe either.' It is now 9 p.m. Tim's second statement relates how Christie had arranged with Beryl to perform an abortion on her, and he had gone to work after telling Christie that his wife was ready for him.

'When I came home in the evening he [Christie] was waiting for me at the bottom of the staircase. He said, "It's bad news. It didn't work." . . . I could see that she was dead and that she had been bleeding from the mouth and nose and that she had been bleeding from the bottom part. She had a black skirt on and a check blouse and a kind of light blue jacket on.'

Christie had then offered to dispose of Beryl's body down the drain outside the house, and this is undoubtedly why Tim is unsettled by the fact that it is empty and that three men have been needed to lift the manhole cover. First, Christie has not done what he said he would, and second, he could never have lifted the cover anyway. Tim also tells the police that when he had fretted about what would happen to Geraldine, Christie had said that he knew a couple in East Acton who would be pleased to have her. It is just after midnight when Tim, exhausted, finishes his second statement.

The statement is then passed on to Notting Hill police station, and officers go round to St Marks Road in the early hours of 1 December. Tim also asks the Welsh police to pass a message on to their London counterparts to give to his mother. The police question Thomasina Probert, and she tells them all she knows, which is what the Christies told Eileen and Mary. She admits to the police that Tim is a terrible liar. The officers then pass on the message from Tim: could she speak to John Christie and ask him for the address of the East Acton couple who are looking after Geraldine? Naturally, Mrs Probert is very confused by this request.

Back in Merthyr Tydfil police station Tim wakes up and is questioned again after some breakfast. DC Evans asks Tim about the last time he saw Beryl's body, and Tim replies that it was when she was being taken down into Mr Kitchener's flat on the first floor. As we have seen, Mr Kitchener was away in hospital at the time. Tim tells DC Evans that Christie had told him to stay in his kitchen on the top floor while he carried Beryl's body down, but Christie had not been able to manage and called to Tim to come and help him. Tim came out of the kitchen and saw his wife's body lying on the stairs. He helped Christie carry Beryl into Mr Kitchener's flat, says Tim, and that was the last time he saw her.

At 10 Rillington Place the police are searching the top-floor flat. There is almost nothing there, but they do find a brief-case and confirm that it has been stolen. Also in the flat are some articles cut out of newspapers. They are about the recent murder of Stanley Setty by Donald Hume. Hume had killed and dismembered car dealer Setty for financial gain and then used a small plane to dump parcels containing parts of his body into the English Channel. Why would Tim Evans have such cuttings in his flat – especially as he cannot read? The Metropolitan Police dispatch Detective Inspector Black and Detective Sergeant Corfield to Merthyr Tydfil to arrest Tim over the stolen briefcase.

1 December 1949, late evening, Notting Hill police station

John Reginald Halliday Christie of 10 Rillington Place has been called in for questioning. Christie's weasel-like face carries an honest expression, and he wastes no time telling the policemen that he used to be a special constable. When the officers tell him about the accusation Tim Evans has made against him (that of causing death by illegally carrying out an abortion), Christie scowls and tells them it's crazy. 'At no time have I assisted or attempted to abort Mrs Evans or any other women,' says Christie. 'I cannot understand why Evans should make such accusations against me, as I've been very good to him in a lot of ways.' He goes on to say that Tim and Beryl were always at each other's throats and the marriage was hardly stable, even that Beryl had once told his wife Ethel she was frightened Tim might kill her in one of his rages.

Meanwhile, Ethel Christie is being interviewed at 10 Rillington Place. She backs up everything her husband has said. She also adds that there has been trouble between Beryl and her friend Joan Vincent, who had recently come to the house, and Beryl had refused to come out of her kitchen to see her. The picture being painted is of an unstable marriage with violent arguments and interfering friends who cause more problems.

It is later that night. There has been no progress in locating Beryl, and as Tim has said she is dead, the police are concerned. The top floor flat of 10 Rillington Place has already been searched, but no sign of the twenty-year-old mother is found. After finishing with Ethel, the police conduct an extensive search of the property, just in case. They meticulously examine every nook and cranny inside the house. Nothing turns up. There is only the garden and wash house left. If they are going to dig up the garden, it will have to wait until it's light. Little do they know that if they do, they will find the bodies of Ruth Fuerst and Muriel Eady, who have been buried there for over six and five years respectively. But would they find Beryl there too?

Using a torch, the officers go outside to the wash house. It's a tiny space, ramshackle brickwork crumbling, mildewed and damp. It's not used; the outside lavatory is separate, behind it, and washing is done inside the house. It's very cold, and the policemen are relieved to be wearing their capes. They prod around, looking for any possible clue or shred of evidence, expecting nothing. But they have to tick the outhouse off their search list. Some wood is leaning against the large cracked white sink. An officer removes a couple of pieces, then a few planks. What's that? he asks himself. It's a long object wrapped in cloth. More wood is removed. Ethel Christie is called out of her living room. She doesn't stop to put a coat on. The torch is pointed down at the find, still mostly covered by wood.

'What is that, Mrs Christie?' says a policeman.

'I've no idea. I've never seen it before,' she says. She tells them that, as far as she knows, the last people to have been in the wash house were the two builders who had recently done some work in there. The policemen wonder how decrepit it had been before the work was done. An officer makes a note to get the names of the workmen when they go back inside. Ethel Christie reaches out and touches the object. She has no idea what it is.

Two policemen drag the object clear of the wood. It's not light. They have it on the stony ground outside now. The torch is shone on it. It's a very big long package, not wrapped up in paper but in a green tablecloth, bound by rope. A policeman unties the rope.

It all happens so quickly. As soon as the rope is untied, the tablecloth loosens and two feet fall out. Ethel Christie lets out a little cry, and the policemen gasp. The tablecloth is pulled back further. Mrs Christie almost shakes with terror. It's Beryl. A big question has been answered. Beryl has not been in Brighton or Bristol. Or down the drain. She's been in the wash house.

An officer goes back into the wash house, and another points a torch after him. There's more wood behind the door. The wood is moved away. What they see is enough to make the most hardened policeman cry. There on the dirty stone floor is the tiny body of fourteen-month-old Geraldine. She looks just like a doll. She has not been wrapped up like Beryl, just left. Also unlike Beryl, Geraldine has a man's tie around her neck.

The Home Office pathologist Dr Donald Teare will soon

examine the two bodies, mother and baby daughter. Beryl
has bruising to her vagina, and her upper lip and right eye
are inflamed. Both she and Geraldine have been strangled.
They have been dead for around three weeks.

Two policemen escort Tim Evans back to London from
Wales. Arriving at Paddington station, he is snapped by a
photographer, looking tiny next to his tall escorts, being
roughly held under the arm by one of them. Officially, he is
not being brought back to answer a murder charge but for
stealing the briefcase found in his flat. But he confessed to
murdering Beryl in his first statement, and he is being treated
as a wife-killer. Now that his baby is also dead – which he
does not know yet – he is possibly a child-killer too. Wearing
his camel hair coat, his hair characteristically neatly slicked
back, the look on his face is one of stunned submission, the
old expression 'like a rabbit caught in headlights' the best
one to describe his countenance. Almost illiterate but far
from stupid, worldly in his own streetwise way, events have
spiralled out of control and are about to get worse.

   At Notting Hill police station, not far from Rillington Place
and his favourite haunts the KPH and the Elgin, Tim is taken
into yet another interview room, where he faces DCI
Jennings. On the table between them are the rope and the
tablecloth used as Beryl's shroud, and next to them the
necktie used to strangle little Geraldine. DCI Jennings informs
Tim that the corpses of both Beryl and Geraldine have been
found in the wash house at his former address. Jennings is
sure that Tim already knows this but he is winded by the
news. Then Jennings tells Tim that he thinks he killed both

his wife and baby daughter. 'Yes,' says Tim, his nerves shot, exhausted already by his previous interrogations and the journey down, but above all by pain and sadness. Or guilt? DCI Jennings thinks so.

As Edward Marston pointed out in his book on John Christie, compiled from the National Archives, the two statements that Tim Evans made on the night of 2 and 3 December 1949 were almost definitely not taken down verbatim. Marston highlighted the following part of the first statement Tim made at Notting Hill police station hours after arriving back in London, in which he confessed to killing both Beryl and Geraldine:

> She [Beryl] was incurring one debt after another and I could not stand it any longer, so I strangled her with a piece of rope and took her down to the flat below the same night while the old man [Mr Kitchener] was in hospital. I waited till the Christies had gone to bed, then I took her to the wash house after midnight. This was on Tuesday 8 November. On Thursday evening after I came home from work I strangled the baby in the bedroom with my tie and later that night I took her down to the wash house after the Christies had gone to bed.

Would an illiterate man have said 'incurring'? It is very doubtful. The statement is very fluent and not how Tim Evans spoke at all, but, more importantly, it contains obvious lies. Mr Jones and Mr Willis, the builders, had been in the wash house working from 8 to 10 November. How could they have missed not one but two dead bodies? Moreover, the wood behind which Beryl was hidden were the ground-floor hallway floorboards removed by the carpenter and given to John Christie for firewood on 14 November, and so could not have covered Beryl's corpse since 8 November. In his second Notting Hill statement Tim also said that he had locked the wash house, although there was no lock on the wash-house door . . .

So, why was Tim lying? He no longer wanted to protect Christie, as he now knew that his 'kindly' neighbour had lied to him, and Tim must have strongly suspected that Christie had murdered his beloved Geraldine. Was it guilt that he had allowed Geraldine to fall prey to Christie? Was it that he now felt he had nothing to live for?

At his trial defence counsel Malcolm Morris – tall, urbane and with a distinctive voice – cross-examined Tim in the witness box. Part is worth quoting here, as it shows that Tim was quite possibly led in his statement by DCI Jennings and DI Black at Notting Hill police station, the police supplying the information that Tim Evans needed to hang himself.

MORRIS: 'He [DCI Jennings] told you that your wife and baby . . .'

EVANS: 'Had been found dead, sir.'

MORRIS: 'Did he say where?'

EVANS: 'Yes, sir. Number 10 Rillington Place in the wash house . . .'

MORRIS: 'Did he say how it appeared they died?'

EVANS: 'Yes, sir, by strangulation.'

MORRIS: 'Did he say with what?'

EVANS: 'Well, a rope, sir, my wife, and my daughter had been strangled with a necktie.'

Later in the cross-examination Malcolm Morris made his point:

MORRIS: '. . . before he told you, had you any idea that anything had happened to your daughter?'

EVANS: 'No, sir. No idea at all.'

MORRIS: 'Did he tell you, when he said the bodies had been found in the wash house, whether they had been concealed or not?'

EVANS: 'Yes, sir. He told me they had been concealed by timber.'

The police charged Timothy Evans with the murder of both Beryl and Geraldine, following his two statements at Notting Hill police station admitting the crimes. He was held on remand in the hospital wing of Brixton Prison, in the same ward as Donald Hume, the murderer of Stanley Setty. In a letter Tim wrote that he was frightened of Hume, who was by all accounts an extremely unpleasant individual. With no funds to pay for his defence, Tim was allowed legal aid. Baillie Saunders, the chief clerk at the firm he chose who gathered information to support his case, was elderly and not at all thorough. The police, on the other hand, were gathering evidence fast, even if it was to fit their prime suspect rather than the crime itself. They managed to persuade Joan Vincent that she had visited Beryl the day before her death (Ethel Christie said the same), but this was not true. John Christie had clearly told his wife what to say, as she was plainly lying, and later events would suggest that she was not culpable in his murders, although it will never be known how much she knew about her husband's activities. Did she suspect him? If she did, this would surely have increased her fear of him. It is important to remember that, although Christie had not been charged with any offence, Tim's second statement at Merthyr Tydfil stated that his failed abortion attempt on his wife had led to her death. So if Tim was acquitted, the focus would shift to John Christie, who had more to lose than anybody knew, as a search of the garden at 10 Rillington Place would reveal. So Christie stuck to his story and ensured his wife backed him up.

The police also asked Mr Jones and Mr Willis and the carpenter Robert Anderson if they were sure they had their dates correct. The dates that the workmen were in the wash house and when the carpenter gave Christie the wood were key in the prosecution of Evans on the basis of his confessions at Notting Hill.

In the end, the police decided to prosecute Tim Evans solely for the murder of his baby, as such a crime was sure to horrify any jury and elicit no sympathy. Also the strained domestic situation and the fights between Tim and Beryl could have been brought up in mitigation if he were tried for Beryl's murder. Without a doubt, the hardest evidence the Crown had on Tim Evans was the confession to double murder that had come from his own mouth at Notting Hill police station on 2–3 December 1949, which in retrospect seems far from fairly obtained and certainly not watertight.

On 15 December Tim Evans was brought before

magistrates to hear the charge against him, and both John and Ethel Christie gave evidence to the court. Ethel was plainly very tense and began crying in the witness box. Did she know more than she admitted about the deaths of Beryl and Geraldine, or was she just stressed? It is possible Christie had told Ethel that Beryl had died during an abortion, and to save him she did what he told her. But surely if she had had any suspicion that her husband had committed a murder, especially that of tiny Geraldine, of whom she was very fond, she would not have supported him. At a second hearing a week later Tim heard the evidence against him and was told he would be tried at the Central Criminal Court.

The prosecution of Tim Evans had now caught the attention of the media, but it inspired far less press coverage than the recent cases of Neville Heath and John George Haigh. It was a very tragic case, but a domestic one, and without the lurid details that had sent the tabloids into a frenzy over Heath and Haigh. But Jock Rae of the *News of the World*, doyen of Fleet Street crime reporters, did cover the story of Evans. John Christie cut out clippings of Rae's coverage of the case, and this would lead Christie to speak to Rae several years later, in very different circumstances. Christie's habit of taking newspaper cuttings suggests a possible source for the clippings about Donald Hume found in the Evanses' flat which had served to incriminate Tim further.

The trial of Timothy Evans for the murder of his baby daughter Geraldine, aged fourteen months, opened at the Old Bailey on the morning of 11 January 1950, just over five weeks after Tim had been brought back to London from

Wales. The judge was Mr Justice Wilfred Lewis, whose drawn face showed that he was a very sick man, and he would in fact die just weeks after the trial ended. Mr Christmas Humphreys KC led for the Crown, and Malcolm Morris led Evans' defence team. After Tim had pleaded not guilty to Geraldine's murder, Morris raised an objection, complaining that the prosecution was going to use evidence relating to Beryl's murder, even though Tim was being tried for just the murder of Geraldine. The jury was excused while the judge considered the objection. Mr Justice Lewis decided that the evidence was admissible, and so although Tim was theoretically tried for just Geraldine's murder, the extensive evidence raised in court relating to Beryl's death meant that both murders were brought before the jury. Of course, just one murder conviction would result in a death sentence.

It was obvious before the trial started that Tim's confessions would be the main thrust of the prosecution case against him, and that was exactly what transpired. In his opening address Christmas Humphreys KC relied heavily on Tim's third and fourth statements made at Notting Hill, in which he confessed to both murders. Christie was hardly mentioned, and not in connection with either murder. Humphreys built up a picture of a very strained and sometimes violent marriage, and the financial troubles that culminated in Tim losing his job, which put him under so much emotional strain that he committed murder. Tim's inaccuracies and the changes in his successive statements were also pointed out.

When the Home Office pathologist Dr Donald Teare was called, he said that no vaginal swab had been taken from

Beryl, and no reference to possible vaginal penetration was made in court. Teare had found bruising in Beryl's vagina, but this was not pursued by the defence. The bruising was hypothesised to have come from injections Beryl had apparently made with a syringe in her efforts to abort her pregnancy. In his 1961 book *Ten Rillington Place* Ludovic Kennedy wrote that if Teare had taken a vaginal swab, 'he would almost certainly have found traces of Christie's spermatozoa'. This would have shown that Christie had raped Beryl, as she would never have had intercourse with him by choice, and Tim had not had sex with his wife for some time. However, in his 1978 memoirs *Forty Years of Murder* Professor Keith Simpson argued that this was a very 'reckless' statement, although it should be pointed out that Simpson and Teare were very good friends, and Simpson could have been defending his friend's oversight.

John Christie was called next. He looked frail, older than his years, and spoke modestly and very quietly. Although he was in fact a sick and neurotic man, telling the jury that he had been suffering from debilitating fibrositis and enteritis at the time of the murders, if Dr Odess had been called to give evidence, he could have told the court that the fibrositis attack came days after Beryl's body had been carried downstairs, and that this might have caused the attack. Christie made sure that he got the jury on his side by recounting that he had been gassed in the First World War, which was why he spoke in a whisper. His police service in the war also helped him appear a respectable and reliable witness.

On the second day of the trial Morris cross-examined Christie for the defence. Morris attacked using Tim's second

statement at Merthyr Tydfil, which had heavily implicated
Christie.

Morris: 'Well, Mr Christie, I have got to suggest to you,
and I do not want there to be any misapprehension about
it, that you are responsible for the death of Mrs Evans and
the little girl. If that is not so, that you know very much
more about the deaths than you have said.'

Christie: 'That is a lie.'

Morris then brought up Christie's past criminal record in
an effort to show that he was a dark character but did not
emphasise the attack with a cricket bat on the woman he
had lived with twenty years earlier while separated from
Ethel. The judge at his trial for that incident had called it 'a
murderous attack', and this could have destroyed the image
that Christie had slyly built up in the witness box the previous
day. Also, Christmas Humphreys managed to limit the
damage to Christie's credibility by making the point that he
had had no criminal convictions for seventeen years. He was
a reformed character, respectable and a good citizen.

The defence then called Tim Evans into the witness box.
Tim was very nervous, clearly under enormous pressure,
and some in court that day thought him shifty. Morris asked
questions that allowed Tim to state that he had not murdered
either Geraldine or Beryl. Morris also emphasised Tim's
second statement from Merthyr Tydfil, in which he had
directly implicated Christie in Beryl's death. When Morris
asked why he had confessed to the murders if he was innocent, Tim replied that he thought that the police might beat
it out of him. Tim added that he had been distraught when
he gave his statements at Notting Hill police station – after

all he had just been told that his beloved baby daughter was dead. When Morris asked Tim if he had anything left to live for, he said that he did not.

Christmas Humphreys showed Tim Evans no mercy when he examined him, ripping him apart in the witness box. Tim was wrongfooted several times, confusing his various statements and giving a poor impression, but he was completely out of his depth. Humphreys asked Tim to say why Christie would want to murder Beryl, and he could only manage, 'Well, he was at home all day.' Of course no one but Christie knew about the skeletons of Ruth Fuerst and Muriel Eady in the back garden at 10 Rillington Place, and that he was a necrophiliac.

The case for the defence over, Humphreys summed up for the prosecution, speaking for just under ten minutes, a very short closing statement. Morris then stood to make the defence's final plea to the jury. He suggested that Christie might have been attempting an abortion when Beryl became unconscious. In a panic, Christie had strangled her and then decided to let Tim Evans take the blame, knowing the couple's troubled marriage would cause him to be suspected. Morris closed by appealing to the jury's sense of fairness.

The following morning, 13 January, Mr Justice Lewis summed up. His speech was firmly against Tim Evans in inference, and when the jury retired, they were only out for forty minutes. The verdict was guilty. Tim replied that he had nothing to say when asked and was sentenced to death. In the dock Tim was shaking. John Christie started crying. Was it sadness for his former neighbour or relief for his own neck?

According to Ludovic Kennedy in *Ten Rillington Place*, there was an altercation between Tim's mother and the Christies as they left the court. Thomasina Probert pointed at John Christie and screamed, 'Murderer! Murderer!' Ethel Christie said, 'Don't you dare call my husband a murderer. He's a good man.'

Awaiting execution, Tim Evans spent his time looking at comics and playing dominoes and other games with his guards. One guard would later say that he 'seemed so harmless'. In letters to his mother and his sisters Eileen and Mary, dictated to guards, Tim maintained his innocence, insisting that John Christie had strangled his wife and baby.

An appeal was mounted on Tim's behalf by his solicitors, but this was rejected on 20 February. Tim's only hope now was a reprieve from the Home Secretary. A petition containing 1,800 signatures was delivered, but no reprieve came. Shortly before his execution Tim was taken back into the Roman Catholic Church. Albert Pierrepoint hanged Timothy Evans, who had been assessed in prison as having a mental age of ten or eleven, at eight o'clock on the morning of 9 March 1950 at Pentonville Prison. Like all executed prisoners, he was buried in the unconsecrated grounds of the prison.

CHAPTER
11

John and Ethel Christie have just returned from Sheffield in the north of England, where they spent a few days with Ethel's relatives. 'A change is as good as a rest,' Ethel had said, and John, or Reg as she calls him, certainly needed some respite. Unknown to his wife, he had come close to being exposed for what he was. Ethel has no idea about her husband's depravity, or the depth of it. His years as a petty criminal are long behind him, and Ethel feels little sympathy for Tim Evans, waiting for his date with Pierrepoint in Pentonville. Tim had tried to palm off responsibility for Beryl and Geraldine's murders on Reg at the trial. Reg, a killer! But she feels deep sadness about the deaths of Beryl and Geraldine, especially the baby. Tim had never seemed the type. If only she knew about Ruth and Muriel, killed by her husband while she had been visiting those same relatives in Sheffield years earlier . . . But she is very worried about Reg today. His nerves are still not right, his diarrhoea playing up again, fibrositis and enteritis his constant companions.

That's why John Christie is at the doctor's today. Dr Odess has been their GP for some time now. Christie sits in the waiting room in Colville Square, where he has been countless times since moving to 10 Rillington Place twelve years before. His head is bowed, and he does not reach for the tatty and well-fingered magazines on the table in front of him. Christie is coiled so tight that he could break down at any moment, his eyes intense behind the wire-rimmed spectacles. Dr Odess opens his door, and the previous patient, an elderly woman – not one that Christie would leer at, says goodbye. The welfare state that William Beveridge designed is less than two years old, but what a difference it's making – free visits to the doctor. Although the Labour government that introduced Beveridge's brainchild won't last much longer. Sir Winston Churchill, the biggest hero of them all, will soon be back in Downing Street. Few people remember that it was Churchill, in the heat of the fight against the Nazis in 1941, who commissioned Beveridge to investigate ways to improve British social conditions.

That same elderly woman had tried to start a conversation with Christie before she went in to see Dr Odess. Won't next year's Festival of Britain be exciting? Christie nodded but said nothing. Next May will be so gay. Christie managed a weak smile and was relieved when the doctor called her in, at the same time acknowledging Christie with a nod. Now it's Christie's turn. Dr Odess beckons him in.

'How have you been, Mr Christie?' Dr Odess knows immediately that Christie is not well, as he looks even thinner than normal, and the dark rings under his eyes, magnified by his strong glasses and washed-out look, indicate that his patient has not been sleeping well. Dr Odess is no fool and knows that in the past Christie has come to him when there was little or nothing wrong with him, but then, like most doctors, he has a number of hypochondriacs on his list. But it is obvious now that Mr Christie is really not well, and Dr Odess, like many members of the public, is fully aware of the trial of Tim Evans and Christie's role in it. Soon after sitting down, Christie begins to cry.

'I advise that you take a holiday, Mr Christie. You've been through a lot,' says Dr Odess.

Christie says nothing. His nerves are bad, and he is depressed, hardly able to face the Post Office Savings Bank, where he works and to which he must now return.

John Christie was let go from his job at the Post Office Savings Bank soon after, as a result of the exposure of his criminal record at Evans' trial. This did little for his state of mind, and he became glummer. On 10 March 1950, just twenty-four hours after Tim Evans was put into the ground at Pentonville, Christie went back to Dr Odess. Could he have been feeling guilt about what had happened to Tim, knowing that he was culpable for one or both murders? Or was it just his nerves breaking down after being stretched for weeks, realising how close he had possibly come to the hangman's noose?

What really happened between 8 and 10 November 1949 at 10 Rillington Place will never be known with absolute certainty. However, using what Christie would later say (although, just like Heath and Haigh, Christie was manipulative and his words must be read with extreme caution) and the known facts, a fair guess can be made. Tim Evans can never be completely absolved of all guilt for those tragic and terrible events, and there are some who think that both Christie and Evans were murderers. However, it can be said with conviction that Christie definitely murdered twenty-year-old Beryl Evans, and it is almost certain that he killed fourteen-month-old Geraldine too.

Christie would give two versions of what happened on 8 November 1949. One is reproduced below, as told to and transcribed by Harry Procter of the *Sunday Pictorial*. Christie begins his story on the day before, 7 November 1949.

One afternoon I went to her flat and found Mrs Evans lying on a quilted eiderdown on the floor of her small kitchen. When I went to the flat she was semi-conscious on the floor and I turned off the gas and she started to come round [the inference being that Beryl had tried to commit suicide by gassing herself]. I opened the window and door. She recovered quickly and was sick. I gave her a drink of water, and approximately a quarter of an hour later she wanted a drink of tea. I made one for her and had one myself. I do not think she would have succeeded at the time because the [gas] pipe was a little distance away from her. There was a small fire in the grate at the time, that is why I turned the gas off and opened [the] door and window, otherwise there probably would have been an explosion. But for the thought of

that happening I should no doubt have allowed the gas
to take its course and help by putting the tube nearer
again. I had a headache as a result of that incident. I
believe I told her not to say anything to her husband
about it and that the following day I would come up to
the flat and if she still felt as depressed I would help her.
This I did the following day after we had some tea which
she made. She did definitely tell me on that fatal day
that she wanted to go through with it [suicide] and said
she would I asked if only I would help her [sic]. I think
she knew I felt like making love to her and she got down
on the eiderdown in front of the fire and said I must
promise to help her after. This I did and afterwards when
she said she was prepared to go through with it and was
ready I got the tube and put it near her and was talking
to her and she told me to keep on with the gas. She
then started to become unconscious and convulsive and
I strangled her at that moment. I believe I made love to
her again just then. I am not certain, but think I did. I
removed the stocking from her neck and put it on the
fire, straightened her clothing again so that it looked
like suicide when her husband came home. I told him
[Timothy Evans] that what she had done and he believed
it. Evans picked her up and put her on the bed in the
next room and covered her over. He must have brought
her downstairs that night or the next one and put her
in the outhouse. I did not help him in any way. He said
he would be taking her away in his motor van and I
thought he had done.

Christie makes it sound like a mercy killing, him helping a depressed Beryl (who was also prepared to have sex with him) to end her life, but is that likely? First, Beryl was not suicidal at that time, just anxious to abort her new baby. Why would she want to kill herself? Also, no evidence of carbon monoxide or any other gas poisoning was found at her post-mortem. And why would she ask Christie to help her commit suicide? Second, would Beryl, an attractive young woman, have offered herself to middle-aged Christie, hardly the most appealing of men? That is very difficult to believe. Third, would Tim Evans have simply accepted it when Christie told him that Beryl had killed herself? Tim was an emotional man and prone to losing his temper, and this would have been totally out of character. Substitute 'abortion' for 'suicide' and replace the offer of sex with rape or more likely necrophilia, and you have a much more likely scenario.

Christie's second version, also published in the *Sunday Pictorial*, is probably closer to the truth, at least regarding Beryl.

As I felt at the time of the Evans affair normally I could not have done it, but if I was ill mentally I could possibly have killed her, using force that came to me without feeling the pain in my back. I believe actions like that are known to occur. What draws me to the conclusion is the thought that without realising it I could have been attracted to her, and, if not, why did I go out of my way to help her (known to my wife and in full agreement with her) and to strongly advise not to take things which injured her health? I realise now that most of these helpful suggestions came from me. But I did not attack the baby. My wife and I were far too fond of it to harm it, and we both wanted to adopt it. And Evans admitted it in court to the police when and how he did it and there is no mistake about that. The charge against his wife was not proceeded with. I did not – most emphatically I say this – harm the baby. Doubts have come into my mind about the wife of Evans. Weighing all things up I could be [guilty of Beryl's murder].

This account refers to Christie's abnormal and predatory sexual impulses but makes his role passive rather than active, as if he was not in control. This is a smokescreen used by many serial killers, often citing voices or a chemical reaction within them. Christie distances himself from the events in this version, not even naming Beryl, referring to her as 'the wife of Evans'. It is known that Christie was sexually excited by Beryl, as the records of Dr Odess clearly show. Christie went to see him complaining of 'nervous diarrhoea' at precisely the same time as Beryl was trying to find an abortionist, something she had confided in Christie. It seems that Christie's symptoms were a side-effect of his mounting sexual excitement as he contemplated the possiblity of intimate contact with Beryl. He had not murdered since 1944, over five years previously, and he was full of sexual tension, which was affecting his stomach.

Whether Christie went into the top-floor flat of 10 Rillington Place on 8 November 1949 with the premeditated intention of killing Beryl can never be said for certain, but it is highly likely. This was so that he could have sex with her after she was dead, giving him the power he so craved. He did not have the knowledge or skill to carry out an abortion; that was his way to get Beryl at his mercy so he could kill and violate her. It is also highly probable that there was a struggle, and that Beryl fought back, as the bruising to her eye indicates that Christie hit her.

Regarding the murder of Geraldine, it seems extremely doubtful that Tim Evans would have killed the baby he doted on, fretted over, played with and fed with love. He bought her a teddy bear in Wales when she had already been dead for some time. If Christie murdered Beryl then he almost definitely killed Geraldine too, as their bodies were both found hidden in the wash house. Tim's mistake was to be taken in by Christie – to hand over Geraldine and leave 10 Rillington Place – but there was never a couple in west London to take care of Geraldine. The baby was just an inconvenience for Christie, and he killed her. That is why Christie was so shocked when Tim suddenly came back to Rillington Place to ask after his daughter.

So it is very probable that by the end of 1949 Christie had murdered four people. Five if Tim Evans being hanged for Geraldine's murder is included. Just how long could he last before taking a fifth or sixth victim?

During the early summer of 1950 the landlord of 10 Rillington Place decided to sell the property. The tragic events that had occurred there the previous late autumn were undoubtedly a major factor in this decision. The 'murder house' had also become a must-see for morbid sightseers, who gawped through the dirty windows, some having their photographs taken in front of number 10. This attention made John Christie angry and Ethel unsettled. Mr Kitchener had recently moved, and so the Christies were alone in the house. For Ethel, the idea of perhaps having to move out of their home of twelve years was the worry, but her husband had a far more pressing anxiety. Ethel knew nothing about the presence of the bodies of Ruth Fuerst and Muriel Eady in the back garden. If 10 Rillington Place were sold, how long would it be before his first two victims were discovered in their makeshift graves?

Christie had had two macabre reminders about Fuerst and Eady several years before. A femur bone belonging to Muriel Eady had appeared in the garden, either dug up by the Christies' dog Judy (the Christies also had a cat) or brought to the surface by the weather. With total lack of respect, Christie had used the bone to help prop up the garden fence. His burial of Eady must have been less than thorough because, as Christie would later say, Judy had been digging in the garden during the police's first search of 10 Rillingon Place in late 1949, when they had been looking for Beryl Evans, and Eady's skull had been half-visible in the earth. With this reminder Christie had been more circumspect, taking it to a nearby bombed-out house and depositing it there. If it were found, it would be thought to belong to a victim of the Blitz. The police had not made an extensive search of the garden in December 1949 as, after finding the bodies of Beryl and Geraldine in the wash house, they had no need to.

Although this was troubling, Christie's state of mind did

improve. As Edward Marston recounts in his 2007 book on Christie, the serial killer visited Dr Odess in June 1950, his ailment being 'loss of memory'. However, after that he did not go back to Colville Square for nearly a year, a very long absence for Christie. Later that summer Christie was also well enough to take up a new job – with British Road Services, where he was a clerk. He seems to have got on well there, and his improved state of mind was mirrored by better physical health, as Christie refereed matches played by a football team set up by his co-workers. But Christie's mental and physical problems would return.

Prospective buyers sometimes came to take a look at 10 Rillington Place. One of them, Ernest McNeil, ironically an undertaker (a fact that apparently disturbed Christie), would later tell Ludovic Kennedy that Christie tried to put him off by telling him about the horrors that had occurred there. The Christies' dog sniffed around McNeil as Christie told him about Beryl and Geraldine's bodies being found, and McNeil asked why the dog had not smelt the bodies in the wash house, as they had been there for several weeks. Christie provided no answer. But it was when McNeil, still interested, brought in a surveyor to produce a report on the house, that he was finally deterred. The report stated that the house was infested with bedbugs and in a state of some decay. This makes it easier to understand why Beryl Evans had become unhappy and was adamant about not having a second baby there. She would have been stuck inside most of the day, every day. For the Christies it was different, coming from an older generation. They had been living like that for a long time.

In August 1950, the house was finally sold to Charles Brown, a Jamaican immigrant who worked as a commissionaire in a hotel. Within a short time Mr Brown had rented out the middle and top flats, formerly occupied by Mr Kitchener and the Evanses, to fellow Jamaicans. This upset the Christies, who displayed the racist attitudes common in white Britons at that time. Notting Hill was very different to what it is now. It was a poor area, and inhabited by some sinister characters. Slum landlord Peter Rachman, who owned a string of properties in the area and badly exploited his tenants, his henchmen threatening violence if the extortionate rents were not paid, and the Black Power leader Michael X, who would later be hanged for murder, were notorious local faces. Notting Hill attracted immigrants, and many were coming from the West Indies to fill low-paid jobs, especially on London Transport. The racist tension would culminate in riots at the end of the 1950s.

The Christies resented sharing their house with 'coloureds', especially the outside toilet. Christie would later say that Ethel was traumatised and intimidated by their new neighbours, and made complaints about them at the Poor Man's Lawyer Centre numerous times – to no avail, even alleging assault, which probably meant that one of the new tenants had brushed past his wife in the hallway. Ethel was the only real constant for Christie, and he would later call her the love of his life. He sounds so sensitive to his wife's feelings; however, the unthinkable was going to happen just a couple of years later.

Sunday, 14 December 1952, about eight in the morning

It is ten months since the death of King George VI, who was genuinely popular with the people, and almost six and a half months since the coronation of Queen Elizabeth II, when street parties had swept the nation, the public needing a cause for celebration. But John and Ethel Christie hardly feel like the king and queen of 10 Rillington Place now, the upstairs tenants not subscribing to Christie's pecking order like the late Evanses and old Mr Kitchener had. John Christie is no longer the king of his castle, and his mental and physical deterioration is partly due to loss of the control he craves. The fibrositis and enteritis periodically return, as do his loss of short-term memory and the inability to sleep. Ethel too has been on anti-depressants for months now, to calm her nerves when awake and to sleep. She is asleep now, having taken her pills, but her beloved Reg is wide awake, nervy and staring at the mildewed ceiling of their bedroom above him. Christie is sexually frustrated, almost to breaking point. He and Ethel have never had a very active sex life, but they have not had sex at all since Tim was hanged. Ethel makes fun of Reg about this sometimes. 'Can't-do-it-Christie' has returned, for it is he who cannot perform, and this upsets him. Perhaps if he could find new outlets for his mounting sexual tension . . .

Earlier this year, in July, a month after the coronation, Christie was referred to a psychiatrist for treatment, as he had an acute anxiety disorder. Dr Petit at Springfield Mental Hospital in south-west London observed him and thought Christie so anxious that he wanted him to stay at the hospital for some time. Christie said no, as he could not leave Ethel with the 'blacks'. He told Dr Petit that his anxiety had started when Tim Evans accused him of the murders of Beryl and Geraldine. Before that, in June, Dr Odess had sent Christie to see a consultant at St Charles Hospital in Ladboke Grove as, on top of his fibrositis and diarrhoea, it was obvious that Christie was severely strung out. Christie spent three weeks at the hospital, sleeping there and receiving visits from Ethel. The consultant at St Charles had referred Christie to Springfield, to which Christie went back in August, claiming to be much better. However, the experienced Dr Petit was not hoodwinked and could see that Christie was still dangerously strained.

Since then only Dr Odess has treated Christie – for his usual physical illnesses, plus catarrh – but he last saw him in September. His main problems remain psychological: the intense stress of almost being uncovered as a double murderer and the possibility of being unmasked as a quadruple killer at the root of his problems, his impotence and loss of status at 10 Rillington Place added factors. As he lies there, his mind racing, insomnia claiming him for yet another night, Christie wonders if he will ever escape from this torture.

But none of this is mentioned in a letter that Ethel writes on 19 October 1952 to her brother Harry Waddington (he had changed his name from Simpson), which can be found in the National Archives. Ethel is clearly putting on a brave face to the outside world. She says she is feeling better, Reg is back at work – although he had a nasty cold on his first day – and also, 'The landlord could not get anyone to do the cracks in our front room ceiling so Reg has done it, quite good too.'. Clearly Christie is not so physically incapacitated that he cannot carry out household repairs, and he is working. This coincides with the period when he is no longer visiting Dr Odess. However, in the letter Ethel writes (probably because of the new tenants), 'But if only we could get somewhere else to live it would be better for us.' Little does she know that Reg cannot leave due to the two young women decomposing in the back garden.

But this early morning, 14 December, Christie has other more pressing things to think about. Things have been building to a climax for over a week. Eight days ago, on 6 December, he resigned from his job as a clerk at British Road Services, telling his boss that he has a new job in Sheffield, where his wife's family live. Then on Wednesday, 10 December Ethel wrote a letter to her sister there, asking Reg to post it as she didn't feel up to going out. Christie kept the letter, knowing it would be useful for his plan. Ethel has not left 10 Rillington Place since Friday, 12 December, when she dropped off some washing at the launderette. She was seen there. The washed clothes will never be collected.

Everything has been building within him: Ethel's impotence jibes, the other tenants, who walk all over *him* – John Reginald Halliday Christie, former special constable, a man of importance who had worn his police uniform and carried out his tasks with such pride and efficiency; Boy Scout and former soldier who had survived being gassed; reformed citizen who had given up a life of petty crime and come through cross-examination at the Old Bailey – reduced to this, a quivering wreck, a shadow, the shell of his former respected glory. But he can still kill, he knows. That's why he has one of Ethel's stockings close by. It's time to take control again.

She's still asleep, the pills doing their work, as he straddles her and puts the stocking around her neck. Christie will later say that his wife woke in a convulsive fit, and that he strangled her in an act of loving mercy, but that's not how it happens. Ethel does wake up, but because she feels the constriction that her husband of thirty-two and a half years is exerting on her throat. Christie is taut with the effort, his back hurting, and when Ethel stops fighting he is relieved that his task is over, his wife's lifeless body beneath him. His sobs come from a mixture of relief and sadness. There's no attempt at post-mortem sex.

Christie will leave his wife in their bed for two days, trying to decide where to put her. The garden graveyard is far from perfect, and the wash house is a definite no-no. Then he decides to conceal Ethel under the floorboards of the living room in the flat. Pulling up the boards isn't difficult, as they are damp and beginning to rot. Ethel is laid under the floor wearing only loose stockings, but wrapped in a blanket, a nightdress and one of her frocks, an undershirt between her legs like a nappy and a pillowcase over her head. Then the wood is replaced, and a rug laid over the grave.

The previous day, with his wife still in the bed where she had died, Christie changed the date to 15 December on Ethel's letter to her sister Lily Bartle in Sheffield and posted it. A few days after putting Ethel's body under the floor, Christie will write a short letter to Lily himself, adding a note at the top: 'Don't Worry She is OK/I Shall Cook Xmas Dinner. Reg.' This will be put into a card and posted, the letter stating that Ethel can't write because of her rheumatism playing up, and that he is posting it from his workplace – from the job he had already left.

Christie is pleased with himself now, and even the other tenants cannot darken his manic yet excited mood. He tells the neighbours that Ethel has 'gone away'. He has freedom, which he achieved by himself with yet another of his ingenious plans, perfectly executed. Now he must make plans to enjoy the fruits of that freedom. When the stench of Ethel's rotting corpse becomes too much, Christie will sanitise the air of the ground-floor flat with cleaning fluid, his wife reduced to just a background smell.

Christie's main immediate concern was money. With no wage coming in any more, all he had was the weekly sum of two pounds and fourteen shillings from the Labour Exchange, now one of the many beneficiaries of the infant welfare state. But the rent still had to be paid, and he was soon feeling the pinch. Alone with his half-breed dog Judy, which he doted on, and a disloyal and roaming cat, Christie had to find ways to get money. First, Ethel's wedding ring – for which he got one pound, seventeen shillings – and wristwatch were disposed of, gaining him a few valuable pounds. Second, when things really started to bite, on 6 January Christie got round Robert Hookway of Portobello Road, the same furniture dealer to whom Tim Evans had sold his and Beryl's hire-purchase items. Christie received just under thirteen pounds for his furniture, much less than Tim had got just over three years earlier, but then Christie's furniture was really his and the late Ethel's and not still legally the property of a hire-purchase company. As the receipt in the National Archive shows, Robert Hookway had Walter Hildreth Ltd, Removal Contractors take away the Christies' furniture, at a cost of one pound, seventeen shillings and sixpence, on 7 and 8 January 1953.

Christie now sat in a deckchair in the kitchen, the same one in which Muriel Eady had taken her last breaths almost a decade earlier, and was sleeping on a musty mattress. Scraping by, hardly leaving the house, this was not the life he wanted. He knew that he had to get out again, as women wouldn't come knocking on the scuffed and creaking front door of 10 Rillington Place. It was time to cast his net again.

Just before or soon after Ethel's murder, Christie had gone with two young women to a room, where one of them had stripped for him and allowed him to take nude photographs of her – for money of course. But Christie had really wanted to see the other woman's body, the one who had sat there observing. Her name was Kathleen Maloney, and she would be unfortunate enough to meet the thin and nervy middle-aged Christie again. The naked photos had not satisfied Christie; only made him feel more lustful. It was control he wanted: to have an attractive young woman as a plaything, like a doll, allowing him to get an erection and ejaculate, and the only way that he could do this was if she were dead.

In January 1953 Christie met a potential victim in a Lyons' Teashop. These were smaller versions of the Lyons' Corner Houses that had dotted the streets of London for decades, offering wholesome and affordable food. The twenty-six-year-old woman with dark blonde wavy hair and imitation pearl earrings whom Christie got talking to in his whispering, sometimes breathless voice was Rita Nelson. Rita had a strong Northern Ireland accent, and this was no wonder, as she came from Belfast. She was attractive and soon had Christie licking his lips. Rita had worked as a waitress at the teashop, but she also had a shadier life as a prostitute, and had a criminal record for public drunkenness, theft and soliciting for male trade. That day she was a customer, and was sitting with a friend.

Christie would later say that they had started chatting when Rita asked for a match. It is very likely that Rita made the fatal mistake of confiding in Christie that she was pregnant, in fact twenty-four weeks gone, and did not want the responsibility of a baby, especially as she was thinking of going back to Belfast. Repeating the offer he had made to Beryl Evans just over three years before, Christie told Rita that he could help her. Christie said later, as he did with most of his victims aside from Ethel and Beryl, that Rita Nelson had acted aggressively towards him, shouting obscenities at him in the street, stalking him, finding where he lived and provoking him into a fight in which she came off worse. This is certainly untrue, and Christie almost definitely planned Rita's visit to 10 Rillington Place meticulously, going back to the wartime modus operandi he had used on Ruth Fuerst and Muriel Eady. The exact date of Rita Nelson's visit to his flat is unknown as, unlike John George Haigh, Christie did not take note of dates. For Haigh his murders had been business; for Christie they were driven by depraved lust.

It cannot be said with cast-iron certainty that Rita Nelson was Christie's first victim after Ethel was killed, but it is very probable. It is known that Rita Nelson went to Rillington

Place on or just after 12 January 1953, the last time her land-lady saw her – she reported her missing on 19 January. Rita never came out.

Rita Nelson knows Notting Hill well. She has plied her street trade there for a while now, especially since leaving her job waitressing at Lyons. Notting Hill is a good hunting ground for a prostitute like Rita; the women offering themselves at nearby Marble Arch are of an altogether higher calibre. More central still, in Soho, most prostitutes are foreign, from the Continent, and run by Maltese pimps the Messinas, the women who work for them often being tattooed with their mark, a kind of ownership stamp.

Rita is sitting in Christie's kitchen deckchair, now even more frayed than when the late Muriel Eady used it almost a decade earlier. Muriel's complaint was her terrible catarrh, a far from life-threatening illness but one that had proved indirectly fatal for her. Rita sits there, glad to be out of the cold outside and happy for Mr Christie to help her escape from her problem. The inhalation device is on the table in front of her, one of the only other pieces of furniture left in the spartan room. Mr Christie has told her that his apparatus will make her drowsy, allowing him to relieve her of the burden of the unwanted coming child. She won't have to go to the Samaritan Hospital for Women now.

Rita sighs as she begins to inhale. She has no idea about the house's dark past. Ruth Fuerst, Muriel Eady, Beryl Evans, Geraldine Evans, Ethel Christie – their lives are unknown to her, their terrible fates a secret. Christie is attaching the gas pipe now. Rita is already slumping, her neck drooping.

Christie gives her a little shove to check she is quiescent and then turns off the gas. He takes a rope from under the sink – put there earlier – places it around her neck and tightens. It takes some force, but not as much as the stocking took to strangle Ethel. Soon Christie knows Rita is dead. He is excited now, beginning to tremble a little, shivers going up and down his spine. He removes the pipe. Picking up Rita in his arms, he carries her into the bedroom, puffing and wheezing, his back shooting with pain but a very small price to pay for the ecstasy to come.

On the stained and dirty mattress Christie pulls up Rita's dress and runs his hands over her smooth legs. Her knickers come off next. He has an erection, his first proper one for years, helped by the fact that Rita is at his mercy. He is the master, the king of the moment. When he penetrates her, the lifeless expression on Rita's face doesn't deter him but makes Christie more excited. He thrusts inside her, and it doesn't take him long to ejaculate. Sperm will later be found in Rita's vagina.

After Christie has enjoyed Rita, he wraps her in a mottled woollen blanket, binding her ankles with a length of plastic flex. Then he puts her in the alcove behind the cupboard in the kitchen. Not far from the old cooking range, the alcove is actually a small room without a door, originally meant to store coal, a hiding place already chosen during his planning. But Rita won't be alone in that dank space for long.

Kathleen Maloney came from Southampton, where she had been orphaned and spent her childhood in a convent. Kathleen had run away from the institution and made her way to London, where she descended into prostitution, a common fate for those who arrive in the metropolis with no friends or money. She had also developed a taste for alcohol. A photograph of Kathleen taken a few years before she met Christie shows a good-looking young woman, but by now she was heavy in the face and somewhat bloated by alcohol. Having gone with Christie to a room in early to mid-December 1952 and watched as he took pornographic pictures of her friend, Kathleen would have not been a major part of Christie's terrible story if she had not run into him again in a pub.

The kind of pubs he went to, the less-than-salubrious kind, offered potential victims. There were prostitutes and transients, as there were in the greasy-spoon cafes he also frequented. Striking up a conversation was not difficult. Some of the young women were looking to make a pound, two if they were lucky. Christie was shabby, had an air of loneliness and was obviously part of an older generation: at the age of fifty-three, he was around thirty years senior to the women he chatted to in his soft voice with the slight Yorkshire accent. He was a nonentity. Such pubs were full of men like him, standing quietly by the bar or sitting at a table, open to conversation with strangers, some of them prostitutes. The men did not always have to make the first move, as the women had a service to sell. Little did Kathleen Maloney know that she would not be hiring her body to Christie for a short time, as she usually did, but giving him her body and soul for ever.

Twenty-six-year-old Kathleen was a little drunk that evening when Christie ran in to her again. He may have planned to do so, just wanted to, or possibly it was pure fate, which Christie embraced enthusiastically.

Back at 10 Rillington Place the more-than-tipsy Kathleen was soon seated in the deckchair. There is no evidence as to why she agreed to inhale the gas through Christie's murderous apparatus, but her drunken state undoubtedly helped Christie. Using the same rope to strangle her, Kathleen was soon at Christie's ecstatic mercy, and once again he violated his victim after death. Before hitting his filthy mattress, Christie placed a piece of cloth between Kathleen's legs as a nappy. He left her slumped over in the deckchair. The next morning Christie wrapped her in a blanket and put her in the kitchen alcove room after moving the cupboard aside. She was placed directly in front of Rita Nelson, closer to the doorway, her legs up the wall.

Temporarily fulfilled, Christie was soon on the hunt again.

Margaret Forrest would later count herself very lucky indeed. Soon after Kathleen Maloney was murdered, Forrest met Christie in the Panda Cafe, Westbourne Park Road, not far from the Ladbroke Grove end of Notting Hill. When Margaret Forrest told Christie that she had to endure debilitating migraine attacks, he was quick to ask if she suffered from catarrh. She replied that she did. Christie, again pretending to have medical knowledge and that he could help her – as he had with Muriel Eady (catarrh), Tim and Beryl Evans (abortion) and Rita Nelson (abortion) – said he had just the remedy, obviously referring to his breathing equipment. Margaret Forrest was impressed, and Christie gave her his address and set a time for her to visit. Christie would have had everything ready, but Margaret did not keep her 'appointment', as Christie termed it. Christie was frustrated and enraged, and he went out to look for her. When he did come across her, she said sorry and a new appointment was made. Forrest seems to have had no fear of Christie and did not feel wary of him. It was her forgetfulness that saved her life, as she then lost the address.

On 26 January Christie, enclosing her bankbook, forged Ethel's signature on a letter to the Yorkshire Penny Bank in Sheffield asking for her account to be closed. Christie received the much-needed ten pounds, fifteen shillings and twopence it contained.

Christie would not have to wait too long for a new victim, although some weeks would pass after Kathleen Maloney had been killed. Initiating contact in a cafe again, this time the problem that Christie could help a young woman with was finding somewhere to live. Hectorina MacLennan was twenty-six years old and from the Hebrides. She had been in London for almost five years, having moved down with her parents. During that time she had had two daughters outside wedlock. Her parents had decided to go back to Scotland in 1952 and took Hectorina's daughters with them. She was now a prostitute, and the Christie files at the National Archives show a string of convictions in her police file, many for soliciting.

It was at the very beginning of March 1953 that Christie met Hectorina MacLennan in that cafe. She looked sullen, and it can be imagined that Christie was sympathetic and sensitive to her, employing his best manner. Hectorina, a tall brunette known as Ena, told him that she was going to be homeless soon and couldn't find a flat or room. Christie seized his chance, still undoubtedly smarting from missing out on Margaret Forrest, and told her he knew of a flat. Hectorina thanked him and arranged to meet Christie outside Ladbroke Grove Underground station early that same evening.

Hectorina MacLennan showed up, but Christie was shocked to see that she had brought somebody with her. A man! To add to his frustration, she introduced the man, Alex, as her boyfriend. Alexander Baker was a lorry driver by trade but currently out of work. He was also married, though separated from his wife. Christie had no doubt intended to take Hectorina back to Rillington Place, incapacitate and then murder her using his tried and tested method, and there was no flat to show her. Now he had no choice other than to take them back to his own flat and say he would soon be moving out and they could have it. In fact, Christie may have already started thinking about subletting the flat, as his financial worries were mounting, and covering the rent was becoming increasingly difficult. Unlike Haigh, Christie's murders did not enrich him.

The unemployed Christie told Hectorina and Alex that the company he worked for was about to send him somewhere else, which was why his flat was almost empty. The couple were satisfied with the space, and as they headed back to their lodgings that evening believed they would soon be taking over Christie's flat. But when they arrived, they found the locks had been changed and they could not get in, evicted more quickly than they had expected. Hectorina and Alex went back to 10 Rillington Place, having nowhere else to go. This must have given Christie quite a jolt, as he liked to be firmly in control of everything around him. Added to that, there were now five dead people in the flat and garden. Ruth Fuerst and Muriel Eady were now just bones in the earth, but Ethel Christie under the living-room floorboards and Rita Nelson and Kathleen Maloney in the kitchen alcove were recent corpses. No amount of Jeyes fluid could cover the horrible stench of decomposition for long, and if Hectorina and Alex stayed, the smell would surely be noticed at some point.

In fact they ended up staying for three nights, although Christie made it clear that they could not sleep together, which no doubt would have made him uncontrollably jealous and even more frustrated. Alex Baker took the mattress in the bedroom, while Hectorina slept in the kitchen deckchair, the alcove where Christie planned to put her just feet away, Judy the dog sometimes sniffing around. Christie slept in the other chair. As he sat in the kitchen talking to her until she fell asleep, Christie doubtless imagined what he would do to her, undressing her and worse in his mind. If only Alex wasn't next door, he'd be having his way with her now. Christie suffered this mental torture for three nights and must have disinfected the flat while they were out during the day. His daily disinfecting ritual did not go unnoticed among the other tenants. Mrs Brown, wife of tenant Beresford Brown, who lived in the top-floor flat, saw Christie using Jeyes fluid in the inside hallway and in the backyard of the house.

After they left, Christie could not get Hectorina MacLennan out of his warped mind. He had been so close to having her, and an ex-Boy Scout, soldier and special constable did not give up easily. Christie's murderous focus was on Hectorina, and he had to have her.

6 March 1953, late morning

There is one place Christie knows he might find Hectorina and Alex, the Labour Exchange in Notting Hill, where Alex goes most days to look for a job. Christie sets out from 10 Rillington Place, cleaning the flat and feeding Judy before he goes, leaving a little milk out for the prodigal cat. The predator doesn't have to wait long for his prey. Christie sees Hectorina hanging about outside the office, waiting for Alex. There's a queue as always, and Hectorina wonders how long he will be today.

Christie walks up to her, asks her how she is, how funny to bump into you, etc., then invites her back to Rillington Place (it has never been discovered how he enticed her). She agrees, but first she must tell Alex, she says. Hectorina goes into the Labour Exchange building, finds Alex, tells him she has run into Mr Christie and he has asked her back to his flat – for whatever reason. Alex nods, and they agree to meet later at a favourite cafe. Hectorina then rejoins Christie outside, and they walk off together towards Rillington Place, looking possibly like father and daughter.

Once inside, they go straight into the kitchen. Christie makes them a pot of tea. Hectorina is back in the deckchair. Christie can hardly control himself as he waits for the tea to brew. He goes to remove the safety clip from the pipe through which the gas will flow, but Hectorina sees him. 'What are you doing? *What are you doing?*' The second time she says this, there is real fear in her voice. Christie is moving fast now, and the weak older man has disappeared. His eyes are fierce with concentration and sexual desire. He brings the pipe near her nose and mouth, holding her off with the other hand.

Hectorina soon becomes drowsy. Taking out the rope, Christie pulls it tight around her neck, and then tighter, so tight that the exertion makes him groan. Hectorina is dead very quickly. Christie wastes no time, removing most of her clothes and violating her right there in the kitchen. Once this is over and he is sated, Christie wastes no time preparing Hectorina for the alcove. He knows Alex might come looking for her.

Christie knows that all trace of Hectorina must disappear. He doesn't bother with wrapping her up or a nappy. He pulls the cupboard away from the wall again, revealing the alcove behind, then picks up Hectorina. Christie gasps with the weight, but he is pleased that he only has a few feet to go, half-carrying, half-dragging his victim. He puts the corpse in the alcove behind Kathleen Maloney and Rita Nelson, in a grotesque conga line of death. He uses Hectorina's bra to ensure she remains semi-upright, her back to the alcove doorway, her head slumped forward. Hectorina is the last to go into the alcove and so will be the first to be found later.

In the early evening Alex Baker comes to look for Ena, as she did not turn up at the cafe. Christie tells Alex that in the end his girlfriend did not visit the flat. As he has a cup of tea with Christie, Alex notices an offensive smell. Christie blames it on the drains. Christie also seems worried about Hectorina and goes with Alex to look around the nearby streets. For the rest of the week Christie will find Alex at the Labour Exchange, to see if Hectorina has turned up. No, Alex will say. But then Christie could tell him that.

CHAPTER
12

Christie knew that his time at 10 Rillington Place was coming to an end. Impoverished, all his possessions sold, his Labour Exchange payments covering the rent but offering little scope for any kind of life, he was now unable to frequent pubs and cafes to find new victims and began to consider subletting his flat and leaving. He must have known that if he moved out the risks of the four corpses in the house and eventually the two sets of remains in the garden being discovered were huge. Perhaps he felt satisfied now, having killed three times after disposing of his wife. Possibly he was frightened that Alex Baker would return to look for his girlfriend, perhaps with the police. Or maybe he just could not face life alone there without Ethel. Whatever the reason, on 13 March, a week after Hectorina MacLennan had breathed her last, Christie showed the ground-floor flat to a Mr and Mrs Reilly. The couple would later say that they had noticed a terrible smell but decided to take it anyway.

Some time during the next week Christie crudely wallpapered over the kitchen alcove, meaning there was just a sheet of paper behind the cupboard between three dead young women and the world.

By the terms of his lease Christie was not allowed to sublet the flat, but he was desperate for money and to escape the graveyard he had created around him. Flight must have seemed the only way to relieve the constant pressure of being caught. On the other hand, perhaps he knew it was the end of the road. By leaving he was inviting discovery – a subconscious act of surrender. There is some dispute about when Christie finally left Rillington Place, but the subletting 'contract' he typed, giving a copy to the Reillys, is in the Christie files at the National Archives, and shows the date 21 March 1953.

> The tenancy of Ground Floor of 10 Rillington Place W.11. has this day been transferred to Mr Reilly who is now the Sub-tenant & has agreed to pay the sum of seven pounds, thirteen shillings being 12 weeks rent in advance to date of 21 March 1953 & hereafter each 12 weeks during period of tenancy.
>   Signed by tenant,
>   John R. Christie
>   Received the sum of . . .

Before leaving, carrying an old suitcase lent to him by Mr Reilly with a few things inside (strangely some ladies' clothes and photographs and frames), Christie had taken his dog Judy to a vet and had her put down. Now with the seven pounds and thirteen shillings in his pocket (the equivalent of an average weekly wage at the time), Christie was homeless after almost fifteen years at 10 Rillington Place. He may have felt relief, but his next actions were erratic, and for once Christie seemed at a loss.

21 March 1953, early evening, King's Cross, London

In the shadow of the train station and the once-glamorous Gothic monolith of the St Pancras Midland Hotel, Christie walks down the street. Fog is descending, and the remnants of the rush hour melt away as the last office workers make their way home. Against the stabbing chill of the wind, Christie wears an overcoat, double-breasted with padded shoulders. Under his jacket beneath the coat he is wearing a pink shirt with stripes and a blue tie, a belt with a large buckle holding up his trousers. His brown shoes are scuffed and have seen many other, better days. The trilby on his head, light brown in colour, makes him even more anonymous as he drags the borrowed leather suitcase, with scuff marks to match his shoes, up the King's Cross Road. He walks past a hotel, wishing he could stay there but knowing that his meagre budget will not stretch to it. No, there is only one place for him. He has heard of it. Most Londoners have.

Walking up the steps to Rowton House, hostel for the dispossessed, Christie is glad to be anonymous. He is no nonentity like the others who stay here, but needs must. He is a man worthy of respect, once looked up to and respected around Rillington Place and its environs. Now in reduced circumstances – temporarily – they can't take who he is away from him. He will muck in with these lowly men, but never sink to their level. He is John Reginald Halliday Christie, a man of intelligence, capable of many things.

Meanwhile, back at 10 Rillington Place, things are moving fast. As Christie opens the suitcase on the tiny musty-blanketed bed in his shared dormitory room, snores and coughs around him, the owner of that suitcase is remonstrating with Mr Charles Brown, landlord of 10 Rillington Place. Who are you, and what are doing here? Brown asks Mr Reilly, as Mrs Reilly stands confused behind her husband. Mr Reilly takes out the 'contract' typed out by Christie, which also serves as their receipt for the advance they have paid on the rent for the flat. He also tells Brown that Christie had said he was going to Birmingham to join his wife, who was already there.

Brown cannot believe what he sees. Christie has no right to rent out this flat, Brown tells Reilly. Besides, Christie still owes him three weeks' rent. The Reillys are despondent and bitter at being tricked. Mr Christie had seemed so matter-of-fact, a little preoccupied but a 'good sort'. Charles Brown takes pity on the Reillys. He tells them they can stay tonight but must leave tomorrow. But what about the twelve weeks' rent we paid Mr Christie? asks Mr Reilly. You'll have to take that up with Mr Christie, says Brown – wherever he is, perhaps in Birmingham.

22–24 March

Christie is walking aimlessly, seeing parts of London he has never visited before. From the dingy streets around King's

Cross – prostitutes under the railway arches offering a quick one against greasy walls or a trip to a filthy room if a client can stretch to it – Christie walks on. Head down, mind racing, he feels lost, and his actual location at any given time of the day is not the cause. His life has no structure. Ethel, his backbone and only constant for so many years, who gave him a feeling of being somebody, is gone. Now he can only dawdle with no direction, filling up the daytime hours, taking breaks in cafes for steaming cups of strong tea. Rationing has ended now, but a hot meal in a cafe is still a treat, not that Christie can afford one. But he is still on the lookout. In a cafe on Pentonville Road he chats to Margaret Wilson, just as he had Rita Nelson, Kathleen Maloney and Hectorina MacLennan. When Wilson tells him that she is pregnant, Christie offers her an abortion, even though his apparatus is no more.

As the evenings set in, and the pea-souper smogs, caused by pollution, smother all around him, leaving a slimy sheen on his overcoat, he walks on, a man in the crowd. Nobody gives him a second glance. His bald head is covered by his trilby hat; his glasses steam up and need to be removed and cleaned from time to time. He takes the Underground out to the suburbs but sometimes returns to Notting Hill. A resident of Rillington Place will later say that she sees him shiftily peering around the corner at the entrance to the cul-de-sac. Little does Christie know that his anonymity will soon be a thing of the past, and that events inside 10 Rillington Place will make him a very wanted man.

24 March

The Reillys have left 10 Rillington Place knowing that they may never get their money back, but there has been another development, one that has implications for Christie. One of the tenants of the top flat, where Tim, Beryl and Geraldine Evans once lived, has had a chat with Charles Brown. This flat is now rented out to two individual tenants, one of whom is Ivan Williams, the other Beresford Brown, a handsome Jamaican with a thin moustache, who lives there with his wife. As the ground floor is now empty, Beresford has asked his namesake Charles if he can make use of the kitchen in the Christies' old flat. Charles Brown has agreed, provided Beresford cleans up the kitchen a little. Christie has left it in a disgusting mess.

Beresford Brown is making a start today. It really is a state. He decides to do the hard labour first. He carries all the old newspapers and accumulated rubbish out into the yard, making a pile of it just outside the wash house, very close to where Beryl Evans was laid out and her blanket-shroud unwrapped three and a quarter years earlier. Then he moves the furniture, so that he can strip off the wallpaper and repaint the walls. The kitchen is now a shell. Beresford is not a man who does things by halves, and he decides to do up the kitchen as well as he can. But he likes to work to music. He gets his wireless set from the top floor and looks around the kitchen for a place to put up a shelf for the radio. Reception is so much better higher up.

Just behind where the cupboard was, there is a new-looking section of wallpaper that looks like it doesn't need replacing.

He wastes no time. Holding a bracket in one hand and a hammer in the other, he gently taps a nail into the wall. That's strange, thinks Beresford. The nail goes right through the paper and there seems to be nothing behind. He feels the wallpaper. It gives under the slight pressure of his fingers. There is only one thing for it, he thinks, poking a hole in the wallpaper and then tearing a strip down. Behind it is just a hollow space. But the smell, oh the smell. He's never smelt anything like it.

Beresford rips the wallpaper down and across, revealing what looks like a doorway, but he can't see anything. He grabs a torch and trains it into the void. What he sees is almost impossible to believe. It's too horrible to imagine. It looks like a human back, but the skin is darkened and putrid. Beresford runs from the room and up the stairs, shouting as he reaches the middle floor, 'Ivan! Ivan!' His fellow tenant Ivan Williams looks down at him from the top floor, over the banister. 'Come quickly!' says Beresford, offering no other explanation. Williams follows him down. Back in the ground-floor kitchen, Beresford shines the torch on the grisly contents of the alcove, the torn wallpaper jagged and flapping. Williams's face contorts in horror. 'It's a body,' he says. No other words are needed. Beresford rushes out of the front door, sprinting to a telephone box to call the police.

While Christie continues his nomadic travels around London, the police arrive at 10 Rillington Place. Chief Inspector Griffin and two constables come first, to be followed by more high-ranking officers – the address has immediately rung alarm bells, recalling the events of December 1949. A call is put through to Home Office pathologist Dr Francis Camps, who is just about to have his dinner. A workaholic and known for his speed with post-mortems, Camps is at the house by 7.30 p.m. The alcove is then investigated more fully, and it is soon obvious that there is more than one body inside. A police photographer takes crime-scene photos, and then the bodies are slowly and carefully removed. Hectorina MacLennan is wearing only a blue bra, its hook in the blanket wrapped around the body behind her, Kathleen Maloney. Finally, Rita Nelson is taken out last, also shrouded in a blanket tied up at the feet. The policemen cannot believe what they are seeing. The bodies are soon taken away to Kensington mortuary.

But that is not all. A thorough search of the flat is ordered. At just after one in the morning on 25 March, about eight hours after Beresford Brown first peeled back the wallpaper, an officer calls out from the living room. He has found that some of the floorboards are loose. These are pulled up one by one, and the wrapped body of Ethel Christie is found in the floor cavity. The blanket around her is held together by a large safety pin, and inside it she is only wearing stockings. Dr Camps asks for the body to remain there until later in the morning. A police guard is put outside 10 Rillington Place.

At dawn Dr Camps and senior police officers rendezvous back at the house, and Camps supervises the removal of Ethel Christie's body to Kensington mortuary, to join the three others already there. Dr Camps wastes no time getting to work. Once the pillowcase is removed from Ethel's head, he quickly discovers the cause of death – asphyxiation by ligature. Camps estimates the date of death as approximately twelve to fifteen weeks previously, with the proviso that this is based on his experience. It is a good educated guess, as Ethel Christie has been dead for almost fourteen weeks. There is no sign of intercourse, and Camps finds no gas in Ethel's lungs. When he examines the bodies of Rita Nelson, Kathleen Maloney and Hectorina MacLennan, he pronounces the cause of death in all three as asphyxiation by ligature. However, signs of gassing and sexual intercourse are present in all of the women taken from the alcove, and sperm is present when vaginal swabs are taken. Not all of the bodies have been identified.

The press is immediately on to the story. An early report calls the gruesome finds 'the most brutal mass killing' in London's history. It is certainly the worst since Jack the Ripper in terms of numbers. Haigh had killed more, but of course only the sludgy remains of his last victim Mrs Durand-Deacon were ever found due to his modus operandi. However, what nobody but Christie yet knows is that there are two skeletons in the back garden, and the newspapers will soon start asking questions about the murders of Beryl and Geraldine Evans.

On 25 March, while 10 Rillington Place is being taken apart by the police, and Dr Camps carries out post-mortems on the four dead women found there, Christie sees the front page of a newspaper and becomes aware of the discovery of the bodies. There are few details in the report, but it's enough to send Christie into a panic. When he arrived at Rowton House he booked in for a week but now knows it's too risky to stay there. He packs the few things that he brought with him in Mr Reilly's suitcase into one of the hostel's lockers. Christie will never return for them. Pulling his trilby further down over his face, he walks out of Rowton House with only the clothes he is wearing into the mass of nameless faces on the street. For the next few days Christie will be homeless and his existence increasingly miserable as his last pennies dribble away, his desperation mounting.

A police report dated 26 March 1953 in the Christie files at the National Archives states that on that day, two days after the four bodies were discovered at 10 Rillington Place, only two had been identified with certainty. It is addressed to the chief superintendent of F Division (Notting Hill), which had dealt with Neville Heath almost seven years earlier. 'Of the three bodies in the cupboard two have been identified, one as Hectorina MacLennan . . . and the other, by finger prints, as Kathleen Maloney . . . The remaining two have not yet been positively identified, but the fourth body, found under the floor boards, is believed to be that of Christie's wife Ethel.' It goes on to say that Ethel had last been seen 'early in January, 1953', but the witness was clearly mistaken, as Ethel had been dead for more than two weeks by then. It ends: 'It is anticipated that identification of the third body will soon be effected.' This was Rita Nelson, the first victim to go into the kitchen alcove after Ethel Christie's murder.

A statement given by Detective Sergeant John Shorto of F Division on 8 April 1953 explains how Hectorina MacLennan, Christie's last victim, was identified. It seems that her boyfriend Alex Baker was involved. DS Shorto wrote, 'On

25 March 1953 [the day after the bodies were discovered], I went to 10 Rillington Place W.11, and searched a quantity of rubbish which was in the yard at the rear of that address.' He found some items with the name of Alexander Baker on them, which had presumably been dumped in the back garden by Christie – left in the flat by Alex when he and Hectorina stayed there for three nights. The items included Baker's driving licence. But that was not all. DS Shorto recounts that some of Hectorina's clothing was also found: 'At about 4.30 p.m., on 25 March, 1953, I was present at Notting Hill Police Station when . . . showed Mr Alexander Pomeroy Baker a white blouse, a black woollen pullover, a brassiere and a suspender belt. Mr Baker identified the blouse, pullover and brassiere as being the property of Hectorina MacLennan, and the suspender belt as being similar to the one worn by the same woman.'

This would not be enough to formally identify the body as Hectorina's, but as she had a criminal record her fingerprints were undoubtedly on file. Rita Nelson was identified by fingerprints too, and perhaps dental records.

The police were completely gutting the ground floor of 10 Rillington Place, pulling up all the floorboards, as well as searching the rest of the house. The strangest find was a tobacco tin which contained four tufts of pubic hair later found to be from four different women, but who they belonged to has been the subject of much debate. Like many serial killers, Christie had kept perverse trophies of his murderous career. Overall, the disruption at the house was so great that the landlord, Charles Brown, would later make a claim against the police for the cost of damage and loss of earnings from his property. Contemporary photographs show the extent of the police activity. Even the chimney was prodded with rods, dislodging decades of soot and dirt. However, nobody knew if more bodies would be discovered, and with four corpses, on top of those of Beryl and Geraldine Evans at the same address several years before, no effort was spared.

The house had no more bodies to give up, but the garden was a different matter. Digging commenced there on Saturday, 28 March. It did not take long. The first few shovel loads of earth contained bones. They were of course the skeletal remains of Ruth Fuerst and Muriel Eady. Some of the bones were in fragments and the skeletons were not complete. The police also spotted the human bone that Christie had used to prop up the fence. It was still there. The police obtained old tea chests from the proprietors of local shops to transport the bones back to the pathology laboratory, where Dr Camps and police surgeon Dr Shanahan got to work. The bones would take some piecing together (some had been burned, presumably by Christie in an attempt to dispose of them), and some were animal in origin. Seemingly Christie had buried bones gnawed by his dog Judy in the garden, perhaps thinking that this would confuse anyone who came across the human remains. As already mentioned, Christie had had Judy put down, but the Christies' semi-feral cat appeared in the garden while it was being dug up. The cat was reportedly so unsettled by the digging that it had some sort of fit and had to be put down too. In his memoirs Dr Camps would write, 'The descriptions and identifications of Christie's first

two victims are outstanding examples of what really system-
atic, properly controlled and directed scientific examination
can yield when closely associated with good police
investigation.'

Ruth Fuerst was identified fairly quickly, as her teeth
included a crown of German or Austrian origin, and when
missing persons records were checked, the proportions of
her reassembled skeleton matched her description. It would
take years for Muriel Eady to be identified (to the suffering
of her family), but this was eventually accomplished on the
basis of her age when she disappeared and the fact that she
had had diseased adenoids. It was Muriel Eady's skull that
Christie had dumped in the rubble of a nearby bombsite,
after Judy had brought it to the surface. The site had since
been cleared, and the lack of a skull made identifying her
that much more difficult.

A major find was a newspaper found in the earth in the
vicinity of the bones. It was dated 19 July 1943, almost ten
years previously and in the middle of the Second World War.
Christie had put it there when he buried his first victim, the
Austrian prostitute Ruth Fuerst, in August 1943. Was it some
kind of macabre time capsule? There was no other apparent
reason for its presence.

The *News of the World*, which sold for twopence-halfpenny
and had a circulation every Sunday in 1953 of over eight
million (it had peaked at 8.4 million in 1950, and by 1959
would fall to 6.5 million) was on to the story. As Matthew
Engel wrote in *Tickling the Public*, his history of Britain's
popular press, 'When there was a murder, the *News of the*

World was still *the* paper.' Under the editorship of Arthur
Watkins, who had also been editor in 1950 when the paper
covered the arrest, trial and execution of Timothy Evans
and reported on Christie's evidence at that trial, crime was
a mainstay of the tabloid. Watkins would die on the job
later in 1953, but his chief crime reporter, Jock Rae, would
remain on the beat for some time to come. Rae was unques-
tionably the main reason for the *News of the World*'s
reputation for covering crime, especially murder. Many other
crime reporters were in awe of Rae, and some rookies simply
terrified of him. Abrupt and to the point, he went not just
'straight to the bone' but sometimes right through to the
marrow.

By the early 1950s readers knew what to expect from the
News of the World. It was titillating and sometimes downright
crude by the standards of the time, while Rae had the best
contact book on Fleet Street, and everyone knew it. He had
intimates within the police, judiciary and the underworld. If
there was a story to be got, Rae could be expected to get it,
and if he did not, then Harry Procter of the *Sunday Pictorial*
would. Police detectives would sell titbits of inside knowledge
on fresh cases, and Rae was usually first on their list. The
Sunday nationals paid more for such gems than the dailies,
so police contacts would hold on to their information until
later in the week, to pass to Rae or Procter.

In his memoirs Harry Procter would write of Rae and the
Christie case, 'During the first week of the Christie murder
investigation . . . Jock Rae swept the floor with the lot of
us . . . he had beaten me hollow . . . So I sent my rival a
telegram saying "Congratulations on your magnificent story

– you have beaten us all."' Procter was referring to Rae's
News of the World front-page scoop of Sunday, 29 March 1953.
Bylined in large type 'By NORMAN RAE, Our Crime reporter',
the headline was 'THE HOUSE OF MURDER YIELDS UP MORE
GRISLY SECRETS: BODY NO. 5 IN THE GARDEN: NOW THE ORDER
IS "DISMANTLE THE BUILDING."' There was also a photograph
of 'The Four Faces of John Christie', including how he might
look with and without his glasses. Harry Procter was just
one of millions who read the *News of the World* that day;
John Christie was another.

Sunday, 29 March 1953, 11.20 p.m., *News of the World* offices, 30 Bouverie Street, London EC4

The offices are quiet, at least compared to twenty-six hours
ago, when that day's edition was being put to bed. Then, the
subeditors' office next door had been buzzing, all of them
around the table with the paper's editor Arthur Watkins. As
the subs, some immaculate in suits, others waistcoated with
sleeves rolled up, cigarettes dangling or burning in ashtrays,
went over the copy yet again, Watkins stood behind them in
his dark blue double-breasted suit, cigarette between the
fingers of his right hand, attentive, ever ready to give direction and answer queries. Nobody knows that Watkins only
has months to live, but then many bodies have been carried
out of these offices. The paper is now 110 years old, and its
telegram address 'Worldly, Fleet, London' is almost universally
known.

The cleaners have been round to empty overflowing
ashtrays and straighten dictionaries and paperwork, throwing

away numerous screwed-up balls of paper that never made
the bins. In the reporters' room there are only three people.
A trainee reporter is being shown the ropes by a veteran
over in the corner, the young man's spectacles steaming up
with his nervous breath. Behind the far desk sits a burly
man, his suit single-breasted and well cut, but not the best,
his hat on the empty desk beside him. Even as he leafs
through a leather-bound book with 'CONTACTS' embossed
in gold on the front, he looks as if he can handle anything
thrown his way – and he has had a great deal hurled at him
in his time.

Norman 'Jock' Rae is fifty-six and has been on the paper
for over two decades, having secured more crime scoops
than most had Sunday roast dinners before the war. Rae is
old school, and despite his seniority still does the legwork.
Contacts need cultivating; contacts mean leads, and leads
need chasing. Most of the other reporters will not be back
here until Tuesday morning, to start on next Sunday's
edition, but Rae wants more on Christie and the 'murder
house'. His scoops are sensational, but the way he gets them
is methodical and low key. A nod from Rae is as good as a
handshake from others, a grimace as good as a smile, and
a smile really means something. He knows how criminals,
especially murderers, think. They are just like you and me.
Some young reporters coming through have made the
mistake of underestimating Rae, thinking he's past it. But
they soon learn that he is sharper than anyone, one of the
greatest tabloid reporters of his or any other generation.
He also has honesty and integrity, and in this cut-throat
world that means a great deal.

People call the switchboard downstairs at all times of the day and night. Rae isn't expecting a call tonight, and the other reporter stops his mentoring to pick up the telephone. 'It's for you, Jock.' Rae moves slowly towards the phone, his head bald but not shiny. 'Rae speaking,' he growls in his easily impersonated Scottish accent. As soon as he hears the voice, Rae knows who it is. He spoke to John Christie when he was covering the Timothy Evans case. The voice is almost a whisper, sometimes a little raspy, but tonight it sounds strained, almost broken. Rae is not surprised – Christie is on the run, the whole country looking for him.

'You recognise my voice?' says Christie.

'That I do,' says Rae.

'I can't stand any more,' says Christie. 'They're hunting me like a dog, and I'm tired out. I'm cold and wet and I've nothing to change into.'

'So why are you calling me?' says Rae.

'Give me a hot meal, a smoke and a warm place to go, and I'll give you my story,' says Christie.

'That can be done, Mr Christie. But I'd have to inform the police immediately after,' says Rae.

'That's understood,' says Christie.

Rae arranges to meet Christie outside Wood Green town hall in north-east London in two hours' time, at 1.30 a.m. Christie has been wandering around that area tonight.

Rae does not betray any excitement. He tells the switchboard to get his driver round. They will drive north through the rain and darkness, but at the appointed time a policeman will walk past, and Christie will run away, thinking it's a set-up. When Jock Rae hears the rustling in those bushes, he will know that he has lost the biggest scoop of his long career, perhaps topping that of John George Haigh.

Tuesday, 31 March 1953, a little after nine in the morning, south embankment of the River Thames, near Putney Bridge

Christie stands looking into the murky water. Thirty-two hours have passed since he abandoned his hiding place in the bushes outside Wood Green town hall at the sight of a passing copper. Rae had been his last hope. The water laps at the keels of cargo barges and boats tied to the posts of the jetty. Timber is stacked in large bundles in several piles just down from where Christie is hunched over, some of the stacks almost as tall as he is. The large building to his left flies the Union Jack, and Christie knows that it is a pub, as 'COURAGE' is emblazoned in gold lettering across the first floor, below smaller letters giving the pub's name, the Star and Garter. If Christie had enough energy left to appreciate the irony, his thin lips would perhaps purse. Courage is what he needs, but he has no more reserves to fall back on.

Soaked through, ravenously hungry and with just two shillings, threepence-halfpenny in his damp pockets, the cafe next to the pub and the shops in the parade round the corner have stopped tormenting him. At first, the sight of refreshment and normal life had irritated him, increasing his hunger and thirst, but now he is resigned and fatalistic, the brim of his trilby pulled out of shape, his state of mind similarly warped. Unshaven and unwashed since leaving Rowton House six days ago, Christie has nothing left. He has seen the headlines of the papers already this morning, as he walked past a news-stand, which talk of the 'murderer on the loose'. His face is on most front pages, and if Christie bought a paper he would be able to read an ex-police colleague's reminiscences of him.

'He was always secluded and reticent and never mixed with the boys. But he knew his job,' the man had told the Murder Gang. 'In his time, he had brought to justice thieves, blackmailers, fraudsmen and men who were found guilty of sexual assaults on women.' Christie's apprehension of the latter was perverse now, and readers knew it. At Saturday's football matches his picture had been displayed everywhere. Police forces up and down the country have his photograph. Christie knows that it won't be long now, as he peers into the dark Thames, almost wishing that he could be within the river, but suicide is not on his mind. He's too good a man for that, he knows. But he is resigned now, listless and unable to think clearly through hunger and fatigue, after days of wandering over much of London.

Christie is so wrapped up in himself that he doesn't hear the footsteps behind him, and if he had would not have time to get away, even if he had the energy to do so. 'What are you doing?' says a voice. Christie is woken from his mental ramblings, but does not start, turning round slowly. 'Are you looking for work?' says a man with a small moustache. His dark trenchcoat, black tie and tall helmet with its badge and chin strap register with Christie. To the young PC Thomas Ledger, number V400 in the Metropolitan Police, Christie is a vagrant of the kind he daily encounters on this, his regular beat.

'I . . . I'm waiting for my employment cards to come through,' says Christie.

'Can you tell me who you are?' says PC Ledger.

'John Waddington, of 35 Westbourne Grove,' says Christie. Ethel's brother Harry changed his name to Waddington, and he had visited 10 Rillington Place, Ethel writing to him sometimes. Christie has had this alias and an address not far from Rillington Place ready for days. But PC Ledger is having a good look at Christie's face now. There is something familiar about this man's penetrating eyes.

'Can I ask you to remove your hat for me, sir?' says PC Ledger. Christie complies, taking off his trilby, causing water to drip onto his coat. The top of his almost bulbous bald head is revealed, and PC Ledger is glad he was alert. 'I need you to come with me, sir,' says the constable, not saying that he has recognised John Christie of 10 Rillington Place from the front pages of every newspaper and from the *Police Gazette*. Christie offers no resistance and meekly comes along, as PC Ledger takes him by the arm away from the river. A police van soon comes to take him away.

In the back of the van Christie is asked to empty out his pockets. As well as the few coins he has left, there is a report cut out of the *News of the World* from 1950, tattered and yellowed after three years. Written by Jock Rae, it is a report on Christie giving evidence at the trial of Timothy Evans. The report is undoubtedly one of the reasons Christie got in touch with Rae the day before yesterday. Also on Christie are both his and Ethel's old ration books, their marriage certificate, a St John's Ambulance badge, some pawn tickets, his Rillington Place rentbook and his union and identity cards.

Confirmation of identity could not be firmer, and Christie is taken to Putney police station. A call is made to Notting Hill: 'We have Christie.'

Chief Inspector Griffin and Detective Inspector Kelly interview Christie, who is exhausted. DI Kelly writes down his first statement. Christie opens with an attempt to gain sympathy: 'I have not been well for a long while, about eighteen months. I have been suffering from fibrositis and enteritis. I had a breakdown in hospital.' The policemen remain impassive. DCI Griffin tells Christie that his wife Ethel's body has been found at 10 Rillington Place. Christie begins to sob. He then says that he strangled his wife as an act of mercy, and that she had attempted to kill herself by taking phenobarbitone tablets. He found a bottle with only two tablets left next to the bed. 'I knew then she must have taken the remainder,' says Christie. Dr Camps had found no phenobarbitone in her body.

Regarding the three bodies found behind the kitchen cupboard, Christie begins with Rita Nelson but does not think she was his first victim (at least in the alcove); that was Kathleen Maloney. However, Rita Nelson was at the back, so unless for some reason Christie swapped the bodies around, logically she was the first alcove victim. Christie says that Nelson was abusive and threatened him in the street outside his flat, demanding money. 'She forced her way in. I went to the kitchen and she was still on about this thirty shillings. I tried to get her out and she picked up a frying pan and hit me . . . there was a struggle and she fell back on the chair. It was a deckchair. There was a piece of rope hanging from the chair. I don't remember what happened, but I must have gone haywire. The next thing I remember she was lying still in the chair with the rope around her neck.' Christie does not mention that she was gassed, or that he had sex with her.

Next, Christie talks about Kathleen Maloney, saying that she had come to look at his flat but then made a pass at him. When he rebuffed her, she became abusive, threatening to get someone round to beat him up. Christie sees himself as passive, Maloney the aggressor: 'I am very quiet and avoid fighting. I know there was something, it's in the back of my mind. She was on the floor.' He goes on to say that he 'must have' placed her in the alcove immediately. Again, there is no mention of gassing or intercourse, or indeed strangulation in this case.

He speaks about Hectorina MacLennan and her boyfriend Alex Baker. He doesn't like Baker and says that when they stayed with him Baker was 'unpleasant', and that the police were after Hectorina. Christie says that she came back to 10 Rillington Place on her own, and that he told her to go, but she got angry. 'I got hold of her arm and tried to lead her out of the kitchen,' he continues, saying Hectorina struggled fiercely, her clothing 'got torn', and she then 'sort of fell limp'. He thinks some of her clothing 'must have' been pulled tight around her neck when they struggled. She wasn't breathing, so Christie says he must have put her in the alcove too. There is no mention again of gas or sexual intercourse.

In all four cases Christie is not to blame, and even if he was, he was only trying to help. Ethel was killed as an act of compassion, Nelson, Maloney and MacLennan in self-defence. Then Christie adds a postscript: 'I wish to state that I am grateful to the police in charge for the kindly way in which I have been treated at Putney police station.'

Christie is now moved to Notting Hill police station by van. When the police van arrives at Notting Hill, it is driven round to the back entrance of the station. His capture has already leaked to the press, and there are reporters and photographers at the front. A uniformed constable holds open the heavy wooden gate while two plainclothes officers from Putney sandwich Christie as they go through. Christie is now without his coat, and his crumpled jacket and trousers are damp. Not handcuffed, Christie holds his hat up to the side of his face to hide it. Bowed over and using his right hand to support himself on a wall, he looks a broken man. Christie does not notice that an enterprising press photographer has secured a vantage point in a building next door, and so he is snapped from above, crystallising this moment for ever. The evening editions of the papers carry the news of Christie's capture, one headline screaming 'CHRISTIE IS FOUND AT PUTNEY', the smiling face of his captor, PC Ledger, in a photograph underneath, now a hero.

At Notting Hill police station this evening, 31 March 1953, John Christie is charged with the murder of his wife. After a brief appearance at a magistrates' court in west London tomorrow morning, 1 April, Christie will be taken on remand to Brixton Prison. When the press try to take his photograph, Christie will shield his face again, shy for a man who shows no remorse and who will actually display some pride in his murderous achievements.

CHAPTER
13

In Brixton Christie soon began to feel better. Regular meals, cups of strong tea, sleep and being able to wash and shave restored his 'dignity'. He showed no remorse, and his old arrogance returned. Christie saw himself as better than the other inmates, revelling in his notoriety. When he went back to the magistrates' court on 15 April 1953 to be charged with the alcove victims, Rita Nelson, Kathleen Maloney and Hectorina MacLennan, however, his public shame returned. Christie this time shielded his face from public view with a newspaper. The crowds outside the court were large and not full of admiring women, as they had been with Heath and Haigh. In fact, a newspaper had compared Christie to the horror actor Boris Karloff. Christie told other prisoners in Brixton that he was 'more like Charles Boyer'. Boyer was a famous romantic actor of the 1940s and 1950s, very popular with women for his passionate and romantic roles. Nobody else could see any similarity between Christie and Boyer, however.

Psychiatrists were observing Christie in the prison hospital. None of them found him at all personable or likeable. Their evidence would be very important at the trial, as his legal team were already telling Christie that his only chance was to be found guilty but insane. But just like Heath and Haigh, Christie would have to be proved so under the M'Naghten Rules. If that was the result, the sentence would be life in Broadmoor; if not, Christie would of course be hanged. Christie boasted to other inmates that he was better than John George Haigh, hanged in August 1949 and already a macabre legend. Interestingly, Haigh had also declared himself superior to Neville Heath.

Press interest in Christie was intensifying. Rae had got the most detail in the first days after the discovery of the bodies at 10 Rillington Place but had missed his opportunity to get Christie's inside story. (Their aborted meeting was not public knowledge as Christie had been on the run.) Now Harry Procter took over the running. Christie would not go with Rae now, and Procter began reporting on him every Sunday, using his contacts to get as full a story as possible, a prelude to Procter getting the real nitty-gritty from Christie himself.

On consecutive Sundays, 19 and 26 April, the *Sunday Pictorial* splashed with Christie. A large front-page photograph showed Reg and Ethel, she holding his arm, Christie in a dapper suit and holding a trilby, looking stiff, not unlike his future Madame Tussaud's waxwork, while Ethel smiles, stout and homely in a flowery print dress. Christie was accused of murdering 'his wife and three other women', and there was no mention of the two garden victims, Fuerst and Eady, or indeed Beryl Evans. The following Sunday there was a photograph of Christie with his dog Judy at 10 Rillington Place, and Christie was quoted talking about the kindness of prison staff and the little treats of fruit and cigarettes they allowed him.

Sold at twopence-halfpenny, the *Sunday Pictorial* had a regular circulation in 1953 of just over five million, three million less than the leader the *News of the World*. There were ten Sunday national newspapers, and the *Pic*, as it was known in Fleet Street, ranked alongside the *People* on the second tier. The editorial director / editor in chief of both the *Sunday Pictorial* and its sister the *Daily Mirror* was the veteran news-paperman Hugh Cudlipp. This was an executive post, but Cudlipp had previously been editor of the *Pic* three times, his last reign ending the previous year, 1952, when he was kicked upstairs amid boardroom machinations. Harry Procter had settled in well at the *Sunday Pictorial*, managing a series of crime scoops, but unlike Rae wrote lighter pieces too. In his memoirs Procter would say that he preferred other reporting but, as previously at the *Daily Mail*, he was felt too talented a crime reporter not to use on major murder stories. Procter realised that the Christie case was going to be perhaps the biggest murder story of the century, particularly with the Tim Evans connection, and he went all out to get the exclusive on it.

On 17 May the *Sunday Pictorial* carried a page 3 article entitled 'The Riddles of Rillington Place – Do You Know These Women?' Alongside it were photographs of Ruth Fuerst and Muriel Eady, showing that both were considered likely candidates for the garden victims, even at this early stage. But, as mentioned earlier, Eady would not be definitely identified for some time, although the police obviously had a strong hunch that the skeleton without a skull was her, and a police contact had shared this information with Procter. However, the article stated, 'The police have no actual information that they [Fuerst and Eady] were acquainted with John Reginald Halliday Christie.' Under the second subheading 'AND . . . RIDDLE NO.2' there was a picture of Beryl Evans, looking very young – as she indeed had been when she died three and a half years earlier – smiling innocently, and captioned 'The Woman To Be Exhumed Tomorrow'. Procter had brought the link with Beryl and Geraldine Evans into the public domain, opening up a whole new angle on the already extraordinary story of 10 Rillington Place.

In fact, Christie had admitted to killing Beryl Evans almost three weeks earlier. Dr J. A. 'Jack' Hobson was observing Christie, which meant them having long conversations. When Dr Hobson gently brought up the subject of Beryl Evans, Christie opened up on the matter for the first time, saying, 'I felt really bad about that, sir. I must have been intimate with her then strangled her.' This initiated a debate that would continue for decades, with many calling the 1950 hanging of Timothy Evans one of the greatest miscarriages of justice ever.

Monday, 18 May 1953, just after 5.30 a.m., Roman Catholic cemetery, Gunnersbury Lane, Chiswick, London

It is going to be a balmy almost-summer day, but at this time of the morning it is cold and the wind carries a chill.

Exhumations always take place very early, to make them as private and as least distressing to the family of the exhumed as possible, but this morning there is a large contingent of Fleet Street reporters and photographers on the bank outside the cemetery on Bath Road. There are also the usual morbid sightseers, who read Harry Procter's piece in the *Sunday Pictorial* yesterday, although some are disappointed, as Procter gave the exhumation time as later – at six o'clock. Four gravediggers have already cut into the common grave where Beryl Evans and her baby Geraldine are buried.

There are thirteen people in the exhumation group altogether, including the undertaker and mortuary superintendent, as well as Home Office pathologists Dr Francis Camps, Dr Donald Teare and Dr Keith Simpson. Dr Simpson, who had worked on the Heath and Haigh cases, will later write in his memoirs that they are known as the Three Musketeers. They are the leading pathologists of their day, all based in London. Simpson has been hired by the defence team to represent Christie. Camps has been given the task of performing the post-mortem on Beryl Evans, having done the same for the six bodies at 10 Rillington Place. Teare is present because he performed the original post-mortems on Beryl and Geraldine in December 1949. There are police representatives, and Christie's lawyers have brought along Dr Hobson, the psychiatrist who recently got Christie to admit that he strangled Beryl Evans.

The reason the defence has requested that Beryl Evans be exhumed is to help with Christie's insanity plea. It is already obvious that he has killed six women, and adding another to the count can only make Christie appear madder. Such are the straws that Christie's lawyers have to clutch at to offer any kind of defence at all.

Beryl and Geraldine are in one coffin, fortunately the top one in the common grave, which contains six. To retrieve it, the gravediggers have only had to go down five feet. Before it is pulled out, the coffin lid is wiped clear of sodden earth, and the nameplate confirms that it contains Beryl, aged nineteen, and Geraldine, aged fourteen months, although the baby's name has been spelt 'Jeraldine'. As Dr (later Professor) Simpson will write in his memoirs, 'We were pleased to see that the wood, which was one-inch elm boarding and kerfed, was in good condition, with the lid only slightly warped.'

Dr Simpson asks for one corner of the coffin lid to be opened slightly, so as to let the gases out. It is then loaded into the back of the waiting hearse and driven by the undertaker to Kensington mortuary, where examination of the bodies – it has been decided to have a look at the remains of tiny Geraldine too – will take place. The exhumation party disperses. Dr Simpson and his assistant, who will become his wife three years later, go to the De Vere Hotel in Kensington for breakfast.

There is some friction between Dr Simpson and Dr Camps at the post-mortems, which start at 8.15 a.m. Both are strong characters, and they do not see eye to eye. Under the 500-watt bulb above the mortuary table, they work on the bodies, with Dr Teare, a close friend of Dr Simpson, observing, as well as DCI Salter and DCI Jennings from the Metropolitan Police. DCI Jennings had taken down the statement of Tim Evans in December 1949 in which he confessed to killing both Beryl and Geraldine, when he had just been told that his baby daughter's strangled body had been found.

No evidence of gas or carbon monoxide poisoning is found in Beryl's body, scuppering one of Christie's later statements in which he said she had tried to gas herself, and he had killed her because she asked him to. The post-mortems confirm that Dr Teare had been correct in December 1949 – both Beryl and Geraldine had died from asphyxiation, strangulation by ligature. After some deliberation, it will be concluded that none of the four tufts of pubic hair found in the tobacco tin at 10 Rillington Place could have come from Beryl, due to the way it had been cut.

The evidence put in jars (lungs and perhaps other organs) and examined by Dr Simpson over the next few days will be the subject of debate for years to come. Only Dr Camps will give evidence at Christie's trial – for the prosecution. Dr Simpson will not be called. The fact that Dr Teare took no vaginal swab at the first post-mortem will be controversial, as it leaves open the question of whether Christie's sperm may have been present. Beryl and Geraldine's bodies are reburied in the same common grave that evening.

On 5 June Christie made the second of his Brixton Prison statements to DCI Griffin and DI Kelly, the officers who had taken down his very first statement at Putney police station on the evening of his arrest. DCI Griffin told Christie that two skeletons had been found in the back garden of 10 Rillington Place, and Christie immediately admitted that he had killed the two women. Christie said that he had had sex with and strangled Ruth Fuerst but again made her out to be the sexual aggressor, with him trying to ward off her advances, as if he was irresistible to women. Regarding Muriel Eady, Christie said that he had had sex with her 'at the time I strangled her'. At his trial the question of whether Christie had sex with his victims before or after their deaths would arise, although necrophilia could not be mentioned openly in a 1953 courtroom. However, it is almost impossible to believe Christie was able to have sex while simultaneously strangling the women.

Three days later, on 8 June, Christie made a third statement, and in this one he admitted killing Beryl Evans as an act of mercy because she wanted to die. He said that he did not have sex with Beryl, as his back was bad then. But Christie would go on to give other versions of Beryl's murder, two later published in the *Sunday Pictorial*.

On Sunday 21 June the *Sunday Pictorial* reported 'RUSH FOR CHRISTIE TRIAL SEATS'. It said that although Number 1 Court at the Old Bailey held 200 people, there were only thirty-six seats in the public gallery, and revealed, 'Court officials say they have never known such a rush of applications for seats or standing room.'

The trial of John Reginald Halliday Christie for the murder of his wife began on the morning of Monday, 22 June 1953, before Mr Justice Finnemore. There were huge crowds outside the Old Bailey as expected, the queue for the public gallery snaking down the road. The van in which Christie arrived and left court each day was surrounded by a police escort, and officers held back the crowds as the van pulled in and out of the rear entrance of the biggest court in the land. All kinds came to gawp: women holding babies, old men in cloth caps, boys on bicycles and City gents dressed for business. Inside there were celebrities, including Robert Sherwood, the New York playwright and Hollywood screenwriter, and the English playwright Terence Rattigan, author of *The Browning Version*. Number 1 was the courtroom in which Christie had given evidence against Tim Evans over three years before and in which Tim had been sentenced to death. It was also where Tim's mother Thomasina Probert had called Christie a murderer. Ethel had defended her husband vehemently that day, but now Reg was on trial for her murder, having strangled her and put her under the floorboards.

The attorney general Sir Lionel Heald led the prosecution, and Derek Curtis-Bennett QC headed Christie's legal team. It soon became clear that Curtis-Bennett was going all out for an insanity verdict. Christie, although dressed in a natty blue suit with a pinstripe, looked broken in the dock, gazing down at his feet, a pathetic figure. The man who had pushed out his chest in his special constable's uniform showed what a nonentity he was, even though his crimes were some of the most horrible and seedy ever heard even in that chamber, which had witnessed the trials of hundreds of murderers.

After the prosecution opening statement, witnesses were called against Christie: the jeweller who had bought Ethel's wristwatch and wedding ring; Dr Odess, who gave evidence that Christie had not had fibrositis when he had said he had at the trial of Tim Evans; the Portobello Road furniture dealer Robert Hookway, who had bought the Christies' furniture, and earlier the Evanses'; Hectorina MacLennan's boyfriend Alex Baker; DCI Griffin, who had taken Christie's statements; and Dr Camps, who had carried out the post-mortems.

Although Christie was being tried for only Ethel's murder, evidence relating to other crimes was admissible. It was tacitly accepted by all concerned that Christie was guilty of all the killings (except perhaps that of Geraldine Evans) and Curtis-Bennett was happy to have Christie associated with as many murders as possible. The more people he had murdered and could be included in evidence, the more likely the jury was to believe in Christie's insanity. He was certainly very abnormal, as Heath and Haigh had been, but was he insane? On the second day, in his opening statement for the defence, Curtis-Bennett told the court that Christie had not known what he was doing or that it was wrong at the time of the murders: 'You can have no doubt, doctors or no doctors, that at the time he did each of these killings, including that of his wife, he was mad in the eyes of the law.' This was a classic definition of insanity under the M'Naghten Rules.

There would only be two witnesses for the defence, and the court fell silent when Curtis-Bennett called Christie himself into the witness box. Neither Heath nor Haigh had given evidence at their trials. The thinking was that Christie's tormented countenance was more likely to elicit sympathy from a jury (if any sympathy were possible) than the debonair Heath or the slick Haigh. Christie was visibly fighting back sobs as he shambled into the box, head bowed, and then faltered and stuttered as he read out the swearing-in oath, taking an inordinate length of time. His whole bearing was nervous – more than that, neurotic – fidgeting, gripping one hand with the other, running his fingers over his domed forehead. Before the third day commenced, a microphone was attached to the box so that Christie's whispering whine could be heard by everyone.

Curtis-Bennett wanted to create the possibility in the minds of the jury that the body count might be even higher. He asked Christie why there had been a long gap between the sets of murders, and if he had killed anyone else between the two women in the garden and Beryl Evans.

It was not in the defence's interest to admit the possibility that Christie had killed the baby – if he did, which seems very likely. No sympathy could possibly be gained by such an admission. But Mr Justice Finnemore picked up on Christie's evidence at the trial of Tim Evans, who had of course been hanged for the murder of Geraldine.

FINNEMORE: 'You were not lying about the baby, but why did you lie about Mrs Evans?'

CHRISTIE: 'Well, I was accused of killing both of them.'

Christie was by turns broken and vague but at moments like this very sharp. Would a truly insane man have been able to be so lucid when it was necessary to serve the purposes of his defence? Christie might have been a psychopath, but that did not mean he was insane under the M'Naghten Rules. The judge also picked up on the fact that Christie had not mentioned the victims buried in the garden or Beryl Evans in his first statement on the evening of his arrest.

FINNEMORE: 'You say that you killed Mrs Evans, and that you had discussed with her husband about disposing of her body and the danger he stood in. He was charged with her murder and the murder of the little child. You gave evidence in a murder trial in this court. Do you mean that you had forgotten all that?'

CHRISTIE: 'Yes, sir. It had gone clean out of my mind.'

Next he was cross-examined by the attorney general for the prosecution. Sir Lionel Heald asked Christie why his wife Ethel had been placed under the floorboards, and not in the alcove or the garden like his other victims. 'I did not want to be separated from her or lose her, and that is why I still had her in the house,' said Christie. This was perhaps the most truthful answer he gave at the trial, as he had loved his wife, despite killing her. The attorney general then tried to show that Christie had known that what he was doing was wrong. He fell right into the trap.

HEALD: 'If there had been a policeman present when you killed your wife, would you have done it?'

CHRISTIE: 'I do not suppose so.'

Heald then elicited that Christie had told lies to explain his wife's disappearance to neighbours and her relatives, demonstrating that he knew what he had done was wrong in the eyes of the law.

The next and only other witness for the defence was Dr J. A. Hobson, attached to Middlesex Hospital, who had observed Christie over eleven sessions, and to whom Christie had first confessed to killing Beryl Evans. Hobson said that in his opinion Christie had not known what he was doing at the time of the murders, which would make him 'M'Naghten mad'. Hobson said that Christie suffered from 'gross hysteria', that this affected his train of thought and that Christie also had an 'abnormal memory'. 'I think he has tried to be as cooperative as possible. I believe that these tricks of memory, or avoidance of getting down to disturbing topics, is to preserve his own self-respect.' The inference was that Christie was not trying to save his own skin but had a mental block preventing him from telling the truth about the more depraved details of his crimes, and so had to skirt around them.

The prosecution had to refute Dr Hobson's opinion, and Dr Matheson of Brixton Prison's hospital wing, who had also observed Christie, was called to the box. Dr Matheson said that Christie was 'a man of weak character' and 'not a man suffering from hysteria, but a man with an hysterical personality'. This was very different to being insane.

DR MATHESON: 'He is immature; certainly in his sex life he is immature. He is a man who in difficult times and in the face of problems tends to exaggerate in an hysterical fashion . . . He spoke quite freely, but when it came to what might be incriminating facts . . .'

Dr Curran, a psychiatrist at St George's Hospital, was then called to the witness box. He had also spent time with Christie in Brixton Prison for the prosecution. Dr Curran said that Christie was 'an inadequate personality' and 'a very extraordinary and abnormal man'. Dr Curran's evidence is very enlightening. After saying that Christie was 'emotional' and 'fearful' when he first arrived at Brixton Prison, he told the court that Christie had soon adapted to his new surroundings.

DR CURRAN: 'He has been meticulously clean and tidy in his person and habits [a lifelong characteristic]. He has always kept himself well occupied; he has mixed freely with the other patients. He has been noticeably egocentric and conceited. He keeps a photograph of himself in his cell. He has been a great talker and has seemed to enjoy discussing his case, bringing the conversation around to it. He has been cheerful and boastful; he has compared himself to Haigh . . . He appears to be above average intelligence; he has always been polite and well behaved. He has slept well, his appetite has been good and he gained eleven pounds in weight . . . I do not believe that Christie's alleged loss of memory is genuine. It is in my opinion too inconsistent, variable, patchy and selective to be genuine . . . He is a man with a remarkable capacity for self-deception.'

The next day, Curtis-Bennett summed up for the defence. He said that Ethel was 'the person he [Christie] loved best in the world', that her murder had no motive and was an insane act. As we have seen, Christie did not have sex with Ethel before or after he strangled her, but Curtis-Bennett brought in evidence from the other murders to support his contention that Christie was insane: 'You may think that a man who had intercourse with a dead or dying body is mad, and that I think has been proved here on one occasion at least.'

Sir Lionel Heald then closed for the prosecution: 'We have to prove, and have very clearly proved, that Christie did deliberately and intentionally kill his wife . . . and he knew perfectly well what he was doing.' Heald admitted that there was no evidence to show that Christie had killed Geraldine Evans. In doing so, he was trying to separate the two murders – to ensure the lack of proof against Christie for the death of Geraldine did not dilute the strength of the case against him for the murder of Beryl. The murder of Geraldine would not go away, however, and the end of Christie's trial was far from the end of the question: Had Christie killed baby Geraldine, a crime for which her father Tim Evans was hanged?

Christie's trial came to a close on Thursday, 25 June 1953, after Mr Justice Finnemore had summed up for two and a half hours. It was a complex case. The judge noted that even if a man 'acted like a monster' it did not necessarily mean he was insane in the eyes of the law. The jury went out at 4.05 p.m. and came back eighty-two minutes later. Meanwhile, Christie was reportedly calm in the cells below, asking for the score in the Lord's Test between England and Australia. The jury filed back in. The verdict was guilty. Mr Justice Finnemore asked Christie if he had anything to say. He did not reply. Finnemore pronounced the sentence of death on Christie, who was led out of the court, still saying nothing.

'The life story of John Reginald Halliday Christie, the Monster of Notting Hill, the man who – in my opinion – murdered at least seven victims, has been told fully to the world. The story was obtained and written by me, exclusively, for my newspaper; it was told in full to a horrified world.' These are the words of Harry Procter of the *Sunday Pictorial*, taken from his memoirs.

Procter had first met Christie while collecting information about Tim Evans in December 1949. Procter had called at 10 Rillington Place, and Christie invited him into his kitchen. The bodies of Beryl and Geraldine Evans had been discovered in the wash house just the day before, and Tim Evans was awaiting trial in prison. Christie had already murdered Ruth Fuerst and Muriel Eady in that room, over six and five years before respectively, and he would go on just over three years later to murder three more women in the kitchen deckchair – Rita Nelson, Kathleen Maloney and Hectorina MacLennan – plus of course his wife Ethel in the bedroom next door. That evening Procter was after background information about the Evans family.

Procter later wrote that shaking hands with Christie was like 'shaking hands with a snake', but of course by then Christie had been exposed as the depraved man he was, and hindsight is not always accurate. In his whisper Christie demanded to see the reporter's press card, and Procter obliged. 'Sit you down. I know you reporters like something stronger, but I can only offer you tea,' said Christie. They spoke about Yorkshire, where they both came from, just as Procter had in 1949 with their fellow Yorkshireman Haigh. Procter was adept at small talk with murderers. Christie told Procter about the Evanses and then turned the tables on Procter: 'Who do you think murdered Mrs Evans and her baby?'

They ran into each other again months later at the trial of Tim Evans, which Procter attended and covered. Meeting outside Number 1 Court at the Old Bailey – seemingly by chance but no doubt engineered by Procter – Christie said of Evans, 'What a wicked man he is.' This must be one of the great instances of ironic projection.

It is not known whether Procter knew about Jock Rae's secret but abortive meeting with Christie outside Wood Green town hall in late March 1953. Procter did not mention it in his memoirs, but in 1958, when they were published, Rae was still active on the *News of the World*. As Christie had been on the run at the time, Rae could conceivably have been prosecuted with obstructing the law or aiding a fugitive even if he had turned Christie in. On the other hand, Rae might have been hailed as the hero of the hour instead of PC Ledger thirty-six hours later. However, Procter may well have known about the planned rendezvous. He was sharp and knew everything going on within the Murder Gang. And Procter would have done the same as Rae if he had received a call from Christie.

Soon after his arrest, Harry Procter was cultivating Christie. Before his second appearance at the magistrates' court, Procter sent Christie, who was in Brixton Prison, a shirt and tie to wear. As Procter wrote later, in court, Christie 'smiled at me as a proud son might smile at his parents on speech day . . . He thanked me for sending him a shirt, but politely complained that it was half a size too big. And he did not like the colour of the tie I bought him.' This was the direct approach, a reporter ingratiating himself with a mass murderer, but official channels were opened too, and Procter kept in daily contact with Christie by short notes and letters through his solicitor, whom Procter described as 'one of my oldest London friends'. Procter did not name the solicitor, but it was probably either Roy Arthur or Ambrose Appelbe, his networking skills again getting results. Procter said that all the notes he sent to and received from Christie were kept in the *Sunday Pictorial*'s safe, along with Christie's handwritten accounts of his murderous life, which would be used in the paper and create a substantial if temporary spike in circulation.

These notes and letters are not available now, and may no longer exist, but the tone of them can be imagined, with

Procter trying to get Christie to feel at ease without condoning his terrible crimes. It seems to have worked as, when Procter attended Christie's last appearance at the magistrates' court, his barrister, the smiling, urbane and bespectacled Derek Curtis-Bennett, took him down to see Christie in the court cells. Procter wrote, 'By this time, Christie regarded me as his friend and champion.' Procter asked Christie if he had murdered Beryl and Geraldine Evans. 'Mrs Christie, yes. I had an affair with her. But not the baby.' Procter recounted that Christie immediately turned his back and 'was ashamed of something'. Presumably not of having an affair with Beryl – the idea is ludicrous anyway – but of killing Geraldine? Procter said that he asked Christie's solicitor, his friend, to get Christie to confess to murdering the baby. This was never achieved, but Procter made it clear in his memoirs he had no doubt that Christie had strangled Geraldine.

Procter had already moved on getting Christie's story while he was on the run. It was an extremely hot story and all the leading lights of the Murder Gang were chasing it, including James Reid of the *Sunday Dispatch*. Procter's problem had been that there was nobody obvious to pay off. Both of Christie's parents were dead, and of course he had murdered his wife. Christie had been estranged from his surviving relatives in the north of England for almost twenty years and had no friends. It is surprising that no money was offered to Ethel's relatives, especially as Christie would later show some sympathy for them, but obviously *the* story could only come from Christie, and he would direct where any money went.

In the end, after making extensive enquiries, Procter found a relative of Christie to approach in the north of England,

and did so. Procter persuaded the unnamed relation – who wanted no money – to speak to Christie by promising the *Sunday Pictorial* would pay all of his defence costs. The fact that Curtis-Bennett, a leading and very expensive counsel, took Procter down to see Christie at the magistrates' court shows that the deal between Procter and Christie had already been done at that early stage. Other Sunday newspapers, perhaps the *News of the World* (Rae) and the *Sunday Dispatch* (Reid), were offering £5,000 for Christie's story. The *Sunday Pictorial* only had to pay for Christie's defence. This was all due to Procter's legwork.

In his memoirs Procter wrote of the method used by the Murder Gang – in his words those 'who dealt in human souls': 'First you contacted a friend – "No intrusion on private grief" says the rule book of the National Union of Journalists – through the friend you contact a relative, preferably a husband, wife, mother or sister. Then you talk, and talk, and talk, and talk . . .' It worked for Procter on the Christie scoop.

The Christie story was considered so important that Procter was accompanied to Christie's last magistrates' court appearance at Clerkenwell by the *Sunday Pictorial*'s deputy editor, the seasoned Reg Payne, with whom he had an uneasy relationship. But in court that day another newspaper did not think that the deal was yet sealed. Competition was so fierce for the Christie exclusive that the *Sunday Dispatch* sent a rival legal team to represent Christie. So in the court lobby that day were two sets of solicitors: those hired by the *Sunday Pictorial* under the agreement with Christie, and those from the *Sunday Dispatch*, the latter not having given up on the story yet.

During the hearing Christie smiled and nodded at Harry Procter. At one point the crime reporters went outside for a cigarette. Procter and Payne were chatting while James Reid of the *Dispatch* stood nearby talking to another hack. Payne turned to Procter and commented that Reid was smiling. At this, Procter said he wouldn't be smiling for much longer, obviously confident that his relationship and deal with Christie was solid. When they went back into court, Procter and Payne were told by their legal team that Christie had been asked to make a choice and had opted to stay with the *Sunday Pictorial*. Procter told Payne that they could get the Christie *Pictorial* advertising poster ready. As they left court that day, Reid shouted after them that he would protest about the decision. He wasn't smiling any more. Procter and Payne looked at each other and shrugged.

On 28 June 1953 the *Sunday Pictorial* had 'CHRISTIE WRITES HIS STORY FOR THE PICTORIAL' splashed across the front page. Christie's trial had come to an end three days earlier, and the paper could cash in on its investment. The editorial introduction ran, 'The life story of John Christie, written by himself, will shock you, but it is important because it is destined to become one of the classic crime documents of all time.' It went on: 'Meanwhile, HARRY PROCTER – who has known Christie for some years – is able to present a picture of this man – the Wickedest Man in the World.' Most of the story that day centred on Procter's own reminiscences of Christie, the build-up to Christie's own story, to come the following Sunday.

Also on the front page that day was a photograph of a young woman and a smaller headline, 'SHE SAYS: I smelled gas in Christie's Kitchen', trailing a story on page 5, where the woman was interviewed by another journalist, Tom Tullett, who would also later write crime books. The woman, twenty-year-old Mary Ballingall from Ireland, claimed to have gone to 10 Rillington Place seven times after meeting Christie at Ladbroke Grove Underground station in January 1953, the same month he murdered Rita Nelson and Kathleen Maloney in his kitchen. Ballingall had been trying to light a cigarette while holding her three-month-old baby, and Christie had offered her a lit match. They got talking. When they got off the train at Hammersmith, he helped her onto a bus and went with her to get her government benefits, and then took her to a cafe and bought her a cup of tea and some cigarettes. He invited her to Rillington Place, and she went. He gave her a pound. During her visits Mary sat on the kitchen deckchair – close to where two women's bodies were stuffed into the alcove – and Christie showed her a photograph album with pictures of his wife. Ethel was of course by then under the floorboards in the living room. Mary said that there were tears in Christie's eyes and he said that he was lonely. On one of her visits Christie tried to touch her, but she rebuffed him. She also smelt gas in the kitchen. On a visit in early February he had dabbed perfume on her dress and put his hand on her shoulder without saying anything, but Christie had not killed her despite apparently having seven opportunities to do so.

The following Sunday, 5 July, the *Sunday Pictorial* featured a large photograph of Ethel Christie on its front page and led with 'My Urge to Kill Women by Christie himself'. It informed readers that Christie had decided not to appeal against his death sentence. His solicitor – and perhaps

Procter's friend – Ambrose Appelbe was quoted: 'Although my client says he does not wish to appeal, in other ways we are doing everything in our power to save his life.' The main thing being done was a letter appealing for mercy designed to put pressure on the Home Secretary, Sir David Maxwell Fyfe, who had unsuccessfully defended the almost undefendable Haigh three years before. But, as would soon become apparent, Maxwell Fyfe was more concerned about Timothy Evans than Christie.

It was also revealed that day that Thomasina Probert, mother of Tim Evans, had written to Christie in prison, begging for the truth. This private letter was not published in the press, but an excerpt can be found in the National Archives (CAB 143/20).

> You are where my boy was three years ago. He knew what was waiting for him and there was no turning back so only the truth would do. He told the priest the truth of his innocence and I will tell you what he said to me the last time I saw him. Mum I loved them I swear before God I never touched them. You did say half the truth last week when you told the Judge you killed poor Beryl but only the whole truth will save you from the wrath of God.

Christie never responded. It is highly probable that he strangled Geraldine after killing Beryl. An untended baby would have drawn immediate attention to Beryl's absence, or Christie may simply have seen Geraldine as a loose end to be tidied up.

Inside the newspaper that Sunday, under the headline 'MY DREAM AND MY FIRST VICTIM', Christie recounted his childhood and the murder of Ruth Fuerst in 1943. There were also photographs of Ethel Christie – on the beach at Brighton, in the park, and 'on a day out at London Airport' – taken from the Christies' album, the one he had shown Mary Ballingall, as reported the previous week. Christie wrote about a recurring dream that he had:

When, as a small boy at Sunday School, I learnt the Ten Commandments, the Sixth Commandment 'Thou Shalt Not Kill' – always fascinated me. In a strange way I was afraid of it. Just as if, even in childhood, I always knew that some day I should defy it. The nearest I ever come to understanding myself and my crimes is in strange dreams at night – when I don't quite know if I am asleep or awake. For instance, one night in Brixton Prison I was restless and half dreaming. This brought vividly to my mind that for years I knew I had to kill just ten women and then my work would be finished. Some unknown force was compelling me to do it.

Just like Haigh, Christie was blaming an outside, other-worldly and therefore unreachable source for the atrocities he had committed. Many serial killers do this. It is a way of detaching themselves from their crimes. Did Christie feel an outside force compelling him to murder or was this a feeble excuse for his inability to control his sexual abnormality, perverted lusts and predatory instincts?

The following day, Monday, 6 July 1953, Sir David Maxwell

Fyfe announced in the House of Commons that he had asked
John Scott Henderson QC, a leading barrister, to head a
special inquiry, aided by the assistant chief constable of the
West Riding Constabulary. Immediately known as the Scott
Henderson Inquiry, it was set up to examine whether
Timothy Evans had murdered Geraldine. Christie's admission
that he had killed Beryl Evans and the trial that had ended
ten days before had thrown up serious doubts as to whether
Tim Evans had killed his baby daughter. Surely there couldn't
have been *two* stranglers living at 10 Rillington Place at the
same time?

Tim's mother, Thomasina Probert, was allotted counsel
and so would be represented, but her lawyer, Bernard Gillis
QC, soon found that his remit in the inquiry would be
severely limited, especially regarding witnesses he could interview. Scott Henderson was very controlling, and for years
afterwards there would be accusations that he had been
cherry-picked by the Home Secretary to ensure that the
decision to hang Tim Evans would not be condemned as
incorrect. Such a conclusion would of course have caused a
massive scandal. The fact that the inquiry was held in private
also rankled with many – would it be a whitewash? – although
of course any inquiry was better than no inquiry. But there
were serious doubts about Tim Evans' conviction, and these
had to be addressed, or at least be seen to be.

Scott Henderson did interview more than twenty witnesses,
although he chose them himself: there was no panel to decide.
On Thursday, 9 July, six days before Christie's scheduled
execution, representatives of the inquiry went to Pentonville
Prison, where he was now held. Bernard Gillis attended, as

did Christie's counsel Derek Curtis-Bennett and also Malcolm
Morris, who had defended Tim Evans at his 1950 trial. But
Scott Henderson would direct proceedings. Under questioning from him, Christie was very vague, saying that he
could not remember details, actions or motivations. However,
he did once again vehemently deny strangling Geraldine and,
more surprisingly, now said that he was 'not sure' if he had
killed Beryl either. Christie disarmingly told Scott Henderson,
'I want to know the truth about it as much as you do.'

On Sunday, 12 July the *Sunday Pictorial* proudly announced
that it had passed Christie's written story to the inquiry as
evidence. The next day Scott Henderson published his findings and presented them to Parliament. The case against
Timothy Evans had been 'an overwhelming one', in Scott
Henderson's opinion. After reviewing all the evidence, he
was satisfied that Tim had killed both Beryl and Geraldine,
and that Christie's confessions to the murder of Beryl were
'not only unreliable but untrue'. He concluded, 'I have therefore to report that in my opinion there is no ground for
thinking that there may have been any miscarriage of justice
in the conviction of Evans for the murder of Geraldine
Evans.' This completely cleared the police of putting words
into Tim's mouth in his statements, and it should be remembered that in one statement Tim *had* confessed to killing
Beryl and Geraldine. However, he had discovered that
Geraldine was dead only moments before. Scott Henderson
was now giving Christie the complete benefit of the doubt
over Beryl's murder.

There was a loud and largely hostile reaction to Scott
Henderson's findings. Many Members of Parliament,

particularly in the opposition Labour Party, called it a
whitewash, and Scott Henderson was driven to submit a
short supplementary report the following day. This would
lead to a debate in the House of Commons on 29 July,
which got very heated, with many MPs calling for a public
inquiry into the Evans case. The Home Secretary refused.

14 July 1953, early evening, the death cell, Pentonville Prison

Christie is tense but quiet. He sits at the tiny desk in his cell,
hunched over a final request he is writing. It is regarding his
sister-in-law, the late Ethel's sister, Lily Bartle. Christie writes,
'The various photographs of my wife to be sent to Mrs Bartle
of 61 Hinde House Lane, Sheffield, together with my
marriage certificate and an apology for any trouble I caused.'
This is the only sliver of remorse that Christie ever shows.
He also writes a letter to one of his own sisters this evening,
to whom he has not spoken for many years. Harry Procter
will offer to publish this letter in the *Sunday Pictorial*, but
Christie's sister will decline.

On the eve of his execution the only thoughts in Christie's
mind are of his own death. Next Sunday the *Sunday Pictorial*
will publish Christie's views on hanging: 'I have always had
the idea for years perhaps since the 1914–18 war that capital
punishment was wrong . . . The more violent ones should
of course be put away in a place where they could not
repeat anything . . . Doctors state there have been "improve-
ments", so it seems a system of treatment over a period
could cause a complete recovery. In that event something

worthwhile could be achieved. Not just the old idea of just – kill him.'

On Sunday, 26 July 1953 the *Pic* will publish the last section of 'Christie's Own Story'. In it Christie will divulge from beyond the grave that he already had another potential victim lined up.

> I do not know her name, I have never seen her close up. She was a smartly dressed woman, a different type to the others. I often watched her driving her car in Ladbroke Grove – a green grey car which looked nearly new. I watched her pull up and go into shops. I never came closer than 50ft to her. But I was in no hurry . . . That woman's face and figure are clear to me even now – I can close my eyes and see her step out of the smart car in smart clothes. She would have been my next victim if I had not been arrested.

Also in that Sunday's edition Christie will reveal: 'I loved my wife . . . It was a once-in-a-lifetime love.' This was the woman whom he strangled and buried under the living-room floorboards.

As Christie gets onto his bunk this evening, to curl up into the foetal position with a warder just outside his cell door, he does not know that his execution notice has already been posted on the prison gates: 'The sentence of the law passed upon John Reginald Halliday Christie found guilty of murder, will be carried into execution at 9.00 a.m. tomorrow.' By that time a crowd of over 200 will have assembled outside the prison, and police constables will be ready to deal with any unrest. But there will be none. No tears will be spilt for Christie. He will fade into the annals of depravity, joining Heath and Haigh as a waxwork in Madame Tussaud's. 'Christie's Own Story' will soon be used to wrap fish and chips. The *Sunday Pictorial* and Harry Procter and the *News of the World*'s Norman Rae will move on to new darkness. Tomorrow a warder will post on the gates a notice that Christie was executed at ten past nine that morning.

That is over twelve hours away. Christie fidgets and squirms on his bunk, resigned to his fate, until just before nine o'clock, when Albert Pierrepoint enters his cell, the man who also hanged Neville Heath, John George Haigh and Timothy Evans.

POSTSCRIPT

Harry Procter only stayed on the *Sunday Pictorial* for another three years. By the time he left Fleet Street after seventeen years – in 1956, aged thirty-nine – he was worn out and his health had started to suffer. He had spent eight years on the *Daily Mail* before moving to the *Pic* in 1952. Procter had asked his bosses at the *Sunday Pictorial* to be moved off crime stories, but they refused, as he was so good at getting them and the stories were so important to the newspaper's circulation. In his 1958 memoirs *The Street of Disillusion*, the title of which summed up how Procter had come to feel about Fleet Street, he wrote, 'But though I was big-time in Fleet Street, I was unhappy. I did not like some of the stories I was writing. A man can have too much of murder and crime, of spending his life with members of the criminal classes.' Procter went back to the *Daily Mail* for a spell, moving to the paper's Manchester offices. A very heavy smoker, Harry Procter died of lung cancer in 1965, aged forty-eight. He would be spoken of in newspaper circles for decades.

Norman 'Jock' Rae remained on the *News of the World*. He continued to get big crime scoops, but its circulation, like that of all newspapers, was in decline by the start of the 1960s. The golden age of the tabloid had been the 1940s and '50s. Rae remained as driven and professional as ever, still a fearsome figure to young reporters coming through. A workaholic, Rae died on the job in 1962, aged almost sixty-six. He never wrote his memoirs, seeing himself very much as a jobbing reporter, even if he had his own car and driver. He remained a Fleet Street legend, even after Fleet Street ceased to be the home of London newspapers – and an atmosphere, a time and a place.

The conviction and execution of Timothy Evans continued to be regarded as a miscarriage of justice by many. In 1955 the Home Secretary at the time of Evans' 1950 hanging, James Chuter Ede, admitted in Parliament that he now felt that a mistake had been made, the clear implication being that Christie had killed Geraldine Evans, the charge on which Tim Evans was convicted. In 1961 Ludovic Kennedy published his seminal book on the Christie–Evans case, *Ten Rillington Place*. At the beginning of the book was an open letter to the Home Secretary written by Kennedy, a plea for the case to be reopened in the interests of justice. Thomasina Probert also continued to press for her son's name to be cleared.

In 1965 capital punishment was abolished permanently in the United Kingdom, the execution of Tim Evans a major feature of the debate that led to the change in the law. During the winter of 1965/6 Sir Daniel Brabin headed a public inquiry into the case that lasted for thirty-two days. Brabin's published conclusion was that it was 'more probable than not' that Tim Evans had killed his wife Beryl, but *not* his baby daughter Geraldine. Many continued to believe that Christie killed both; some agreed with Brabin, a few thought that Tim Evans killed both Beryl and Geraldine. But Brabin's conclusion meant that the 1950 conviction of Timothy Evans had been unsafe, and his execution for killing Geraldine therefore a miscarriage of justice.

On 18 October 1966 Timothy Evans was granted a royal pardon, signed by Queen Elizabeth II and Home Secretary Roy Jenkins, and Thomasina Probert was able to have her son reburied away from Pentonville Prison, in a Roman Catholic churchyard.

Rillington Place continued to be the focus of morbid attention despite being renamed Ruston Place in 1954. The 1971 film *Ten Rillington Place*, based on Kennedy's book, was shot in a house just two doors down from number 10, as the house itself was not practical for filming. The houses were pulled down immediately afterwards, and the area redeveloped. Today, where Rillington Place once was is a gated mews, and the spot where number 10 stood is a small garden.

Albert Pierrepoint retired as Britain's top executioner in 1955, shortly after hanging the last woman to be executed in Britain, Ruth Ellis, for the shooting of her lover. Pierrepoint always denied that her controversial execution was a factor in his resignation, and it seems he retired because of a disagreement with the authorities over payment for his services. However, it had been reported that Pierrepoint was already in discussion with the *Empire News* and the *Sunday Chronicle*, and after he resigned parts of his life story appeared in the newspapers. The Home Office considered prosecuting Pierrepoint under the Official Secrets Act but decided against doing so. However, the government put so much pressure on the owners of the tabloids concerned that the articles did not run for nearly as long as planned. Pierrepoint went on to run a pub, and it was alleged that a sign stood on the bar which read 'NO HANGING ABOUT'. On capital punishment Pierrepoint said, 'In my view, it achieved nothing except revenge.' Albert Pierrepoint died in 1992.

BIBLIOGRAPHY

Primary Sources

Files

At the National Archives, Kew, London.

Neville Heath
As noted in the Introduction to this book, a Freedom of Information request was made for files not publicly available, but was rejected. The only objects available are photographs of the fingerprints of Heath's first victim, Margery Gardner, and of the whip Heath used.

John George Haigh
Files Catalogue PCOM 8/818. These are letters written by Haigh. All materials relating to Haigh's last victim, Olive Durand-Deacon, are held in Crawley, Sussex.

John Christie
Files Catalogue MEPO 2/9535. This consists of several large boxes, including letters, photographs, police reports and other official documents.

Newspapers

At the Newspaper Library, Colindale, London. Thank you to
   the staff.
News of the World: February–August 1949; December 1949–
   March 1950
Sunday Pictorial: May–October 1946; March–July 1953

Website

www.10-rillington-place.co.uk This has many good contemporary photographs relating to the Christie–Evans case.

Secondary Sources

Byrne, Gerald, *Borstal Boy: The Uncensored Story of Neville Heath*, Headline, 1947
Byrne, Gerald, *John George Haigh*, Headline, 1950
Eddowes, John, *The Two Killers of Rillington Place*, Little, Brown, 1994
Engel, Matthew, *Tickle the Public*, Victor Gollancz, 1996
Firmin, Stanley, *Crime Man*, Hutchinson & Co., 1950
Hodge, James (ed.), *Famous Trials 5: Heath*, Penguin, 1955

Hodge, James (ed.), *Famous Trials 6: Haigh*, Penguin, 1962

Honeycombe, Gordon, *The Murders of The Black Museum*, Comet, 1983

Jackson, Robert, *Francis Camps*, Granada, 1983

Jenkins, Alan, *The Forties*, Heinemann, 1977

Kennedy, Ludovic, *Ten Rillington Place*, HarperCollins, 1971

Marston, Edward, *Crime Archive: John Christie*, National Archives, 2007

Phillips, Conrad, *Murderer's Moon*, Arthur Barker, 1956

Procter, Harry, *The Street of Disillusion*, Revel Barker Publishing, 2010

Selwyn, Francis, *Rotten to the Core*, Routledge, 1988

Simpson, Professor Keith, *Forty Years of Murder*, Harrap, 1978

Thomas, Donald, *Villains' Paradise*, Pegasus Books, New York, 2006

INDEX

(key: EC = Ethel Christie; JC = John Christie; BE = Beryl Evans; TE = Timothy Evans; JH = John Haigh; NH = Neville Heath)